INSIDE THE CELTIC TIGER

CONTEMPORARY IRISH STUDIES

Series Editor Peter Shirlow (The Queen's University of Belfast)

Also available

James Anderson and James Goodman (eds)
Dis/Agreeing Ireland
Contexts, Obstacles, Hopes

Paul Hainsworth (ed.)
Divided Society
Ethnic Minorities and Racism in Northern Ireland

Peter Shirlow and Mark McGovern (eds)
Who are 'the People'?:
Unionism, Protestantism and Loyalism in Northern Ireland

Gerry Smyth
Decolonisation and Criticism
The Construction of Irish Literature

Gerry Smyth
The Novel and the Nation:
Studies in the New Irish Fiction

INSIDE THE CELTIC TIGER

The Irish Economy and the Asian Model

Denis O'Hearn

Pluto Press

LONDON • STERLING, VIRGINIA

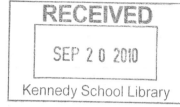

First published 1998 by Pluto Press
345 Archway Road, London N6 5AA
and 22883 Quicksilver Drive, Sterling, VA 21066-2012, USA

British Library Cataloguing in Publication Data
A catalogue record for this book is available from the British Library

ISBN 0 7453 1288 8 hbk

Library of Congress Cataloging in Publication Data
O'Hearn, Denis, 1953–
Inside the Celtic tiger: the Irish economy and the Asian model/
Denis O'Hearn.
p. cm. — (Contemporary Irish studies)
Includes bibliographical references.
ISBN 0–7453–1288–8 (hardcover)
1. Ireland—Economic conditions—1949– 2. Ireland—Social conditions. 3. East Asia—Economic conditions. I. Title.
II. Series.
HC260.5.045 1998
330.9417'0824—dc21 98–24903
CIP

Cover image on the paperback edition from the Book of Durrow, reproduced courtesy of the Board of Trinity College, Dublin.

Designed and produced for Pluto Press by
Chase Production Services, Chadlington, OX7 3LN
Typeset from disk by Stanford DTP Services, Northampton
Printed in the EC by Athenaeum Press, Gateshead

Contents

List of Tables

List of Figures

List of Abbreviations and Acronyms

CAP	Common Agricultural Policy
CORI	Conference of Religious in Ireland
CSO	Central Statistics Office
DEC	Digital Electronics Company
ECU	European Currency Unit
EDB	Economic Development Board
EEC	European Economic Community
ESRI	Economic and Social Research Institute
EU	European Union
FDI	foreign direct investment
FIM	Federation of Irish Manufacturers
GATT	General Agreement on Tariffs and Trade
GDP	gross domestic product
GNP	gross national product
ICTU	Irish Congress of Trade Unions
IDA	Industrial Development Authority
IDB	Industrial Development Board
ILO	International Labour Office
IMF	International Monetary Fund
IRA	Irish Republican Army
IRS	Internal Revenue Service
ISI	import-substituting industrialisation
JETRO	Japanese External Trading Organization
LFS	Labour Force Surveys
MITI	Ministry of International Trade and Industry
NAFTA	North American Free Trade Agreement
NIC	newly industrialising country
OECD	Organization for Economic Co-operation and Development
OEEC	Organization for European Economic Co-operation (now OECD)
OEM	original equipment manufacture
PCW	Programme for Competitiveness and Work
PESP	Programme for Economic and Social Progress
PNR	Programme for National Recovery
PPS	purchasing power parities (or units)
R&D	research and development
TNC	transnational corporation
WTO	World Trade Organization

Do Annette, Sinéad agus Caitríona

Preface

It is sometimes surprising, often annoying, and nearly always dangerous when the public perception of something is informed primarily by a 'received wisdom'. This book is about one such received wisdom, namely, that the southern Irish economy became a miracle economy during the 1990s and was practically transformed, in half a decade, from one of the most peripheral and poorest regions of the European Union (EU) to a fully participating and wealthy member of the European core. Ireland became the 'Celtic tiger' of Europe, the place to emulate, what other peripheral countries should and *could* be.

Around this central received wisdom came many associated assertions that have also, too often, been taken as social fact. One was that this new miracle economy was creating so many high-tech jobs and opportunities that prosperity was there for the taking – *if* one was willing and motivated enough to garner the necessary skills. Some public figures went so far as to imply that if you did not get one of these jobs you were some kind of inferior creature from an impoverished Irish past. The poor were often portrayed as victims of their own making or, worse, encouraged to see themselves in such a failed light.

This was bad enough for the tens of thousands of middle-aged men and women who were the long-term unemployed products of the 1980s, and who had little chance to participate in the 'Celtic tiger'. Worse still is the fact that so many young people will never participate in the 'feel-good factor' and the conspicuous consumption that they see all around them. Too often, they turn to crime or drugs. Always they face a daily dose of despair. Ireland, too often familiar with poverty in the past is, ironically, now facing some of the worst problems of inequality and alienation *because of* its prosperity.

If the recession of the 1980s brought too little criticism of Ireland's dependent industrialisation strategy, the economic expansion of the 1990s brought even less critical thought. Many former radicals, trade unionists and social activists either became swept up in the 'feel-good factor' or became resigned to the inevitability of it all after the fall of the Berlin Wall, the end of history and the global failures of national liberation movements. For

Ireland, neoliberalism and European membership were now simple facts of life where a decade before they had been the focus of struggle.

It was the silence around these issues that motivated this book. Like most Irish people, I was proud that the nation was emerging from its deep inferiority complex of the 1970s and 1980s, which was often displayed in the form of public guilt at being Irish. It was great to be living in a place that was 'hip', even if those of us in Belfast were sometimes pitied for not being in the *real* Ireland of Dublin or Galway. But I was also concerned that the positive media image of the Celtic tiger faced little critical scrutiny. Yes, fundamental changes were taking place in Ireland. But many of these changes were not what they seemed – they were partly illusory, and often had a negative side. Because of this, it is highly questionable whether the underlying basis of recent economic change is sustainable. Perhaps most worrying in the immediate sense is that the process of change has led to increasing problems of social exclusion – rising poverty, inequality, and social marginalisation.

As I wrote this book, rumblings began to be heard in Ireland and doubts began to surface. Most of these doubts were about inequality and poverty, about the fact that so many Irish people were being excluded from prosperity. But a few commentators also began to question the economic basis of the 'Irish miracle' and, especially, how long it could last. These thoughts were intensified with the collapse of the *other* tigers, in East Asia, which happened as this book was being written.

Older doubts resurfaced. Could an economy that depended so heavily on foreign capital ever achieve 'development' in a more holistic and sustainable sense? Were the sources of economic growth – in foreign computer firms, construction, and tourism – simply too tenuous to be guaranteed in the long term? The main beneficiaries of growth – foreign computer firms and Irish professionals – disposed of most of their fortunes in ways that were either fruitless (in the case of profits removed from Ireland) or downright harmful (property speculation that drove the costs of housing through the roof). For anyone who has studied dependent development in other parts of the world, it all looked familiar, although with its own very Irish twists.

It is this comparative impulse that guides most of this book. By comparing the Irish experience to others perhaps we can understand it better. Since Ireland has been called a Celtic 'tiger', it was natural that a starting point of comparison would be with the original 'tiger economies' of Asia. Although the south of Ireland is clearly not Asia, many points of comparison are none the less quite useful. This is especially true when we contrast the broadly strategic patterns of East Asian growth with the narrowly dependent case of Ireland.

To compare Ireland with East Asia is not to say that the latter is a model of how late industrialisers should behave. Nor would I wish my critical analysis of Irish development to be construed as saying that the Celtic tiger is *all* an illusion. Clearly, momentous things have happened in Ireland in the 1990s. Clearly, new companies have arrived in large numbers, new products are being produced, and many young people have been able to find employment in the land of their birth where, before, they had to emigrate. Clearly, many people are better off than they were ten years ago, and some are *much* better off. This book is meant to draw out the limitations and realities of such change, not to deny it.

In analysing the limitations of Celtic tigerhood, I am aware that many Irish people will chafe at my conclusions. 'We're finally doing well, why must you try and spoil our moment of glory?', I can hear some people asking. If I write with a sceptical pen, however, it is out of concern and not derision. Let us keep our renewed sense of pride in being Irish. Indeed, let us turn it beyond this limited dream of Celtic tigerhood, and aspire to something really great for *all* of our people.

Above all, I write critically because I think it is imperative to advertise the dangers that are inherent in the neoliberal development model that has been sweeping the world. The 'miracles' of Ireland or East Asia cannot simply be repeated by any region that follows the World Bank's prescriptions of austerity, privatisation and free trade. The more likely outcome of such policies, as we have seen across the world, is economic marginalisation for the many and riches but for a few. In a world where regions compete for miracles in the form of transnational corporate investment, one region like Ireland succeeds at the expense of many others. For the world, therefore, we must find a better and more generalisable strategy for creating 'miracles'.

Writing about Ireland is always difficult. As a republican (small and big 'r') one is always faced with the problem of balancing the desire to avoid 'partitionist' thinking with the necessity of recognising the reality that the island is divided into two economies and two jurisdictions. I have attempted to analyse important points about Ireland as an island economy, although the book as a whole is primarily about the southern Irish economy. Some readers may find it awkward that I refer to the 'southern Irish economy' or the 'south of Ireland' where many would be content with 'the Irish economy' or 'Ireland'. I apologise to my 'southern' friends in County Donegal, who will always live at a higher latitude than us 'Northerners' in Béal Feirste.

Many people provided advice and support at various stages of this project. Douglas Hamilton, Peadar Kirby, and Ronnie Munck read drafts of most if not all of the chapters and made invaluable and supportive comments. Roger van Zwanenburg of Pluto Press encouraged me to consistently draw out the comparisons of Ireland with other tiger economies throughout the text. Others who contributed at various points along the way include Roberto Franzosi, Stephen Bunker, Boa de Sousa Santos, Gay Seidman, Andrew Schrank, Patrick O'Hearn and participants in seminars from Dublin to Oxford to Madison, Wisconsin. Of the many librarians and statisticians who helped at various stages of the research, I am especially grateful to the staff of the Irish Central Statistics Office who, on many occasions, went out of their way to get data to me at a moment's notice. Go ralbh maith agat to Robert Ballagh for the 'Celtic tiger'.

I am deeply grateful for the friendship, advice and support of Vincent Tucker, who died tragically just as this manuscript was at its beginning. His insights and, hopefully, his humanity inform the book from start to end.

Finally, I'd like to dedicate this book to Annette and to Sinéad and Caitríona, who sacrificed many happy hours with Freddi Fish so that Daidí could work away at his computer.

1 Comparative Tigerhood

Ireland became a tiger economy on 31 August 1994. The country was busy celebrating the Irish Republican Army (IRA) cease-fire that went into effect the same day, so there was a muted immediate reaction when the American investment bank Morgan Stanley published a bullish 'Euroletter' on the Irish economy. One author in the report half-jokingly asked, with obvious reference to East Asian tiger economies like South Korea and Taiwan, was Ireland a 'Celtic Tiger'?[1] In support of the claim, he cited growth rates well above the European average, low inflation, growth of exports, and a firm exchange rate. Despite the fact that the investment bank was primarily interested in selling Irish stocks to its institutional investors, after including Ireland in its stock index in 1993, there could hardly have been a more authoritative voice on the matter than the quintessentially capitalist House of Morgan.

Morgan Stanley was not the first to trumpet the Irish economic revival. Former Irish Taoiseach Garret FitzGerald was writing in early 1994 about Ireland's 'spectacular' economic performance. Over five years, the country had experienced the highest economic growth rates and lowest levels of public borrowing in the EU, an increase in average purchasing power second only to Portugal, the lowest death rate in the world for mothers and for children under five, and high levels of food consumption and home ownership. Yes, the country still had low living standards relative to the rest of Europe and sky-high unemployment rates. But these, argued FitzGerald, were merely an artefact of Ireland's historic high birth rates. Since the country had halved its fertility rates over the preceding decade, this demographic anomaly of such large numbers of young people flooding the job market would eventually disappear, and the country's rapid economic growth would be matched by full employment.

As a tiger, southern Irish economic growth indeed looked good. The country had sustained its high (by European standards) growth rates for possibly the longest period since the establishment of the Irish Free State in 1922. Real gross domestic product (GDP) grew by 4 per cent in 1993, by 5.3 per cent in 1994, and by a whopping 7.5 per cent in 1995. The Organization for Economic Co-operation and Development (OECD) and other experts were forecasting more high growth during 1996 and 1997. If these predictions came true, the southern Irish economy would have grown by more than 5 per cent annually over a five-year period, all at a time when the rest of the EU was in recession.

What a turnaround! In 1988 Ireland was the laggard of Europe, proof to some critical development analysts of their claims that countries that depended on transnational corporate investment were likely to face economic stagnation (O'Hearn 1990a, Munck 1993). Even in early 1993, after some spotty boom–bust years since 1989, Irish economic experts went into a funk after the value of the punt plunged by 10 per cent in an EU monetary crisis. And as late as May 1994 a correspondent in the *Financial Times* began her article, 'Whither the economy of Ireland? Or should that be "wither"? ...'[2]

After the bullish Morgan Stanley report, word spread from the business press to the popular press. Pundits whose knowledge of East Asia amounted, at most, to watching Bruce Lee films on their Samsung videotape recorder suddenly found copy in Ireland's new-found status. The name 'Celtic tiger' stuck.

But how apt is the comparison between Ireland and the East Asian 'tiger economies'? Many epithets that are first applied half-jokingly subsequently take hold. Their image, however superficially, contains a kernel of truth that appeals to the name-callers. Such name-calling can be revealing or obfuscating. Usually, it is both. The case of the 'tiger economies' reveals layers of instructive and confusing imagery. In the first layers, comparing Ireland to the East Asian economies reveals some instructive similarities. It also reveals equally instructive differences, which complacent Irish pundits and policy makers ignore at their peril. At a deeper level, the very tiger image *as applied to the East Asian economies* is problematic. Not only does it ignore important differences among these economies but it fails to recognise very serious limitations to the East Asian models of economic development. This last point became especially clear as the Asian economies went into serious economic crisis in 1997.

This book, then, aims to use the concept of the 'tiger economy' to examine illusion and reality in southern Ireland's recent 'economic success'. It explicitly compares the different Asian and European tiger economies as a way of exploring the nature of Irish economic change. By unpacking the multiple meanings of being a 'tiger economy', both in the Asian and the European contexts, we can hopefully achieve a better understanding of the processes that drive and limit economic change in those countries, like Ireland and the East Asians, which try to achieve economic success by industrialising long after their larger and more powerful neighbours in Europe, North America, and the Pacific Rim.

What is a Tiger?

We all remember the story of the blind men and the elephant. One man, feeling the elephant's tail, concludes that 'an elephant is like a rope'. Another, feeling its leg, says 'an elephant is like a tree'. The same could happen with tigers. Someone looking at South Korea might conclude that a tiger has giant world-class corporations, like Hyundai, Samsung and Daewoo. Another, observing Taiwan, might observe that a tiger has multiple networks of small to medium-size enterprises, producing machine tools, or parts for big Japanese firms. A third, in Singapore, would see few private indigenous companies and would conclude that a tiger is full of the best and biggest foreign electronics companies – Philips, Texas Instruments and Fujitsu. And yet a fourth, in Hong Kong, would find that a tiger is a massive collection of the biggest banks, alongside countless networks of small and nameless textile and electronics producers. An Asia expert from Harvard University was probably understating matters when he insisted that 'there are at least three models of East Asian development' (Perkins 1994).

What, then, *is* a tiger? It certainly is less tangible than an elephant. Several economies, now including Ireland's, have earned the name. Yet the few widely agreed characteristics of tiger economies are largely descriptive and superficial. The deeper one goes into their economies, the more disparate the 'tigers' appear to become. Once one attempts to explain how they *achieved* their economic success, the disputes deepen.

It has been widely understood at least since the 1980s that the original four 'tiger' economies (sometimes also called the four 'dragons') included the East Asian states of South Korea, Taiwan, Singapore and Hong Kong – probably in that order of importance. Some authors would also include Japan, on the basis that it was the original East Asian ascendant whose economic successes paved the way for the other four. More recently, authors have referred to wider groups of Southeast Asian countries as 'newly industrialising countries' (NICs) (Grimwade 1989, Chowdhury and Islam 1993), 'high performing Asian economies' (World Bank 1993, Page 1994), the 'next Asian NICs' (Tan 1993) or, popularly, the 'tiger cubs'.[3]

Despite their differences, the original four East Asian successes share some core economic characteristics. The most important of these is sustained high economic growth rates (Table 1.1). Ireland's rapid economic growth in the 1990s was the primary reason why pundits began to compare it to the East Asian economies. Other common characteristics include rapid demographic transitions to highly urban, low-fertility, low-mortality societies; dynamic agricultural sectors; and unusually rapid export growth. Finally, some economists have associated rapid economic growth with rapid growth in personal savings (whether voluntary or forced), high rates of investment relative to national income, and high levels of skill-formation through education and training (Page 1994:616–17).

Table 1.1 Economic characteristics of the East Asian tiger economies

Economy	*Average annual GDP growth rate 1960–70*	*1970–80*	*1980–89*	*Average annual per capita GNP growth 1965–89*	*Annual growth of mfd. exports 1970–85*
S. Korea	8.5	8.7	9.2	7.0	28.0
Taiwan	9.2	9.7	8.0	7.0	26.4
Singapore	8.8	9.0	6.9	7.0	24.8
Hong Kong	10.0	9.5	8.9	6.3	15.0

Source: Chowdhury and Islam (1993: 8, 14, 17).

With the exception of Hong Kong, there are important characteristics that the other three tigers share. The most important are their interventionist and generally authoritarian states. Each of the three states has intervened heavily in their economy, although with different strategies, to promote exports and economic growth. Each has limited the activities of their populations, especially popular movements like trade unions, in order to control wages and create the stability that they viewed as a necessary prerequisite to economic growth. Each has introduced forms of control over markets that have led social scientists to refer to them as 'central planners'. And the three East Asian tigers, along with Japan, have been largely responsible for the popularity of the concept of the *developmental state* among sociologists and political scientists (Evans 1995).

Although some Western pundits compare Ireland with the East Asian economies on the basis of its rapid economic growth in the

1990s, few of them seriously consider just how sustained East Asian growth has been. Each of these countries sustained rapid economic growth over several decades. Over the three decades of the 1960s, 1970s and 1980s all four maintained average annual economic growth rates of more than 8 per cent. Even on a per capita basis, their annual economic growth rates averaged 7 per cent.[4] Such sustained rapid growth is all the more remarkable when one considers that the annual growth rates of OECD countries (including Ireland) during the same period were in the region of 2–3 per cent.

These rapid and sustained growth rates are usually associated with even more rapid growth of exports, particularly of manufactures. Thus, over the 15-year period from 1970 to 1985 manufactured exports grew annually by more than 25 per cent in South Korea, Taiwan and Singapore. The conventional wisdom is that these rapidly expanding exports *drove* higher economic growth rates in general. Orthodox economists like those in the World Bank have turned this association into a purported relationship, where export growth *causes* economic growth. They have used this largely unproved assertion to convince late-industrialising countries throughout the world that they should abandon any attempt to encourage their local industries by protecting them on national markets. Rather, the orthodox economists argue, they should open their economies to international markets and seek to export as much as possible, in the hope that such export growth will create broader economic growth (World Bank 1993). Such has been the rationale for the resurgence of free trade agreements, including global agreements like the Uruguay Round of the General Agreement on Tariffs and Trade (GATT) and regional agreements like the North American Free Trade Agreement (NAFTA). On the other hand, a large number of experts have argued that East Asian successes were largely the result of effective state interventions, which strategically protected key industries to build them up until they were able to compete in export markets. From a comparative standpoint, the question of what causes economic success is much more interesting than the mere descriptive identification of certain economies as 'successful'.

How they became Tigers

One of the most vibrant debates in development studies has been about the causes of economic success in late-industrialising countries. Positions in this debate largely break down between orthodox neoclassical economists and those who take institutional approaches to economic change. The former argue that economic success depends on 'getting the prices right' so that markets alone can do their work and encourage efficient economic activities. The latter contends that most of the East Asian states have intervened quite heavily to influence markets in their favour. Indeed, their interventions have often been 'market-distorting' and even protectionist. Some analysts add that global factors – geopolitics and the specificities of Asia's regional economy – affected the economic 'success' of the tiger economies, both recently and through the socio-economic foundations that were laid down under Japanese colonialism.

It is important which of these factors we associate with economic 'success', because some of them can be copied by other late industrialisers while others cannot. 'Getting the prices right' should, in theory, be the easiest strategy to emulate because it mainly involves removing policies or practices that interfere with markets. Effective state intervention is less easy to emulate since it can be difficult to establish efficient states with the capacity to intervene in economic arenas. Finally, to the degree that success depends on global factors, it is practically impossible for small nations to recreate the fortuitous conditions that favoured the four East Asian tigers.

Markets

I have already indicated that the most popular conservative explanation of East Asian successes is their adherence to strict market principles. From the point of view of neoclassical economic orthodoxy, the surest route to economic success is to allow markets to set prices freely so that each product will be produced in the optimal quantities and in the most efficient way by the most able producers. Market economists rarely distinguish between different time frames, insisting that rapid economic growth (whether for an individual, firm, country or region) results from the efficient *short-run* allocation of resources. This allocation can only be achieved, they argue, by 'getting the prices right' and allowing different producers to produce those things they are best at producing. Moreover, it is claimed that these principles of market efficiency are universal, so that countries at all levels of development must follow them if they wish to ascend to higher levels.

Such free market principles have special ideological importance in the East Asian case because the four 'tigers' have been so widely promoted as remarkable economic success stories. According to the neoclassical perspective, the lesson for other countries throughout the world who wish to follow in East Asia's footsteps is that their states must abandon interventionist attempts to induce development and let the market do its work: *get the prices right*. Neoliberal programmes – open doors to foreign investment, privatisation, austerity, free trade, and export-orientation – are more attractive if it can be demonstrated that they were the secret to success in other countries.

The economist Bela Balassa (1988) makes this point by comparing East Asia to Latin America. He argues that both the East Asian and Latin American states began their post-war attempts to industrialise by following the typical strategy of *import-substituting industrialisation* (ISI), where local markets are protected from imports in order to induce national capital to produce things that were previously imported. But when this strategy reached its inevitable crisis, argues Balassa, the East Asians shifted to a market-friendly export-oriented strategy while most Latin American countries attempted to 'deepen' their protected industrialisation by producing machinery and consumer durables instead of just basic consumer goods like clothing and shoes. This, he argues, opened East Asian industries to foreign competition, forcing them to concentrate in producing the things they were best at producing and to produce these things more efficiently so that they could compete in world markets. Moreover, the East Asians preferred to leave industry to private capital, who would respond correctly to market signals, while many Latin American states fell into the trap of establishing or taking over industrial activities and then running them inefficiently.

More recently, a major study by the World Bank (1993) attributes the 'East Asian miracle' to the four tigers' strict observance of the Bank's 'market friendly' approach by 'getting the prices right' so that markets could be left to do their job of creating growth and prosperity. The World Bank's message for other countries who wish to achieve similar rates of long-term economic growth is quite clear: dismantle protection in favour of free trade, privatise, open your economies to the free movement of foreign investment, and export.

States

There is just one thing wrong with this neoliberal prescription. Aside from the World Bank and a few ultra-orthodox economists, most experts have found that the East Asian tigers succeeded mostly because their states *intervened* so successfully in their economies, not because they let the markets do all the work. Unlike neoclassical economists, social scientists who study institutions recognised very early on that states played an important role in East Asian development. A group of Harvard economists led by Ed Mason, for instance, referred to the Korean state as 'Korea Incorporated', arguing that the South Korean economy was like a huge corporation, with the state as its board of directors (Mason et al. 1980). Although the heights of the economy were dominated by huge *chaebol* (holding companies) like Hyundai and Samsung, these in turn were strategically directed by the state. It used various policy instruments to induce corporations to invest in target industries, to export key products, to introduce new technologies and to spend more on improving their workers' skills. Moreover, the state was involved both directly and indirectly in subsidising some activities while it discouraged others, in rewarding firms which responded to state directions and sanctioning those that did not.

From this point of view, markets are not automatic. For one thing, they are imperfect because *other* powerful states and firms manipulate them, so that prices cannot by themselves direct economic actors in the most desirable directions. But more importantly, the experience of many industrialised countries indicates that competitive advantages are not endowed, as the neoclassical economists would have it, but are built or captured over time. Japan was but a recent example where the state successfully allied with capital to upgrade the economy's competitive advantages over time to more profitable and high-tech activities. Britain did broadly the same, although its policies differed in detail, to reinforce its industries' position against their competitors in the eighteenth and nineteenth centuries (O'Hearn 1994a). Thus, as So (1995:12) puts it in his analysis of East Asia, 'states have a strategic role to play in taming international and domestic market forces and harnessing them to national ends'.[5]

Although East Asian states have typically followed interventionist industrialisation strategies, however, they are anything but socialist. As Johnson (1987) argues, these states pursued economic growth and competitiveness, not social welfare, as their foremost priority; they strongly favour private property to state ownership; and they attempt to manipulate markets rather than eschewing them in favour of central commands. Moreover, most East Asian states have severely repressed their working classes, restricting or outlawing trade unions and other popular movements. In South Korea, for instance, this has created an ongoing dispute between the state and popular classes, which regularly spills over into violent conflict.

Repression has been equally severe, if not as militantly resisted, in Taiwan and Singapore. Indeed, conditions for the working classes have been so severe in these states that some analysts have argued that popular repression may be a major prerequisite to economic growth in developing states. Consider the words of the former prime minister of Singapore, Lee Kuan Yew, quoted in *The Economist* (27 August 1995:15) insisting that ' ... what a country needs to develop is discipline rather than democracy. The exuberance of democracy leads to indiscipline and disorderly conduct which are inimical to development.'

Yet the East Asian states have not blindly supported their capitalists and major corporate powers, as strict free enterprise models might prescribe. Rather, the state's relationship with business throughout East Asia has been one of subsidies and discipline, 'carrots' *and* 'sticks' (Amsden 1989). The South Korean state, for example, extends many advantages such as subsidised credit and foreign exchange to its corporations, so long as they meet targets for introducing new technologies or expanding exports. Yet the same state has been known to completely dismantle a major *chaebol* overnight and distribute its companies to other owners because it was dissatisfied with some aspect of its performance. On a lesser scale, the state sanctions poor performance by withholding credit, industrial licensing, access to technologies or foreign exchange, and so on.

Although the South Korean state is often regarded to be the most interventionist in East Asia, others intervene as well. Taiwan, like South Korea, violated the usual neoclassical prescriptions by keeping interest rates artificially low in order to stimulate investments, protected key sectors from competing imports until they were able to compete in export markets, and subsidised businesses to increase their competitiveness rather than allowing extreme wage cuts. Even in Singapore where, as we shall see, industrialisation depended more on foreign investments and freer trade than Taiwan or South Korea, the state has none the less been 'heavily interventionist'. Among other things, Singapore's 'developmental state' has intervened in the labour market to control wages and consumption; forced savings through price manipulations and its control of banking; and been heavily involved in state-owned industries (Lim 1983, Grice and Drakakis-Smith 1985, Huff 1995).

Despite neoliberal assertions that economic growth requires free enterprise and free trade, then, the experience of East Asian economies actually indicate the opposite. These have been the world's most 'successful' economies since the Second World War in terms of economic growth and industrialisation. Yet their states have also been highly interventionist, manipulating market mechanisms, strategically protecting key sectors, and becoming heavily involved in the planning and execution of industrial strategies and trade. As Amsden (1994:627) points out, the East Asian states *create* competitiveness through 'pervasive intervention'.

It is, perhaps, the unconvincing nature of neoliberal analyses of past East Asian success that explains their reaction to the severe economic crisis that hit Asia in 1997. The crisis, which first appeared in Southeast Asian 'tiger cubs' like Thailand and Malaysia but then spread to large financial institutions in Japan and South Korea, appeared to have conservative Western economists rubbing their hands with glee. Finally, they could argue, these Asian states had overstepped their competencies. Perhaps, they could now safely admit, states could manage their economies when they were smaller. But when South Korea grew to the eleventh largest economy in the world, its economy was simply too complex for a state to manage. Only markets, they argued, could efficiently interpret a large economy's vast array of rapidly changing economic signals. Moreover, state partnerships with business had an inevitability about them: whenever a business ran into difficulty the state simply bailed it out rather than forcing it to adjust to changing realities, as the market would do. Such partnerships became corrupt since state managers and corporate executives had a mutual interest in covering each other's mistakes. States forced banks to lend money to corporations to bail them out of their difficulties and the companies used the money to expand their inefficient practices. When, inevitably, such corporations could no longer pay their debts, both they and the banks faced failure. States like South Korea were forced to call in the International Monetary Fund (IMF) to bail out their economies, but in return they had to marketise them – something for which the IMF, the World Bank and the US government had agitated for a long time. From the perspective of Western states and their corporations, who argued that they had for too long faced unfair competition from state-supported Asian companies, Japan and South Korea had finally got their come-uppance. (Whether or not this is an accurate perception is discussed in Chapter 6.)

Globalisation

The East Asian miracle may be a remarkable story, which has finally reached its conclusion, or an ongoing success which has simply come to a momentary hitch. Regardless, one can hardly dispute that Asia's developmental states have played a central role in the successes of their tiger economies. To recognise the role of state intervention in this long-running success story, however, only partly answers the question of how tigers are made. Other late-industrialising states intervened heavily in their economies, but with much less success (in many cases, with largely negative results in terms of growth and industrialisation). Moreover, other states that tried to intervene, for example, by protecting national industries, encountered strong opposition from global forces such as the US government, the World Bank and the IMF. These organisations have very effectively used coercive programmes like structural adjustment and tied lending to 'persuade' states throughout the world to liberalise their trade, privatise their state sectors, impose austerity plans against the public and open their borders to the free movement of foreign investment (George 1992, O'Hearn 1994a). The East Asian tigers, on the other hand, appear until quite recently to have been relatively immune from such Western coercion. Thus, part of the explanation for their success must account for why *they* were allowed to pursue statist strategies that drew sanctions in other parts of the world. This is a particularly important issue for Ireland and other peripheral European countries because EU rules preclude them from applying most of the instruments that the East Asians used so successfully.

The most convincing explanation of why the East Asian countries were able to get away with protectionism and state intervention centre on geopolitics. First, all of the East Asian tigers benefited from the fact that they were front-line states in the Cold War. Not only did they (especially South Korea and Taiwan) receive substantial amounts of US aid without many of the usual strings attached, they were also left free to pursue unorthodox economic policies that would not have been tolerated in Europe or Latin America, so long as they stood firm against their communist neighbours and supported an American military presence. Aid was useful, although not essential, for funding economic development programmes. But, more importantly, freedom to use interventionist economic instruments gave these states a degree of autonomy from international sanctions and control (Cumings 1984, So 1995). Only recently have American regimes complained bitterly about East Asian (including Japanese) protectionism, and threatened to retaliate.

The geopolitical source of autonomy, however, is only one side of the story. We still have to explain East Asian *state capacity*: why were their states effective in their interventions where many other states have been corrupt and ineffective. A number of explanations have been put forward for Asian state effectiveness in implementing and co-ordinating economic policies, some of them cultural and some historical. Probably a combination of both factors are important. Some experts credit the special nature of Japanese colonialism in East Asia for transforming 'corrupt and ineffective' states into highly authoritarian but effective developmental organisations, while clearing out many of the class interests that might have corrupted post-colonial states. The result, as in the South Korean case, was a highly bureaucratised and penetrating state, which became the dominant partner in alliances with property owners for industrial production and profits, and which also exercised repressive control of the working classes (Kohli 1994). Essentially, the Japanese state, which had itself become a highly effective developmental state, created a series of East Asian states in its own image. Once Japan reintegrated these states in its regional economy during and after the 1960s, these efficient developmental state characteristics were further encouraged.

Time and Development: a Tale of Two Globalisations

Several approaches have dominated thinking about the issue of how 'development' proceeds across time. At the global level, McMichael (1996) refers to two periods following the Second World War: a 'development project' that prevailed during the 1950s and 1960s, which then gave way to a 'globalisation project' in the 1970s, and which prevails to this day. The first period was one of relative optimism about development, with widespread agreement on both sides of the Cold War divide that *nations* could follow the Western route to development through industrialisation. Orthodox modernisation theories assumed that societies could become 'modern' by acting in modern ways and, specifically, by inducing and allowing 'enterprising men' to come forward and follow the Protestant ethic of forgoing current pleasure for future gain. Such individualistic market-oriented behaviour would eventually but inevitably lead to a 'take-off to self-sustained growth' for each country around the globe (Rostow 1960). Many Marxists and other critics argued, to the contrary, that the control of the global market by large capitalist states and firms enabled industrial development in some countries but produced *under*development in others. Therefore, late developers required interventionist states to overcome imperialist power or market distortions and direct development toward modern industrialising ends. Both approaches, however, held that national development through industrialisation was inherently possible.

On the other hand, there was always an ambiguity in practical industrialisation strategies between trying to achieve modernisation through home-grown modernisers or taking the short-cut of inviting transnational corporations (TNCs), as the most modern and expansive institutions, to bring the seeds of modernity through their direct investments. Few countries that practised ISI completely eschewed foreign investment. As Baran (1957) noted long ago, TNCs tend to make their way into even the most protected economies. Latin American crises in ISI a decade later almost inevitably led to a renewed willingness to turn to foreign investors for help. Thus, McMichael and others (Arrighi et al. 1993, Arrighi 1995) argue that the crisis of the 'development project' in the 1970s led to its replacement by a 'globalisation project', which is altogether less optimistic and where countries participate not as nations on their way to modernity but as pragmatic and strategic actors in a much more restricted game. This new game is governed more strictly by global rules of free trade, specialising in what you can do without the aid of protection, privatisation and 'living within ones means'. Of course, it could be argued from the point of view of the industrialised core and its institutions, that the 'development project' was always a 'globalisation project'. But its global character has been strengthened by several decades of core penetration of all regions of the globe, especially through TNC investments, and by the restructuring of world trading and investment patterns after capitalism's crises of the 1970s and 1980s.

However, while the surge of outward movement after the late 1960s included capital from all core regions, the forms of economic change in the Japanese-centred regional economy of Asia were quite distinct from Western Europe and North America. For one thing, Japanese firms tended more than US firms to shed certain economic activities as they upgraded to other activities, leaving more niches for other producers. Moreover, large Japanese firms sourced more inputs and even some final products from external networks of subcontractors while vertically integrated multidivisional firms in the West supplied more of their own inputs. Again, this left wide networks of firms who supplied the larger Japanese corporations. As a result, foreign penetration in East Asia was very different from other semi-peripheral regions like Latin America or the European periphery. Broad sets of activities and subcontracts were moved to the East Asian countries, creating greater chances for them to upgrade their technologies of production and participate in more profitable economic activities over time.

The emergence of the East Asian tigers was based on two interconnected processes: their specific form of integration into the Japanese-led regional Asian economy during and after the 1960s; and their creation of strong domestic economies, directed by developmental states but made possible because niches were opened up within the emerging regional division of labour. These interconnected processes are very different from those which followed the rapid expansion of foreign direct investment in the West, which were far more limiting of local development. Contrary to experiences elsewhere in the world economy, Japanese economic penetration appears to have 'stimulated, rather than retarded economic growth in less developed nations along the western Pacific Rim' (Hill and Fujita 1995:91). In the case of East Asia, 'dependence' on Japan appears to have encouraged rather than retarded the emergence of local industries in the tiger economies, which are widely regarded as the most successful industrialisers on the globe since the 1960s.

One way to understand how regions are affected by globalisation is through the concept of *commodity chains*, where a global division of labour spans distinct core, semi-peripheral and peripheral regions. According to this concept, global production of each final commodity is organised in a chain, where different stages of production form links or nodes which are spatially dispersed throughout the world economy. The world economy as a whole is a vast network of interlinking commodity chains. Yet siting of different kinds of production is not random – rather, core regions engage in the most technologically advanced and profitable nodes, peripheral regions engage in the least advanced, and semi-peripheral regions do intermediate activities or a range of more or less technically advanced activities. Typically, core TNCs imperfectly organise each commodity chain with the aid of their sponsoring states. 'Economic development' generally refers to the ability of a region or country to upgrade its participation in this hierarchical division of labour into higher tech, more profitable activities.

Yet how are these activities distributed among regions? Neoclassical economists explain the division of labour through the concept of comparative advantage, where countries or regions specialise in producing the things they are best at producing given their endowments in natural resources, capital, and human abilities. Radical development theorists and institutional economists assert that different regions have different *economic power* resources – including military forces, access to international regulating bodies like the World Bank or the World Trade Organization (WTO), large corporations, and so on – by which they develop or capture *competitive advantages*. States use their power to protect the abilities of their nationally based corporations and financial institutions to maintain competitive advantages over those from other states. Some experts use the term *hegemony* to denote this ability to exert imperfect but powerful control over the organisation of the world economy and its division of labour (Wallerstein 1991).

This is not to say that all regional core powers and their corporations use the same strategies to attain or maintain profitability and position. Indeed, as Hill and Fujita (1995) argue, there are major differences between US and Japanese corporate competitive strategies, and these lead to important differences in their associated locational investment strategies, regional divisions of labour and, subsequently, in the developmental prospects of semi-peripheral countries that are integrated into those regional divisions of labour and their commodity chains.[6] One difference between the two sets of corporations concerns their main strategies to achieve and maintain profitability. The other is in the structure of the firm itself and, consequently, its relations with other firms.

Corporations gain extra profitability through innovations: in the products they produce and distribute (gaining market advantage) and in the ways they produce them (gaining cost advantages). Yet they can maintain their extra profitability either by extending a product's 'life-cycle' so that it remains highly profitable for a longer time, or by constantly upgrading their techniques of production and introducing new products. In practice, corporations and regional economies use both strategies to maintain profits, but they use them to different degrees.

In recent decades American firms have tended to concentrate on prolonging product life-cycles by maintaining secrecy about technologies and product development, by controlling markets and by cheapening labour costs. Although American ideology emphasises 'free markets', the oligopolistic structure of its major industries leads corporations to use collusive agreements and other protective methods like patents to protect their market shares in the hope of extending the period during which a given product brings extra profit to the corporation. In addition, since the US state equates corporate interests with national interests, it supports its corporations in their efforts to maintain profitability by moving production abroad to cut labour costs. Such, for example, has been the strategy behind the encouragement of American-owned *maquilador* firms in the free trade zones along the Mexican border, eventually leading to the

NAFTA. The result has been the creation of low-cost industrial slums in Mexico as well as vast deindustrialised zones in the US.

Japanese corporations, on the other hand, primarily compete by constantly upgrading their products and ways of producing them. Contrary to prevailing US corporate strategies, the Japanese state encourages its corporations to *shorten* product life-cycles in order to capture the monopoly profits that come from introducing new products and production processes. Because Japanese companies concentrate on such upgrading, once they shift into new higher-value-added activities they are more likely to shed the more standardised nodes of commodity chains to subcontractors. In addition, Japanese companies have been the victims of their rapid success in a relatively small economy. In cases such as cars and electronics, their exports expansion was so rapid that they could not source enough inputs or even final products at home. Thus, they encouraged regional producers to supply them under sub-contracting agreements, as explained below.

This process of upgrading has created a distinct historical pattern of economic change in Japan. As a late-industrialising 'follower', Japan began by importing technologies to produce basic consumer products like textiles that were demanded on the domestic market. As a 'learner', it adapted the technologies to its own production and improved them, increasing productivity and expanding its local production to capture economies of scale. Eventually, it was able to compete in export markets, thereby capturing further economies of scale. Profits from the activity were then turned to new economic activities like steel, machinery and cars, which eventually went through the same cycle from home production to exports. Throughout, the Japanese state was deeply involved in programmes to move the product cycle forward, both through providing business incentives but also by disciplining industry. Amsden (1989) argues that the premise that business must serve the interests of the nation is the opposite of the Western liberal ideal that the state should limit its intervention on the grounds that 'what is good for General Motors is good for the USA'.

Japan's movements through different industrial product life-cycles indicate that Japanese economic change has been marked by a rapid upgrading through new leading sectors: labour-intensive light manufacturing in the 1950s (textiles), capital-intensive heavy machinery in the 1960s (steel, machinery), knowledge-intensive industry in the 1970s (cars, consumer electronics), information technologies in the 1980s (videotape recorders), and 'flexible industry' in the 1990s. As Japanese corporations upgraded, they often 'shed' their old activities to producers in other East Asian countries.

Associated with differences in profit strategies are different structures of industrial organisation in Japan versus the West. The typical North American or West European foreign investor is the large integrated multidivisional firm (Chandler 1962). This firm moves abroad to gain access to raw materials, cheap labour and/or markets, but it generally does so through fully- or majority-owned corporate affiliates. The result is the typical 'global corporation' with many subsidiaries that comprise many links of one or several commodity chains, selling inputs to each other and assembling products for markets throughout the world (Jenkins 1987).

Japan, however, is at the centre of a regional 'multilayered subcontracting system' that has expanded prodigiously into East Asia and Southeast Asia since the 1960s (Arrighi et al.1993:49). Japan's famous corporations like Honda or Mitsubishi are at the top of the system, but they source many of their inputs externally from small and medium-sized corporations. These in turn subcontract from smaller firms, and so on down the line. According to the Japanese External Trading Organization (JETRO), a single Japanese automaker deals with up to 170 primary subcontractors, which in turn consign contracts to manufacture parts to 4,700 secondary contractors, which in turn deal with 31,600 tertiary subcontractors. Below that level, the numbers are too great even to estimate. In 1973, the proportion of value added to cars by the main Japanese automakers was only 18 per cent, as opposed to 43 per cent in the US and 44 per cent in Germany. Subcontracting is even greater in the electronics industry, where 70–80 per cent of inputs are sourced externally by large Japanese firms, as opposed to just 20 per cent in the US and Western Europe (Arrighi et al. 1993:51).

During the 1960s, however, the Japanese economy like other global economies faced a world economic crisis (the same ensuing crisis that led to the rapid expansion of American TNC investments abroad). Not only was there a rising general intensity of competitive pressures world-wide, Japan also faced an increasing shortage of domestic labour for its large and growing industrial networks. In order to obtain labour and raise competitiveness, many Japanese subcontracts went abroad. But this foreign direct investment was very different from the US or Western European patterns that came to prevail in Ireland and elsewhere. For one thing, Japan extended its subcontracting networks, rather than corporate subsidiaries, abroad to East Asia. By one count, in 1971 joint ventures and minority ownerships accounted for some 80 per cent of Japanese foreign investment projects, compared to just 20 per cent for Western TNCs (Arrighi et al. 1993:58).

Moreover, because this outward regional movement from Japan was based in subcontracting networks, it involved more small and medium-sized enterprises instead of the huge TNCs that dominated Western foreign direct investment. With the help of powerful Japanese trading companies (*sogo shosha*), which directed trade between networks of sellers and buyers in Japan, masses of small and medium-enterprise operations moved abroad to the emerging East Asian tigers. The *sogo shosha* located foreign partners, funded joint ventures and acted as agent to locate inputs and find purchasers for exports of finished goods. From the mid-1970s onwards, the larger Japanese firms began to make up a larger share of investors in East Asia, embarking on joint ventures and subcontracting agreements. Unlike Western TNCs, which tended to buy their material and technological inputs from their own subsidiaries elsewhere, these Japanese companies brought networks of smaller suppliers with them and also induced new local suppliers in their host East Asian economies.

Finally, Japanese investments were far more agglomerated geographically than Western direct investment. Arrighi (Arrighi et al. 1993:60) suggests that this was particularly important in the first years of Japanese expansion, the late 1960s and early 1970s, when the four East Asian economies received more than half of Japanese investment in textiles and 80 per cent in electronics. During 1964–74, and mostly in the early 1970s, Japanese investments in the East Asian four exploded by more than 20 times the numbers of the previous decade, to 581 projects for South Korea, 400 for Taiwan, 111 for Singapore and 79 for Hong Kong. Western investments did not begin to agglomerate in this way until the restructuring of the late 1980s and 1990s, a factor which, as we shall see, would become crucial for Irish economic growth. But, even then, they never agglomerated to the degree of Japanese investment. Moreover, the rapid and sustained growth of East Asia is explained not just by the *number* of foreign investment, but by the fact that they created networks of linked economic activities and, most importantly, encouraged the rise of strong domestic industrial sectors. Some corporations in these sectors themselves became competitive on export markets.

As a result of this pattern of industrial upgrading and 'shedding', the Asian regional economy differs from the wider American-led world economy, creating different results for integrated national economies. Rather than 'shedding' activities, American TNCs move discrete parts of their production process (nodes of commodity chains) to other regions, characteristically under their direct control in corporate subsidiaries. Because profitability is seen to depend on oligopolistic advantage, direct ownership enables corporations to maintain strict control over their technologies of production along with proprietary rights to key products, even while they take advantage of cheaper peripheral labour. The result, as Raymond Vernon (1971) noted in his work on *product life-cycles*, is that typical American and European corporations strictly control their technologies, licensing them only after advances elsewhere have eliminated the extra profits from monopolising them, and selling them only after they have become routine. This technology hoarding severely limits the *technology transfer* available to host countries from American foreign direct investment (FDI) while it restricts the opportunities for local economies to become involved in technological upgrading, research and development (R&D), product design and other higher profitability activities.

The characteristic Japanese corporate pattern, on the other hand, has been to 'put out' activities through subcontracts or other means as they upgrade. The Japanese system of *flexible specialisation* in manufacturing relies more heavily on subcontracting than on direct investments in majority- or fully-owned subsidiaries. The Japanese state philosophy in this regard is that regional investment and trade strategies should be linked.[7] By encouraging the East Asian countries to take over certain industries that Japan has shed, it not only has strengthened them as markets for Japanese consumer products, it has also created assembly industries in sectors like consumer electronics that depend on key Japanese high-tech semifabricates and assemblies.

In this respect, the Japanese are said to follow what Akamatsu Kaname called a 'flying geese' pattern of regional development. In his analogy, the countries of the regional economy have formed an inverse 'V' formation, like wild geese, with Japan in the lead. As Japan advanced and concentrated in higher-tech industrial activities, it shed the next-lower echelon of activities and technologies to the East Asian countries. As the East Asian economies took on these new activities, they in turn shed the next lower rank of activities and technologies to the Southeast Asian economies. In this way, as the leading countries advanced, they brought along sets of 'new industrialisers' behind them.

From the Japanese point of view, industrial development in East Asia is desirable because large East Asian corporations have become some of the most important customers for Japanese high-tech products. While many American firms would see vibrant electronics industries in other countries as competitors, Japanese corporations and state bodies like the Ministry of International Trade and Industry (MITI) see them as important potential customers for computer processors and other products.[8] As a result of this strategy, Japanese foreign investors rely much less on majority ownership than American TNCs. In 1971, minority ownerships and joint ventures made up about 80 per cent of Japanese foreign investment projects, compared to less than 20 per cent for American and British TNCs (Arrighi et al. 1993).

Countries like South Korea and Taiwan have been careful to avoid FDI by TNCs and, in doing so, have avoided some of the problems that dependency on them creates. Such TNC investments contributed only 2 per cent to Korea's capital formation during 1976–87, and about 3 per cent to Taiwan's during 1965–85. To put the strength of East Asian local industry into perspective, Japanese and American FDI into the four tigers during the whole period 1980–88 amounted to $11.6 billion, which is just a fifth of Samsung's *annual* sales (Hobday 1994b:336, 337). This does not mean, however, that these economies avoided foreign investment altogether – indeed, foreign investment in these countries has been significant. Yet they have gone into joint ventures and subcontracting networks instead of direct subsidiaries.

These forms of investment have created typically East Asian pattern of industrial upgrading that is not common in late industrialising economies elsewhere. East Asian 'latecomers' have exploited foreign technologies through such processes as learning and reverse engineering, gradually becoming more able to compete internationally in their own rights. They have been able to do this – at least in South Korea, Taiwan and Hong Kong – because Japanese firms have encouraged them to operate under *original equipment manufacture* (OEM) agreements, a specific form of subcontract where they produce goods to the precise specification of the foreign firm, which then markets it through its own distribution channels under its own brand name. This has given Japanese companies the ability to rapidly increase their capacity, but it has also meant that they must provide a great deal more access to technology and training for their foreign partners than fully-owned subsidiaries would provide to host economies.

For example, Samsung (now the second-largest South Korean conglomerate) began as a joint venture with Sanyo of Japan in 1969. It soon allied with several Japanese companies like NEC and

Matsushita to make parts for their products. In time, as Samsung gained technical and engineering capabilities, it graduated to OEM arrangements with Japanese firms and large American retail chains. Such arrangements gave Japanese companies the ability to expand rapidly, while Samsung got crucial training in assembly methods and engineering, links to export markets, and began to reverse engineer electronic products like colour TVs and microwaves. Eventually, with the help of the Korean state trading agency, Samsung became an international electronics exporter under its own name and began its own R&D and product design (Hobday 1994b:344–5).

Similar examples abound in Taiwan and Hong Kong, although they have depended more on learning and upgrading in smaller companies (employing fewer than 300) instead of the huge *chaebol* found in South Korea. In Taiwan, the average firm employs just 24. This included nearly 4,000 exporters of computer products in 1989 (Hobday 1994b:349). Unlike South Korea, only a few Taiwanese firms, like the computer company ACER, have achieved international branded status. More of them are small producers who depend on Japanese and American retailers to distribute their products.

The top-down pattern of technical shedding from Japan has its 'bottom-up' equivalent from the point of view of the later East Asian industrialisers. According to Hobday (1994b:341), the four tigers have followed a typical pattern of industrial upgrading that combines both marketing and technology (see also Wortzel and Wortzel 1981). Many East Asian companies began as assemblers in joint ventures, with competitive advantages mainly in cheap labour and totally dependent on their Japanese partners for distribution (or, more often in the case of textiles, their US partners). In time, they began to compete not just in cheap labour but also in quality and speed of production, and began to actively sell *productive capacity* to foreign buyers under OEM. In their most advanced stages, some local firms began process and product innovation and R&D, marketing more of their own products abroad, eventually under their own brands (for example, Hyundai, Samsung). They achieved these advances, however, through a slow process of learning and reverse engineering, mainly in routine products, rather than by 'leapfrogging' directly into high-tech products (Hobday 1994a, 1994b). And, with a few exceptions, OEM-type arrangements have limited them even today to lower value-added, lower quality products that are produced by relatively labour-intensive means compared to core products in Japan or the US.

Since subcontractors make more of their own decisions about sourcing materials and technologies, they are more densely linked to other parts of their local economies than are TNC subsidiaries to their hosts. Amsden (1989), for example, describes the origins and development of the South Korean steel industry, which began as a turnkey operation organised by a consortium of Japanese companies. As it progressed, the Korean industry reinvested in technical upgrading and expansion of its activities. With the blessing of Nippon Steel, it also progressively moved into more and more activities that were originally done or supplied by the Japanese. Not only did it source more of its inputs locally, it also eventually moved into R&D and product development. This contrasts starkly with the American TNC experience not only of protecting intra-company sources of supply, but even choking off local industries in the countries where they locate.

As the example of electronics shows, there are also clear differences between Japan and the US in the range of activities that are 'shed' from the leading core economy to integrated semi-peripheral regions. Japan encouraged the transfer of a wider range of industrial activities to the East Asian tigers than ever occurred in the West. South Korea, for example, not only became a regional centre for producing textiles, but also for shipbuilding, electronics and, eventually, cars. Taiwan built steelworks to supply Japanese industry and then used the steel in its machine-tool industry. Part of this difference stems from the different sizes of the leading regional economies. Since Japan is small relative to the United States, it reached its labour supply limits relatively early, and was forced to shift a wider range of functions to other countries. This was done not only to cheapen the costs of production in times of difficulty, but also to obtain extra productive capacity in times of rapid expansion. The United States, on the other hand, more or less achieved industrial maturity before it had to turn abroad for major supplies of labour and even many critical raw materials.

Yet the East Asian economies also required a level of tolerance from international bodies not just for their strategic protectionism, but also for their technology borrowing practices which, in other cases, might have been construed by the US as violations of 'intellectual property rights'. The fact that they relied so heavily on such forms of technology access (and continue to do so even today), however, points to a limitation on tigerhood that has come under increasing scrutiny among observers of East Asia in recent years. This is an increasingly apparent problem of *technological dependence*, where the East Asian countries appear to have approached a technological 'glass ceiling', above which they are finding it difficult to upgrade.

While the Japanese regional model, therefore, allows considerably more scope for industrialisation by its semi-peripheral partners, we should be careful to underscore the limitations of this model for the East Asian economies and, especially, for the next wave of 'new industrialisers' such as Indonesia, Malaysia and China. As Bello (1993) points out, East Asian regional integration is still based on an unequal division of labour among its participants. Compared to Japan, South Korea and Taiwan are still mainly sites for relatively labour-intensive production, such as electronic assembly of Japanese components. Even their 'heavy' industries like shipbuilding, steel or machine-tools are relatively less high-tech and lower profit than associated Japanese nodes of the same commodity chains of which they form a part. And even their leading sectors, like computers or cars, are still heavily dependent on Japanese technology.

David Smith clearly defines the limitation in East Asian technological upgrading in his work, based on interviews with major engineers and business elites. He argues that the East Asian economies like South Korea's are still technologically dependent on Japan and the US because the 'technical know-how and organizational innovations critical to commodity production and marketing are controlled by "external" or foreign entities (firms and states)' (Smith 1997). Even in the 1990s, he finds, indigenous Korean companies are still limited to 'backward engineering', where they carefully disassemble leading technologies and copy them (a practice which is becoming more difficult and costly with recent American moves to protect so-called intellectual property). Or, they pay a dear price in the form of joint ventures, royalties or licence fees to obtain access to innovative production and marketing technology. Large companies like Samsung have been forced to set up R&D facilities in American locations like the Silicon Valley or Princeton because Korea cannot generate engineers of sufficient quality. Even the design for the 256K DRAM computer chip, which has been seen as South Korea's great breakthrough into true innovation, was purchased from the American firm Mostek, and Samsung pays massive royalties to American firms for their memory products.

Hobday (1994a, 1994b) has similar findings throughout East Asia. Even today, he finds, 'leading' East Asian sectors like Singapore's electronics sector have made only limited gains in technological upgrading. Not only have they found the 'learning' process to be slow and arduous, but they have also been largely limited to rather mature stages of electronics product cycles, accumulating technology that is largely 'pre-electronic' in character. Electronics firms in Singapore – foreign as well as indigenous – have concentrated their competitive advantages in 'crafts, mechanical and precision engineering, electro-mechanical interfacing and basic manufacturing skills, rather than the software, computer and R&D skills usually associated with electronics' (1994b:831).

Bernard and Ravenhill summarise the limitations of East Asian tigerhood. Sectors like South Korean electronics – the leading Sectors that are usually singled out as the heights of East Asian success – are 'lacking design and marketing capabilities, structurally locked into production hierarchies from which they derive key components and other inputs, and dependent on low-cost production to maintain export competitiveness' (1995:192). Such severe limitations even on the leading tiger economy in terms of technology are crucial to the Irish case where, as we shall see, quite a play has been made of the degree to which the country in the 1990s, unlike the 1970s or 1980s, has made great breakthroughs into high-tech innovation and is reaping the rewards of long-term government strategies to educate engineers.

To sum up, the East Asian economies are now faced with the problem of 'graduating' into the core of high-tech economies that can compete through innovation so that they are not too dependent on core economies for critical technologies. Despite its limitations, however, integration into the Pacific Rim economy has given the East Asian tigers economic growth rates and degrees of industrial and technological upgrading that are the envy of late-industrialising economies around the world.

Tigers and TNCs

So far, our examples of East Asian tigers give little hope that a country or region could attain rapid economic growth and 'development' – in the sense of industrial upgrading to more high-tech and more profitable activities – simply by letting markets do their work or even by attracting transnational corporate investment. Rather, East Asian successes appear to be explained by *differences* between Pacific and Western regional integration; Japanese and Western corporate behaviour; the opportunities available to Asian and Western states; and Asian and Western state capacities to exploit opportunities.

Direct investment by Western TNCs does not appear to be very conducive to development. Even the limited kinds of learning and industrial upgrading achieved in South Korea and Taiwan required encouragement for local industries, first as domestic producers and then eventually as exporters, that appear to be seldom forthcoming from Western TNCs which mainly locate abroad to capture cheap labour or to gain access to markets. Because these TNCs make their decisions on the individualistic basis of what is good for the firm, they see little importance in inducing local development in host economies. Indeed, strong local industries are often regarded as potential competitors, either for the local subsidiary or for corporate subsidiaries elsewhere. The US state, steeped in its individualistic *laissez-faire* philosophy, gives its TNCs encouragement and protection but little strategic guidance, much less discipline.

It appears, then, that Western TNCs are not good candidates as 'engines' of economic growth ... until, at least, southern Ireland's economy emerged as a successful 'tiger' in the 1990s. Here was an economy that, as we shall see in Chapter 3, was highly penetrated by TNCs, mainly from the US. Here was an economy whose domestic industrial sectors had stagnated for nearly half a century. Were there any Asian experiences that accord more closely to this recent Irish experience?

We have concentrated mainly on South Korea and Taiwan, where Japanese firms invested, but mostly indirectly with an eye to encouraging the kinds of regional subcontractors and consumers the new upgraded Japanese industries desired. These were economies where domestic industrial sectors thrived under Pacific regional integration. In the South Korean case, some of the world's leading industrial conglomerates emerged in Daewoo, Samsung and Hyundai. Even in Hong Kong, whose success has concentrated more in its financial sector than either South Korea or Taiwan, industrial successes were largely domestic and integrated into the kinds of regional subcontracting networks that I have described in South Korea and Taiwan.

There is another Asian tiger, however, about whom we have said very little. At least at a superficial level, Singapore appears to offer more instructive comparisons to Ireland. Its population of about three million compares roughly to that of the south of Ireland. But its economy is similar, too, in some important ways. Like Ireland, Singapore set up an industrial board, the Economic Development Board (EDB), to attract foreign investment. Like Ireland's Industrial Development Authority (IDA), the EDB soon concentrated on attracting American TNCs, especially in electronics. Both boards have been very successful in attracting such investment. And, also like Ireland, Singapore's manufacturing sectors are dominated by foreign transnationals. The foreign share of manufacturing investment in Singapore grew from just 43 per cent in 1965 to 75 per cent in 1994, and the foreign share of GDP doubled from 18 per cent in 1970 to 36 per cent in 1990 (Lee 1997). In 1991, Singaporean-owned firms accounted for only 16 per cent of total manufacturing investment, and much less in sectors like electronics (Hobday 1994b:837). At about the same time (1992), foreign companies accounted for 74 per cent of output in manufacturing and 85 per cent of manufactured exports (Huff 1995:740).

Singapore was the first country to successfully base its economic growth on concentrated investments from targeted foreign sectors. In 1959 the EDB was established to create the necessary infrastructure for industry, including industrial estates such as that at Jurong. The Singaporean state recognised two advantages with respect to attracting foreign investment, especially in manufacturing. One was its relatively cheap labour. The second was its historical role as an entrepôt, for trade within the region and between several continents. With these in mind, the EDB set about strategically identifying the most promising sectors to attract foreign investment, and its record of intelligence in this respect is second to none – often, it should be noted for the purpose of this study, preceding similar moves by the Irish IDA by several years. For instance, the EDB identified the potential of electronics in 1966 and began immediately to target TNCs in that sector, some five years before the IDA. The electronics share of assets in manufacturing grew rapidly, from less than 2 per cent in 1965, to 19 per cent in 1970, to nearly 30 per cent in 1980 (Lee 1997:60).[9] The EDB targeted financial and business services in the early 1970s, based on the sector's favourable outlook for sustained growth and Singapore's own historic 'comparative advantages' as entrepôt and banker to trade. This was a decade and a half before the IDA began to target internationally traded services in the late 1980s, mainly because it was having great difficulty attracting foreign manufacturing investments. Indeed, although the Irish IDA has often marketed itself as a world innovator in terms of its programmes for attracting and targeting foreign investment, one would be forgiven for concluding that it achieved much of its success by being the first European country to mimic Singaporean programmes.

Singapore also introduced a series of incentives for foreign investors which closely resemble those introduced in Ireland (see Chapter 2). It has generally foregone any restrictions or regulations on the entry of foreign capital or personnel, or their productive activities while in Singapore. There is no restriction on the removal of capital or on the repatriation of profits, dividends and interest. And the state has provided tariff protection for foreign firms; tax incentives for exporters; duty free importation of machinery, equipment, and materials; industrial estates with full amenities; and various subsidies and grants. It has also enacted laws and regulations to guarantee political stability, peaceful industrial relations and orderly wage increases, while suppressing labour movements (Lee 1997). All of these things have made Singapore, in one expert's words, 'the world's most globalised economy' (Ramesh 1995).

Singapore's economy began to grow rapidly in the 1960s, first as a service and trade centre for the region and, from the later 1960s, based on TNC manufacturing investment and petroleum refining. The ratio of manufactured exports to GDP rose from 12.7 per cent in 1966 to nearly 60 per cent in 1992. The share of manufacturing in total output rose rapidly from 16.6 per cent in 1960 to 29.4 per cent in 1979, with the manufacturing share of employment rising by about the same amount. This sector was superseded by the growth of financial and business services in the 1980s, which rose from 19 per cent of GDP in 1979 to 26 per cent in 1992. Together, these two broad sectors made Singapore the single biggest recipient of foreign direct investment outside of the developed core during the 1980s, receiving nearly 13 per cent of such investment (Huff 1995:738, 739).

Although there is a strong resemblance between Singapore and Ireland, in terms of policies and results, there are important differences. As I have already noted, Singapore's strategies preceded Ireland by some years and, crucially, it received far more investment and employment in the foreign sectors than Ireland has ever attracted. Singapore also differs from Ireland and most other countries because it is a city-state. Little need be said about this structural characteristic except to note that it is much easier to maintain rapid growth in a city than in a country, where hinterlands often suffer at the expense of urban 'growth poles'. This is especially true of an economic growth model that depends on foreign investments. Ireland has consistently faced the problem that its successes in attracting inward investment in and around Dublin cannot be matched in the countryside. On the other hand, any attempt to steer foreign investments to small towns and rural areas risks alienating prospective investor, who are attracted both by the agglomeration of other firms and infrastructure around Dublin and by the lack of red tape and state direction in matters of where and how they invest. Thus, high manufacturing growth and low unemployment in the larger cities (usually with the exception of pockets of high unemployment) is often achieved at the expense of rural stagnation, unemployment, and poverty. Singapore, on the other hand, has skilfully manipulated the surrounding countries to attract labour and other resources in support of its industries whenever necessary, while problems of underdevelopment and unemployment are left to the surrounding areas of Malaysia and Indonesia. Only recently have other surrounding states begun to compete with Singapore in any serious way for incoming foreign investment.

Another difference from Ireland is Singapore's state which, like South Korea and Taiwan, intervenes quite heavily in the economy. As Huff (1995) points out, government control and directives have replaced market price mechanisms in three arenas: the labour market, state-owned enterprises and forced private saving.

Singaporean labour paid a high price for economic growth. Once the state identified wages as being too high for it to compete effectively in attracting foreign investment, it moved decisively to bring them down through the Employment Act and Industrial Relations (Amendment) Act of 1968. Wages were regulated by a National Wages Council. These measures transferred control of trade unions into state hands and gave employers control of bargaining. Subsequently, although labour productivity in Singapore was higher than the US, its wages fell below the other East Asian tigers. Despite this, authoritarian state measures depoliticised the labour movement and work stoppages were virtually eliminated. Even as labour began to go into shortage in the early 1970s, state control of wages held so firmly that TNCs did not bid-up wages to gain access to workers. And even as high-tech TNCs flocked to Singapore during the 1980s, they were chiefly attracted to the country's supply of flexible, unskilled, low-wage, mainly female labour. In 1990, 72 per cent of workers in electronics were female (Huff 1995:742).

In the 1960s, the Singapore state, like South Korea's, recognised direct state involvement in industry as a necessary engine of economic growth. It moved into key support sectors for the export industries it was beginning to target: iron and steel, shipbuilding and ship repair. According to Lee (1997:64), state enterprises produced about 15 per cent of manufacturing output in 1974. The state was particularly active in traded services, such as shipping, banking, transport, and trading. By the mid-1980s, the state owned some 490 companies. According to Huff (1995), this experience showed that state firms can be run efficiently and at a profit, partly because the Singapore state began afresh in key economic activities, rather than taking over loss-making enterprises.

Finally, Singapore's state-forced private saving (through its social security scheme) and added public savings at a rate that made the country the highest-rate saver in the world. A large part of the savings were invested in infrastructure and public enterprise, both of which helped Singapore's attraction of more foreign investment. Together, state investment and foreign investment gave Singapore among the highest fixed capital investment rates in the world (about a quarter coming from FDI). In addition, Singapore's state invested heavily abroad, making it one of the most solvent states in the world, but also opening the way for its own major transnational industry: the provision of infrastructure in other regional states.

In short, the 'Singapore model' of economic growth is based on strict control of labour, heavy state investment in infrastructure financed by forced savings, extensive state enterprise, and high dependence on TNC investment in manufacturing and financial services. It was 'successful' in two major respects, which generally qualify Singapore as a tiger: rapid economic growth and job creation. Real GDP growth averaged more than 8 per cent annually throughout the 1960s and 1970s, and about 7 per cent during the 1980s and 1990s. And total employment in Singapore rose from 472,000 in 1960 to more than 1.5 million in 1992. Within that total, employment in manufacturing rose from 74,000 to 433,000, and in financial services from 21,000 to 172,000.

Like South Korea and Taiwan, however, Singapore has faced barriers to technological development. Although TNCs producing advanced computer and other electronic products give the country the appearance of a high-tech core industrial power, these companies still employ predominantly women at extremely low wages. Even as late as 1990, 72 per cent of workers in electronics were female, receiving wages lower than the rest of manufacturing. High profit stages like R&D and product design remained in the home countries of the TNCs. And the state had been notably unsuccessful at restructuring the economy toward higher-tech activities, since it was unable to create substantial domestic sectors and had little influence over the kinds of projects provided by the TNCs. Ironically, according to Huff (1995:741) 'the reliance on foreigners, together with Singapore's lack of an indigenous technological contribution to manufacturing, marks the Republic as not being a developed country'. Singapore's 'success' appears to lie primarily in its ability to attract a continuous flow of foreign investment that is sufficient to maintain its high economic growth rates and ensure full employment. While this may be possible in Singapore, a city-state, it would be a much more difficult in a country with a rural hinterland such as South Korea, Taiwan or, perhaps, even Ireland.

Finally, it is worth noting that even Singapore has faced increasing competition in its bid to attract foreign investment since the late 1980s. 'Late-late industrialisers' in Southeast Asia, such as Thailand, Malaysia and Indonesia, have been increasingly able to attract major manufacturing investment. Thailand, especially, has succeeded in securing major investment in electronics since 1985. Its economic growth rate (real GDP) nearly doubled in 1985–90 over the previous five years, to 9.9 per cent. This was largely due to an influx of foreign electronics investment, which is reflected in the fact that this sector accounted for a third of the growth of value added in Thai manufacturing during this period, rising to 40 per cent in the 1990s. Moreover, its share of the total rise of GDP rose from less than 5 per cent in the early 1980s to 16 per cent in the 1990s.[10] With respect to its recent influx of foreign electronics production, Thailand compares quite strongly with Ireland, although the latter is even more dependent on electronics investment as a source of growth. We will return to a discussion of the possible consequences of such deep dependency on outside investors in Chapter 6.

Conclusions: Important Points of Comparison

I have given a basic outline of the nature of the East Asian tiger economies – what it means to be a tiger, and how they got there. We have seen that tigerhood is mainly an economic characteristic of sustained growth. Each of the four East Asian tigers achieved high economic growth rates – greater than 8 per cent per year – and maintained them for several decades. This enabled them to achieve rapid upward mobility in the world economy, rising from low-income non-industrial countries to moderate-income highly industrial countries in a few decades after the Second World War. In doing so, they went through rapid demographic transitions, rapidly increased their agricultural productivities, achieved high rates of savings and investment and attained rapid rates of export growth. In achieving the latter, they each went through periods of industrial upgrading where they moved into progressively 'higher' industrial products, in terms of their technologies of production and the skill levels of their workers.

The East Asian tigers achieved these results, however, not through a single model but through several paths. The most well-known are the South Korean and Taiwanese, where industrial development was based on the creation of strong indigenous sectors. Yet even these two countries differed in the degree to which industrialisation was based on large corporations and holding companies following the Japanese model (South Korea) versus networks of relatively small but technologically advanced companies (Taiwan). In both cases, however, indigenous industries were highly dependent on their networked connections with external suppliers, buyers and distributors, such as the Japanese industrial firms which shed activities to subcontractors in South Korea and Taiwan, or the American retailers who contracted the production of their branded products to East Asia. Partly because of this dependency, several analysts have noted a technological 'glass ceiling', above which neither South Korea and Taiwan have been able to rise, leaving the most profitable high-tech activities in R&D and product development to Japan and the US and, in some cases, Europe.

Singapore, on the other hand, appears to have achieved its growth through an entirely different path, which may be more instructive to the Irish case. Like Ireland, it has been highly dependent on direct investment by leading Japanese and American firms, especially in electronics, as well as internationally traded financial services. These investments were targeted by the Singaporean authorities, much in the same way as the Irish IDA later targeted first electronics and then service investors. On the other hand, there are questions about the degrees of success of Singapore and Ireland in attracting these investments – Singapore appears to have achieved a much greater inflow of investment over a much longer period, so that the continuous inflow of investment may have more than counteracted any negative impacts of foreign penetration on the local economy (the connection between foreign penetration and domestic industrial decline in Ireland will be discussed in Chapter 2). Moreover, the Singaporean state played a very central, some would say decisive, role in its overall economic strategy, becoming directly involved in a number of economic ventures including infrastructural industries and trading companies. We will examine the degree to which the Irish government played such a strong state role, or whether its state was more *laissez-faire* with regard to industry, and the effects of differences between the Irish and Singaporean state on economic success. Finally, of course, Singapore is a city-state, so that its ability to maintain rapid growth through foreign investments may be better compared to an area such as Dublin, rather than to the whole Irish economy. It is worth asking whether such dependency can be more successful for certain regions where foreign investment aggregates, but less positive for outlying regions. This will be an important point of discussion in Chapter 5, on poverty and inequality.

This brings us to a final, most important, conceptual characteristic of economic 'tigerhood', and one that is often overlooked. Those economists and business journalists who concentrate on economic growth and what may cause it, generally ignore the social consequences of different forms of economic change. There is a widespread popular assumption that economic growth will 'trickle down', both in terms of creating employment and in terms of creating wealth. It is often assumed that a 'healthy economy' must be good for society as a whole, without adequate consideration not just of the way the new prosperity is distributed among classes in society, but also of the effects economic growth has on *quality* of life, including quality of work. We cannot simply assume that growth will create jobs. And, even if it does, we cannot assume that these will be *good* jobs, better than those that went before in leaner times. The issues of employment and work will be addressed in Chapter 4. We will examine whether 'tigerhood' has brought positive change for Irish workers, in terms of greater access to work, stability of employment and conditions of work.

Tied to the issues of employment and work are issues of equality and poverty. Chapter 5 will examine the effects of tigerhood on general prosperity in Ireland. *If* Ireland is becoming rich, how has this affected the *least* well off in society? Does the whole Irish population have access to the promises that are held out by economic 'prosperity'?

2 Celtic Kitten

> 'Suppose the people just don't like sago, like me?'
> A very low, unmusical laugh escaped from McPherson.
> 'If they prefer starvation they are welcome.'
> 'Well, how will you get this sago plantation going?'
> 'Sago trees will grow anywhere, and two freighters loaded with shoots will arrive shortly. A simple bill in your parliament expropriating the small farmers and peasants can be passed quickly, with a guarantee that there will be no evictions, or at least very few. You are a young man Hartigan. You will probably live to see your land covered with pathless sago forests, a glorious sight and itself a guarantee of American health, liberty and social cleanliness.'
>
> (Flann O'Brien, *Slattery's Sago Saga*)

Ireland's great modern satirist, Flann O'Brien, wrote *Slattery's Sago Saga* in the 1960s after working as a top civil servant in the Department of the Taoiseach (prime minister). In that position, he closely witnessed southern Ireland's transition from an industrialisation strategy based on protecting indigenous industry to one that was highly dependent on foreign investment from the United States. The freighters loaded with sago shoots and the parliamentary expropriations of small farmers and peasants were his images of the arrival of American investment, if necessary at the price of squeezing out Irish producers. His vision of 'pathless sago forests' sagely foretold the arrival of 'pathless' US electronics companies in today's Celtic Tiger.[1] Yet his satirical tone betrays the impression that O'Brien was less enamoured of this vision of the 'American dream' than many of his contemporaries or, indeed, their counterparts of today.

To understand the southern Irish economy at the end of the twentieth century, we need to know how it got there. As in the case of other (Asian) 'tigers', this is partly the story of a colonial past. Ireland's relationship with the British empire left the newly partitioned country not only with developmental constraints and opportunities, but also with an ideological legacy that raised industrialisation to an imperative. The south's short experience of trying to industrialise through self-sufficiency, and its later transition to an outward-oriented foreign-dominated economy, created the economic regime that today vies for 'tigerhood'.

Before and After Colonialism

'Every time Ireland was about to develop industrially, she was crushed and reconverted into a purely agricultural land.' Such was Karl Marx's evaluation of Ireland's colonial history (Marx and Engels 1971:130–3). While historians of today question many elements of the Marxian and nationalist analyses of British underdevelopment of Ireland, there is truth in Marx's conclusion. Whenever the Irish began to compete, or even to look like competing, with powerful English interests in cattle, woollens or cotton, English policies were implemented to channel the Irish into other, non-competing economic activities (although not always 'purely agricultural'). Historians have successfully argued that British policies were not usually intended to impoverish the Irish (although sometimes that was undoubtedly their intent). Usually, English governments encouraged new economic activities like naval provisioning or linen production in place of the ones they discouraged. They have shown that British policies were sometimes disorganised and contradictory with, for example, certain class or state interests in favour of a policy to restrict an Irish activity and others against (for example, Kearney 1959). And Irish developmental outcomes (industrial decline) were seldom entirely the result of English intentions, but generally some combination of English policy and Irish political economy.

Yet all of these provisos hardly matter. By some combination of design and accident, England continually dominated the leading sectors of its regional and Atlantic economies, from woollens to cotton to engineering. And Ireland like other regions was continually peripheralised as a producer of less profitable and less expansive products – semi-industrial goods like linen in a few regions that were increasingly concentrated in the north-east, and export/subsistence agriculture over most of the island. Failures of Anglo-Irish capitalists to industrialise in wool or cotton are the most common historical tales of underdevelopment, but the more important historical memories for the Irish themselves were the removal of native elites from towns and professions under the penal laws, the marginalisation of native populations into the most barren lands through confiscation and evictions, emigration and starvation. At 'independence', like so many other post-colonial states, the south of Ireland found itself with underdeveloped capitalist and working classes, little industry, and relatively impoverished masses on its lands.

After years of struggle, a section of the Irish nationalist movement signed a treaty with the British in 1921 which copperfastened the partition of the island, as set out in the Government of Ireland Act of the previous year. The Irish Free State comprised only 26 of the 32 counties on the island, the new 'Northern Ireland' just 6 of the 9 counties of Ulster. But the 1921 treaty promoted continuity more than change, dependence more than independence. The Free State bureaucracy, for instance, was modelled on the British bureaucracy and many British-appointed officials remained after partition (Commission of Inquiry 1936). The new state remained in the British Commonwealth and gave British forces access to designated treaty ports. Its economic bonds to England continued. Without the semi-industrialised north-east, agriculture made up nearly half of the economy and over 98 per cent of exports went to Britain. The Irish currency, the punt, was tied to sterling so the country could not control foreign exchange and during sterling crises could not even trade freely with non-sterling areas.

At partition, Ireland had a small but growing industrial working class; a relatively large population of small shopkeepers; and a small professional elite. The first census after partition counted 150,000 industrial workers, many of whom were actually small artisans. The Irish Congress of Trade Unions (ICTU) had 189,000 members, but was strongest in transport and services rather than manufacturing (Meenan 1970:156). Irish agriculture was divided into small farmers, a small agrarian proletariat and a few large farmers. Where only 3 per cent of agrarian workers owned land in 1870, 64 per cent owned their farms by 1921 (Peillon 1982:11). Three-quarters of farms were family-owned farms of less than 50 acres, although 60 per cent of the land was still in the hands of large farmers who owned estates of more than 100 acres.

What little industry remained in the south after partition was mainly brewers, distillers and agricultural processing. Very few firms employed more than 100 people and half employed fewer than 10. Most 'manufacturers' were artisans like smiths and small millers. The largest firms were British-based conglomerates like Guinness, which in 1933 accounted for two-thirds of shares on the Irish stock exchange (Department of Industry and Commerce 1933).

Ironically, the election of a nationalist government in 1932 rather than the Constitution of 1922 brought the first significant economic changes to the Irish Free State. Moderate nationalists led by Eamon de Valera promised economic self-sufficiency and the erection of indigenous industry behind protective barriers. British restrictions on Irish industry made such a strategy popular among Irish nationalists long before it became a standard strategy of development economics in the periphery. Nationalists like Arthur Griffith of Sinn Féin ('We Ourselves') were strongly influenced by protectionist economists like the German Friedrich List and Henry Carey in the US. According to Griffith, 'a nation cannot promote and further its civilisation, its prosperity and its social progress equally as well by exchanging agricultural products for manufactured goods as by establishing a manufacturing power of its own' (Griffith 1918).

With this goal, two months after taking office de Valera's government introduced 43 new tariffs. The list of tariffs increased from 68 articles in 1931 to 281 in 1936. With the addition of import quotas, 2,000 articles were protected by 1938. The government also outlawed foreign investment and established an Industrial Credit Company in 1933 to underwrite new industrial projects and expansions. One observer wrote that 'the last surviving example of a predominantly free trading state left in the world' had become 'one of the most heavily tariffed countries that could be found' (Meenan 1970:142).

Despite a hostile British economic war against Ireland, the new strategy was initially successful. Southern manufacturing output grew by 7.3 per cent annually during 1932–39 and manufacturing employment rose from 62,608 to 101,004. Expansion was particularly rapid in metals, chemicals, cement and glass, clothing and footwear. Yet the new industrialisation strategy was vulnerable to chronic structural problems. The government never restricted imports of industrial raw materials or semi-fabricates in order to encourage their local production, so dependence on imports for key factors of production caused balance of payments problems and bottlenecks. Since new tariffs were introduced mainly at the request of industrialists rather than used strategically to induce new industries, Irish protectionism never induced new producers to step in and produce things that were needed by existing companies. Nor did state industry step in where private industry was unwilling. Only two industrial (alcohol and sugar) and three infrastructural (electricity, airline and shipping) state companies were established by 1945. O'Malley (1989) suggests that the Irish state should have followed a policy of inducing backward linkages during the 1940s and 1950s (along the lines of the later South Korean model). This, he argues, would have been preferable to the export-led and TNC-dependent path the state followed after the late 1950s. Yet it is difficult to imagine the Irish state, with its strong free-enterprise orientation, succeeding in such a programme where even strong dirigiste Latin American states were later to fail. As I argued in Chapter 1, it took the special conditions of South Korea or Taiwan – with a different relationship of dependence to Japan and with the US allowing overlooking their protectionism as a quid pro quo for anti-communism – for such a 'capital deepening' programme to work.

Since the state did not induce domestic capitalists to reinvest after they exploited the profitability of a few 'easy' sectors, Irish profits flowed to British financial markets. From 1939 to 1949, Irish assets held abroad rose dramatically and Irish commercial banks' British holdings more than doubled (Whitaker 1948–49). The Irish regime, committed to free enterprise, did nothing to restrict this outflow.

There is little evidence, however, that the local market was 'exhausted'. A 1949 study by the Department of Industry and Commerce identified imported products that could have been made in Ireland creating 45,000 jobs (*Irish Times*, 10 March 1950). The Department compiled a long list of locally demanded basic products like dyes, steel pipes and paper products that had never been made in Ireland. It concluded that 'there is perhaps, more than a suspicion that manufacturers are content to concentrate upon a limited field which will give them the best return with the minimum of effort'.[2]

Successes of the 1930s were thus related to a phase of 'easy industrialisation' when protection enabled profit-taking in basic goods. Thus, southern Irish industrial growth slowed considerably during the 1940s. Meanwhile, imports from the US trebled from $28 million in 1940 to $95 million in 1949, creating huge dollar trade deficits.[3] US officials did not hesitate to remind the Irish government that only 6 per cent of its dollar income came from exports, the bulk coming equally from tourism and emigrant remittances.[4] Meanwhile, over 90 per cent of Irish exports continued to flow to Britain, earning sterling which was not convertible to dollars.

In response to these unstable economic conditions, fiscal conservatives in the state advocated austerity. In 1949, senior Finance official T.K. Whitaker wrote a seminal memorandum ('Financial policy') attacking excessive spending. The whole southern Irish regime supported restraint on social expenditure, but Finance also wanted to hold down *productive* expenditures. As Ireland's balance of payments deficit grew, Finance gained support after 1951 for austerity budgets which abolished food subsidies, cut social services, and restricted wage rises.

By 1955, four years of austerity policies had taken effect. Industrial production fell that year by 3 per cent, agricultural production by 7 per cent, and GNP by 1.3 per cent. Employment fell by nearly 10 per cent between 1951 and 1956, and when census results revealed that population had declined by 2.11 per cent over that period, the state faced unavoidable pressures for economic change.

Two developments helped determine the direction of economic change: one was the erosion of class support for protected industry; the other was pressure from the US. Class support for protectionism dwindled in the 1940s as economic stagnation discredited southern Irish capital. Membership of the main employers organisation, the Federation of Irish Manufacturers (FIM), fell drastically and the government increasingly refused to listen to its suggestions. If there was a united 'inner circle' of large corporate powers, it was comprised of foreign companies that identified with free trade instead of protection.

As stagnation deepened, some southern state officials made proposals to promote industrial growth. Increasingly after 1947, these proposals responded to an agenda set by transnational capital, the US and Europe. After some early proposals to regulate industry and induce reinvestment, sponsored by the Minister for Industry Sean Lemass, were defeated on the grounds that they violated the state's commitment to free enterprise, reforms centred on attracting new export-oriented projects (O'Hearn 1989). These decisive defeats of Lemass by economic liberals in the Irish state may help explain his later conversion as one of the biggest advocates of liberalisation.

Exports promotion was encouraged by the emerging post-war global environment. As a policy to support its major industries, the US state pushed an 'open door' policy for its trade and investment throughout the world (McCormick 1989, Shoup and Minter 1977). This hegemonic strategy allowed vertically-integrated TNCs to rapidly process intermediate products through different stages of production, thus lowering costs and increasing productivity (Chandler 1990, Arrighi 1995). At the end of the production chain, the expansion of markets was necessary to sell this higher throughput and realise profits. The Marshall Plan, in particular, opened doors since the US gave reconstruction aid to Europe in return for freer access to its markets and former colonies. American post-war expansion required a stable, non-communist, integrated, free-trading Europe.

Ireland participated in the Marshall Plan to raise money for development programmes and to fight its balance of payments problem. In return, it had to participate in the rapid liberalisation of European trade. This made it impossible to maintain protectionist industrialisation policies. Moreover, the US strongly pressed the Irish government to introduce unilateral reforms to encourage exports and foreign investment. These included setting up an industrial development authority, providing grants and tax incentives to foreign investors and removing laws that restricted foreign investments and trade (O'Hearn 1990a).

The Irish government quickly responded to pressure. In 1948 it established the IDA, which became the single most important institution charged with attracting new industry to Ireland. In the early 1950s, boards were established to encourage exports (Coras Trachtala) and to administer grants for (overwhelmingly foreign) investors who promised to export their product (An Foras Tionscal). Throughout the early 1950s measures were taken, both unilaterally and in concert with the Organization for European Economic Co-operation (OEEC), to remove import restrictions. In late 1956 the Taoiseach announced a series of investment incentives that would become the hallmark of a new strategy of foreign-led industrialisation. Although he promised to favour home investment over foreign investment, these outward-oriented incentives were tacit admission that domestic industrialisation was dead. Acts of 1956–58 extended capital grants for new investors, gave full profits-tax relief to manufactured exports, removed restrictions on foreign investment and gave the IDA extended powers to seek out and encourage foreign investment. Ireland joined the IMF and World Bank in 1957. But these were only the end products of a new policy direction that irrevocably began with the establishment of the IDA and other bodies in the early 1950s at the suggestion of the US administration, closely followed by the OEEC-imposed programme of liberalising trade.

Foreign Investment and Irish Industry

Large numbers of TNCs responded to the new policies and set up subsidiaries in the south, especially after Ireland entered the European Economic Community (EEC) in 1973. Foreign investment grew by more than 27 per cent per annum during 1974–81, spurred particularly by the arrival of US-owned electronics, pharmaceuticals and health care firms. During the 1970s, nearly half of fixed capital investment in manufacturing came from TNCs who desired duty-free access to the large and growing EEC market. Yet *real* growth rates of foreign investment were lower – much of the 1970s was a time of rampant inflation – and they even fell during periods such as 1971–74 and most of the 1980s. Even the partial recovery of investment in 1991 and 1993, as Ireland became a 'Celtic tiger', was well below the real investment levels of 1976–83.[5]

The absolute levels of investment, however, understate the impact of foreign penetration. Some infrastructural investments associated with foreign manufacturing were made by the state rather than by TNCs. In addition, capital investments in electronic and chemical companies, despite their high-tech character, were low because their production tends to be intensive in materials rather than fixed capital (this 'investmentless' character of dependent industrialisation in Ireland is analysed further in Chapter 3). Overall, TNC subsidiaries directly accounted for about a third of fixed capital investments in manufacturing during 1960–94, and indirectly for an unknown amount of infrastructural investments made on their behalf.

In terms of employment, by the 1960s the vast majority of new manufacturing jobs were in TNC subsidiaries. While early projects produced basic products, American electronics and pharmaceutical firms began to arrive in large numbers after Ireland joined the EEC in 1973 to gain free access to the European market. Even in high-tech sectors like computers, however, relatively unskilled operations like final assembly for re-export to the continent were located in Ireland. As domestic employment fell under EEC-mandated free trade, American TNCs became the undisputed centre of industry in Ireland.

The IDA regularly claims credit for attracting the new post-1973 'modern' foreign investment because it identified electronics in 1974 as recession-resistant and concentrated on attracting American firms in that sector (see, for example, Killeen 1979). In a sense, its success was also its undoing. Employment in foreign companies rose mainly because the IDA attracted ever greater numbers of TNCs to Ireland each year, not because existing projects were expanding and reinvesting. As time went on, the southern Irish state relied more and more heavily on attracting greater numbers of new firms each year to meet its employment targets. The employment problem was exacerbated because electronics and pharmaceutical firms employed fewer people on average than foreign firms in other sectors. The average size of foreign computer firms fell from 509 employees in 1973 to 156 in 1986 with the entry of a new wave of smaller firms. Overall, average employment in TNC subsidiaries fell from 111 in 1980 to 91 in 1985. Thus, when TNCs stopped coming in adequate numbers economic stagnation and widespread unemployment resulted. In 1979, the IDA optimistically forecast that electronics employment could grow to 30,000 by 1985, with over a third in highly skilled job categories (Killeen 1979:14). In the event, according to unpublished IDA survey data less than 19,000 were employed there in 1985, less than a quarter of these in highly skilled jobs. Employment in all foreign sectors fell rapidly in the 1980s and did not recover until after 1990.

Put in its global context, the shift to American investment came during a period when rapidly increasing world-wide investment in high-tech sectors such as electronics coincided with Ireland's accession to the EEC. Free imports of intermediate goods into Ireland and re-exports of final products into Europe were (and are) powerful attractions for American-based firms. Ireland's incentives and lack of governmental regulations made it especially attractive to US producers seeking a foothold or expansion in Europe. The shift to electronics and pharmaceuticals partly counteracted stagnating foreign investment in other sectors during the 1970s. But widespread global restructuring in the 1980s led even leading-sector TNCs either to cut back their Irish employment or leave altogether, causing a severe unemployment crisis.

Despite chronic unemployment, public illusion is often more important than reality in providing legitimacy to economic strategies. As economic growth resurged and emigration halted during the early 1960s, there was widespread feeling that this 'miracle' was caused by opening up the Irish economy to foreign industrial investment, despite evidence that the economic upturn was more a result of Keynesian fiscal policies (see Kennedy and Dowling 1975). A second 'Irish miracle' occurred with the upturn in foreign investment after 1973, giving the illusion that EEC membership would bring prosperity (the image of prosperity was enhanced as EEC price supports raised rural incomes for some years). Yet prominent public announcements of new foreign investment and 'job approvals'[6] were the flip-side of a disastrous but quiet collapse of indigenous industry due to the same EEC free trade policies that attracted the foreign investment.

The removal of protection during the 1960s and 1970s left indigenous industries dangerously vulnerable to competition from imports. Between 1960 and 1980, imports took over Irish markets for virtually every category of manufactured goods. A country which had virtually clothed and shod itself in 1960 imported more than 77 per cent of its clothing in 1980. Imports replaced domestic products in textiles, leather, chemicals, metals and machinery and miscellaneous manufactures. The share of imports in non-electric machinery rose from 55 per cent to more than 98 per cent, a clear difference between Ireland and export-oriented industrialisers like Korea and Taiwan, which eventually succeeded in exporting machinery. Overall, a country which produced 60 per cent of the manufactures it consumed in 1960, imported more than 60 per cent in 1980.

The effects of such a large-scale influx of manufactured imports were predictable, although they were largely ignored by the Irish media and experts. After Irish entry into the EEC, indigenous firms began to collapse. By 1980, employment in Irish firms that were established under protection fell by over 80 per cent in textiles and clothing, and by more than half in chemicals, metal products and miscellaneous manufactures. Only 15 of the largest domestic industrial companies (employing more than 500) remained in 1986, and all but one of these were in sheltered or food sectors.[7] While some job losses were due to the replacement of workers by machines during restructuring, most jobs were lost to closures (82 per cent in chemicals, 72 per cent in clothing, 65 per cent in textiles, and 52 per cent in manufacturing as a whole). Three-quarters of domestic clothing firms, two-thirds of textile firms, and half of metals/engineering firms failed within 13 years after Ireland joined the EEC. Overall, 44 per cent of indigenous firms closed.

Again, the devastation of Irish domestic industry differs from experiences in export-oriented industrialisers in East Asia. What distinguished the Irish regime from these regimes was its near complete adherence to free trade after the 1950s. Since free trade was necessary for the attraction of TNCs, which was considered to be the 'engine' of export-oriented growth after 1960, the destruction of Irish indigenous industry is best viewed as an *external diseconomy* of foreign penetration.

The new domestic firms that were established after 1973 were very small. Average domestic firm size fell from 39 employees in 1973 to 18 in 1986. The modal new domestic 'firm' was a man with welding equipment or woodworking tools in his back yard who serviced domestic homeowners, very much like the situation that prevailed at partition. The rapid decline of larger Irish firms meant foreign industry came to dominate large-scale manufacturing in Ireland while indigenous industry became dominated by the tiny firm.

Foreign Industry: Engine of Modernity or a Periphery Once Again?

Foreign-dominated industrialisation came to Ireland with the promise that it would finally propel Ireland to modernity, where it could take its place among its European neighbours. One hope was that foreign companies, as the most modern and productive economic institutions in the world, would transfer modern technologies and ways of organising production to the general Irish economy. As an early proponent of foreign-led industrialisation claimed, 'by far the most hopeful means of getting good management, technical knowledge and capital all at once is from subsidiaries of large foreign companies ... a plant which is paid for by foreign capital is a great deal better than one which has to be paid for from the scanty savings of the Republic' (Carter 1957:140). Moreover, the new orthodoxy claimed that exports were an engine of growth and that foreign investors, by exporting their products, would earn foreign exchange that could be turned to broader programmes for economic development. In the popular phrase of the day, a prosperous foreign sector would be the 'rising tide that lifts all boats'. These attitudes partly reflected the dominant modernisationist ethos of the time, and partly just recognised that the globalisation and 'Europeanisation' of Ireland was an unstoppable force.

In reality, the strength of the foreign 'tide' to lift the domestic economy, at least before the 1990s, was limited. One chronic limitation, which increased as foreign industrial dominance increased, was the degree to which transnational corporations took away the profits they received from their Irish operations. Levels of profit repatriations increased over time as foreign corporations reinvested very little in Ireland. Of course, the initial foreign investment was a positive economic contribution but low reinvestment rates removed economic 'multipliers' that could have encouraged sustained growth.

IDA surveys show a stark difference between TNC and indigenous profit levels, with foreign companies receiving the vast majority of profits in Irish manufacturing. During 1983–90, Irish-owned firms received averaged profit rates of just 2.7 per cent while TNCs averaged 21.4 per cent (Table 2.1).[8] US companies received even more: pharmaceuticals subsidiaries averaged 45.4 per cent profit rates and all US subsidiaries averaged 29.3 per cent.[9] As discussed in Chapter 3, however, there is increasing concern that a large part of these profits are just an illusion, produced when corporations transfer their profits to low-tax havens like Ireland by manipulating the internal 'transfer prices' at which they sell products from one of their subsidiaries to another.[10] Whether profits are 'real' or just a result of creative accounting, however, the question remains: where do they go? Are they are reinvested to multiply economic growth in Ireland, or are they removed to other regions of the world?

Table 2.1 Profit rates for Irish firms and TNCs (profits as % of sales), 1983–90

			US TNCs: of which			*TNC share of*
Year	*Irish*	*TNCs*	*Computer*	*Pharm.*	*Total*	*total profits*
1983	–0.27	19.03	25.51	36.57	24.17	101.87
1984	1.75	21.73	29.72	47.10	30.82	91.47
1985	1.42	20.27	27.14	48.25	29.27	93.00
1986	2.50	19.73	25.97	48.68	29.17	87.03
1987	3.06	22.58	29.26	42.86	29.54	87.96
1988	4.27	22.62	31.41	40.96	30.28	84.93
1989	5.13	22.10	23.46	49.45	28.97	85.05
1990	3.88	23.48	32.40	49.38	32.18	86.61

Source: unpublished IDA survey data.

The data in Table 2.2 indicate that foreign companies reinvest very little of their profits in Ireland. Indeed, they repatriated an increasing share of their profits during the 1980s and by 1985 they repatriated all of them. In some years, TNCs repatriated more profits than they received. Thus, the high profitability of foreign firms in Ireland does little to increase Irish investment but instead accrues to other regions of the world economy.

Finally, Figure 2.1 compares foreign profit repatriations with total corporate profits received in the south of Ireland. In the early 1970s, TNCs were already repatriating a fifth of total corporate profits (industry *and* services) there. This proportion rose rapidly with the entry of US capital and the demise of large sections of Irish-owned industry. By the late 1980s half of the profits received in Ireland were repatriated abroad, and this rose to 55 per cent in the mid-1990s. Thus, not only did some 12 per cent of GDP comprise of repatriated profits by the 1990s, an amount that is completely lost to Ireland, but half of the capital available for accumulation goes to other regions of the world economy. Most of the remaining 45 per cent accrues to corporations in services, commerce, and real estate and very little of this is reinvested in industry.

Table 2.2 Profits received and repatriated by TNC subsidiaries in the south of Ireland, 1983–90 (I£ million)

Year	*(1) Profits in US-owned leading sectors**	*(2) TNC profits*	*(3) Repatriated profits*	*(4) (1) / (2)*	*(5) (3) / (2)*
1983	678	936	659	.724	.704
1984	1,070	1,372	940	.780	.685
1985	1,097	1,405	1,321	.781	.940
1986	947	1,291	1,358	.734	1.052
1987	1,108	1,712	1,442	.647	.842
1988	1,331	1,958	2,093	.680	1.069
1989	1,281	2,114	2,564	.606	1.213
1990	1,609	2,297	2,507	.700	1.091
1983–90	9,121	13,085	12,884	.697	.985

* US metals/engineering and chemicals sectors. These sectors are dominated by computers and pharmaceuticals, respectively.

Source: calculations from unpublished IDA data.

The problem is not simply that such large resources are removed from the southern Irish economy, but also the distortions this

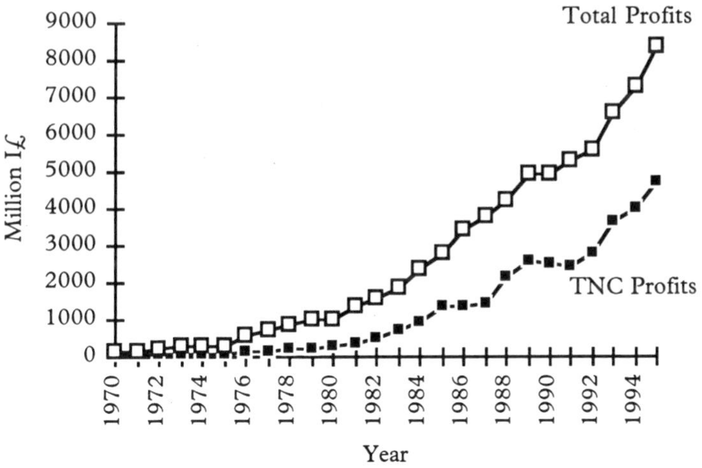

Source: CSO.

Figure 2.1 TNC profits and total corporate profits in the south of Ireland, 1970–95

causes. The development of a diversified industrial structure is impeded because TNCs divert potential industrial resources abroad, while the resources that remain in the local economy are concentrated in non-productive service and commercial sectors.

Their failure to reinvest locally is not the only reason why foreign companies have had limited effects on broader Irish development. In core regions of North America, Europe and Asia large corporations are often centres of innovation – they induce clusters of other activities which aggregate regionally. But TNCs in Ireland do not appear to create *linkages* with other firms, either to supply them with intermediate goods and services or to process their products further. Once this became apparent from some early studies (see, for example, Telesis 1982), the IDA launched a 'national linkages programme' in 1985, which aspired to tie specific American-owned subsidiaries to existing domestic suppliers with five- to seven-year targets for increased local purchases. There were no attempts to induce *new* activities to produce an expanding range of products for the TNCs. Nor, because of EEC free trade regulations, could the state use East Asian-style state policies of protecting and cajoling private capital to enter new activities.

Table 2.3 shows how few inputs TNCs bought in Ireland during the 1980s. Irish firms spent about 44 per cent of the value of their sales on Irish materials, almost three times as much as TNCs (12 per cent) and more than seven times as much as American firms (6 per cent). US subsidiaries in computers and pharmaceuticals, which have dominated the 'miracle' recovery of the Irish 'Celtic tiger' economy in the 1990s, spent the least on local materials (6.7 per cent and 3.25 per cent, respectively).

Further analysis of IDA data for the period shows that TNCs spent so little in Ireland primarily because they import their materials, often from other subsidiaries of their parent company. Both domestic and foreign companies spent about the same proportion of their total costs on material inputs. Thus, foreign companies were not particularly efficient in their use of materials, they simply bought less locally.

Low local spending levels would be more acceptable if TNCs bought more in Ireland over time, as they identified or encouraged local suppliers. But this does not appear to be the case since American-owned pharmaceutical and computer companies bought about the same proportion of their material purchases in Ireland in 1990 as in 1983. This failure to improve after more than a decade of IDA linkage programmes indicates that Ireland has little hope to increase the local buying behaviour of foreign firms.[11]

Table 2.3 Irish-sourced material purchases as % of sales in selected industrial sectors, by nationality of ownership, 1983–90

Sector	*Irish-sourced material inputs as % of total output*							
	1983	*1984*	*1985*	*1986*	*1987*	*1988*	*1989*	*1990*
Food								
Irish	67.78	66.20	65.13	63.67	2.88	60.26	61.57	61.38
TNC	44.13	43.55	35.00	34.39	36.02	37.27	39.18	39.60
Textiles								
Irish	8.42	7.47	8.55	9.92	26.14	25.37	10.61	7.45
TNC	4.49	3.86	8.45	7.84	9.25	9.52	6.45	5.38
Clothing								
Irish	18.75	10.25	11.88	25.20	24.35	10.41	8.32	8.45
TNC	9.70	6.85	5.46	4.20	5.18	7.13	6.77	5.80
Chemicals								
Irish	24.94	17.98	17.39	19.12	20.57	33.43	37.40	31.11
TNC	6.91	4.83	6.42	5.63	5.50	5.88	5.96	6.35
of which: US	*8.67*	*6.12*	*6.23*	*4.53*	*4.76*	*5.42*	*6.52*	*6.95*
Metals/ engineering								
Irish	12.69	11.37	20.36	17.35	14.80	15.43	16.87	15.07
TNC	5.40	4.97	4.71	5.15	5.52	6.08	6.60	6.85
of which: US	*4.59*	*4.45*	*4.35*	*4.93*	*4.90*	*5.15*	*5.85*	*5.74*
Miscellaneous mnfrs.								
Irish	13.50	9.85	10.28	10.90	6.27	7.92	7.33	7.62
TNC	6.98	9.70	9.87	8.45	8.97	9.53	9.85	8.79
Total manufacturing								
Irish	47.96	42.31	44.63	44.54	44.78	40.72	41.94	41.97
TNC	13.30	12.43	11.15	11.23	12.09	12.63	11.66	12.02
of which: US	6.53	5.04	5.17	5.59	5.44	6.49	7.52	7.58

Source: author's calculations from unpublished IDA survey data.

While TNCs buy few materials in Ireland, they do appear to buy local services. In 1990, for example, TNCs spent nearly as much on local services as Irish companies. While Irish firms bought 85 per cent of their services in Ireland, TNCs bought 80 per cent of their services in Ireland, a factor that would be partly responsible for a rapid rise in service employment in the 1990s (see Chapter 4). On the other hand, many of these 'local purchases' are internationally traded services and computer services bought from other foreign subsidiaries. The fact that TNCs encourage local service firms but not local manufacturers, however, reinforces the problem of an imbalance in the southern Irish economy between underdeveloped indigenous industry and oversized indigenous service sectors. Such services are relatively low-wage and low-profit activities.

Little need be said about TNCs encouraging local firms to use their products for further industrial processing, because they export nearly all of their output. American companies come to Ireland mainly to get their goods into European markets. American computer and pharmaceutical firms exported more than 98 per cent of their output (in Chapter 3, I will discuss the relationship of these exports to southern Ireland's recent rapid economic growth). Finally, several studies have shown that TNCs have induced few 'spin-offs,' where their former employees create new firms to produce related products (O'Brien 1985, Eolas 1989).

Overall, the evidence clearly indicates that TNC subsidiaries in the south of Ireland, while concentrated in sectors with especially high profit rates and innovative production techniques, do not transfer these advantages to the local economy. Foreign sector profits are repatriated to other subsidiaries abroad while foreign firms do not link among themselves or with Irish producers. 'Innovative clusters' are bounded by the global firms and the core regions where they operate, but do not extend beyond its subsidiaries to the surrounding sectors or firms of their semi-peripheral host regions.

Exports and Industrialisation

Irish development strategy after 1960 was deceptively simple: attract as much foreign industry as possible, increase exports as much as possible, and economic development will follow (Kennedy and Dowling 1975, chapter 4). In terms of foreign investment and exports, southern Ireland has been highly successful. Exports grew in real terms at an annual rate of 9 per cent from 1960 to 1990. Manufactured exports grew even more rapidly, and exports of pharmaceuticals and computers more rapidly still. Foreign capital investment grew annually by about 15 per cent in real terms from 1960 to 1980. Thus, the 'engine' of growth was running rapidly and smoothly.

But rapid growth in 'target' variables like exports and foreign investments clearly failed to create rapid economic growth, full employment, or general material well-being before the 'Celtic tiger' emerged in the 1990s (Table 2.4). Real gross national product (GNP) grew by less than 2 per cent during 1960–86. Between the time Ireland joined the EC and 1986, GNP growth rates plunged to 0.1 per cent and manufacturing employment fell by 0.4 per cent per year.

During the early 1960s, a number of Irish observers noted Ireland's 'remarkable' growth rates, which they attributed to economic planning and the growth of manufacturing industry. Others since referred to Ireland as a 'high growth' economy (Cypher 1979). Until the 1990s at least, the facts simply did not bear this out. The highest single-year growth rate of per capita GNP in the early 1960s was 5.3 per cent, but the growth rate for three of the five years from 1960 to 1965 was less than 3.5 per cent. After 1965 economic growth declined considerably, remaining below 3 per cent throughout most of the 1970s. In the first six years of the 1980s the south of Ireland experienced unprecedented economic stagnation, unmatched even by the recession of the mid-1950s. During that time, per capita GNP never grew by even 1 per cent in any year and in three years it declined.

Table 2.4 Average annual rates of growth of exports, foreign investment and GNP, 1960–94 (constant prices)

	Policy targets			*Developmental goals*			
Year	*Total exports*	*Ind. exports*	*TNC investments*	*GNP per capita*	*GDP per capita*	*Employment Total*	*Employment Mfg.*
1960–73	8.03	10.46	25.57	3.51	3.63	0.01	2.24
1973–86	8.01	10.37	11.14	0.65	2.01	0.10	–0.43
1986–94	9.69	10.10	1.03	3.96	4.42	1.12	1.29
1960–94	8.41	10.34	14.28	2.63	3.19	0.48	1.06

Source: CSO.

The rapid fall of growth rates after 1973 raises the question of whether EEC membership somehow caused economic stagnation. But particularly low and negative economic growth rates during 1973–76 and the mid-1980s suggest that periods of world recession may have contributed to Irish stagnation. Or, perhaps EEC membership somehow made the south of Ireland more vulnerable to the effects of world-wide recession. O'Hearn (1990a) found that TNC investment flows had positive effects on economic growth, but that the stock of TNC-*penetration* had negative growth effects. In other words, all foreign investment directly caused immediate economic activity and growth, but as the foreign sector got larger it began to have negative effects on the Irish economy. This was mainly an indirect process. Foreign companies require free trade to import the things they need to produce their products, and then to freely export them. But in Ireland's case free trade also brought a flood of foreign products which drove domestic Irish producers out of business and discouraged domestic investment. Similar arguments have been advanced by O'Malley (1989) and Mjøset (1993).

While free trade and foreign investment crowded out Irish industrial companies, thus transferring many of industry's 'developmental' effects outward, they also transformed the Irish economic structure. Textiles and clothing declined after 1973 while food, drink, wood, paper and clay simply stagnated. Yet metals, chemicals and other manufacturing – where foreign investment was highest – experienced rapid growth after Ireland entered the EEC.

If post-EEC economic growth rates were unsatisfactory up until the 1990s, the effects of foreign domination on employment were dismal. Foreign companies generally used less labour for a given level of investment than the domestic firms they replaced; and they did not replace domestic firms in adequate numbers to counteract their low labour-intensity. Thus, the southern Irish unemployment crisis reached its heights in the mid-1980s, when some estimates accounted it at 20 per cent and above (Figure 2.2).[12] By any reckoning, Irish unemployment rates have been among the highest in the EU since the mid-1980s, exceeded only by Spain.

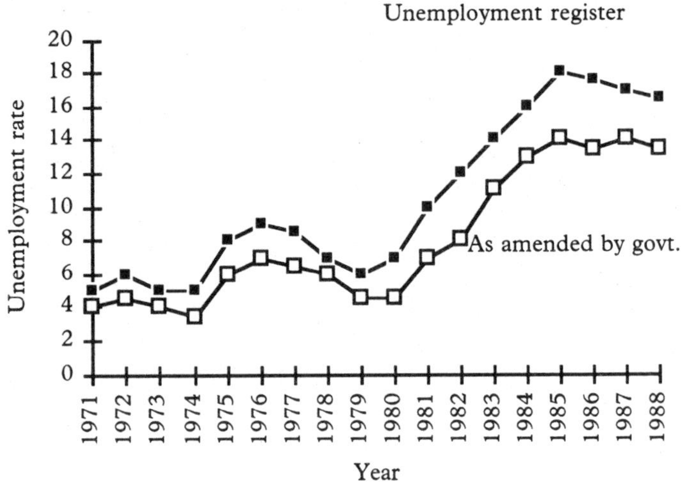

Source: CSO.

Figure 2.2 Unemployment rate in the south of Ireland, 1971–88

Unemployment rates rose and remained high despite rapid emigration. Between 1982 and 1993, some 472,300 people emigrated from the south of Ireland (Courtney 1995:68). If they had remained, the unemployment rate would have been higher still. Unlike the general shame that accompanied high emigration during the 1950s, however, it was actively encouraged as a policy variable to reduce unemployment by the late 1980s. A well-known Irish economic journalist, for example, called emigration 'part of the natural order of things' while the southern Tánaiste spoke approvingly of emigration as a policy alternative in the American magazine *Newsweek*.

Above and beyond its high levels, unemployment became a more serious social problem during the 1980s because it changed from predominantly short-term to predominantly long-term. While 36.9 per cent of the unemployed were out of work for more than one year in 1983, one of the lowest proportions in Europe, 67.2 per cent were long-term unemployed by 1990, by far the highest rate in the EU (OECD 1992a) (in the north, 50 per cent were long-term unemployed in 1992 (Borooah 1993:6,15)).

Northern and Southern Irish Economic Change Compared

As serious as economic problems seemed in the south of Ireland in the 1980s, they were far worse in the north. As limited as southern options were for fashioning an industrialisation strategy, Northern options were limited even more. By the time the south embarked on its new industrialisation policies in the 1950s, it had partially delinked its industrial economy from Britain's, although its agrarian exports still depended on English markets. The new policies shifted southern economic dependence from England to the US.

Although the north was more industrialised and materially better off than the south at partition, it remained politically and economically dependent on Britain. Its economy remained subservient to British economic interests and highly concentrated in agriculture, linen and shipbuilding. These were generally lower-wage and 'lower-tech' than English or even Scottish industries, with severely constrained markets for their products. Linen production had grown in Belfast only because it concentrated there from rural regions – Ireland actually produced more linen in 1830 than in the 1900s. This narrowly based economy was thus precipitously vulnerable to collapse. And its subservience to London limited its alternative strategy choices when collapse came.

Northern economic decline followed British commercial and industrial decline in the early twentieth century. The linen industry collapsed with the introduction of synthetic fibres and shipbuilding was hit by British maritime decline and competition from new producers (Isles and Cuthbert, 1957). By 1940, Northern unemployment stood at 20 per cent, its social services were far below British standards, infant mortality and overcrowding were high and per capita income was half the British average (Rowthorn and Wayne, 1988).

By the 1950s and 1960s, a new set of differences between the southern and Northern economies was emerging. Following the southern example, Northern governments regularly asked London for the power to introduce similar programmes to attract foreign capital, but the British government refused most of their requests. British governments bluntly informed Northern Irish representatives that England had its own deindustrialised regions, so it could not allow the north special status. Northern officials bemoaned the fact that British ministers and bureaucrats felt that 'there is political kudos to be gained for getting a new industry into a "grey" spot on their list [but] there is none if it goes to Northern Ireland'.[13]

Programmes that were allowed were introduced more tentatively than in the south. Northern investment grants, for example, were lower than in the south. Moreover, southern programmes were more stable because they were sponsored by a committed Irish state rather than a lukewarm distant government.

Once its deindustrialisation became intolerable in the 1970s, the north was allowed to extend larger grants to foreign investors with fewer strings attached.[14] Yet it still faced disadvantages, including its 40 per cent corporate tax rate compared to a southern 10 per cent rate. Moreover, foreign investors have been attracted to the south not just by economic incentives but by the political support which has been consistent since the 1950s. The north, on the other hand, never even had a specialised state body like the southern IDA to attract foreign investment until the Industrial Development Board (IDB) was established in 1982. Until then, various state departments shared responsibilities for attracting and administering foreign investment.

Once foreign investors began to agglomerate in the south, as in other regions like Singapore, more followed in their wake. Instead of attracting companies from Europe and the US, however, the north in the 1950s and 1960s attracted mainly English companies in synthetic textiles and other basic industrial products. The synthetic textiles industry in the north was dominated by three English firms – Courtaulds, ICI and British Enkalon – whose collective employment grew rapidly from 1,500 in the 1950s to 9,000 in 1973 (7 per cent of the Northern manufacturing workforce). But it fell just as quickly to 1,000 in 1982 (NIEC 1983:38).[15]

As war made the north an unattractive site for foreign investment, English investment dried up while existing English subsidiaries failed. Competition for new investments increased, not just with the south of Ireland but also with Britain, whose industry had declined so thoroughly that they, too, sought offshore investment. By 1990, Britain attracted 40 per cent of inward manufacturing investment into the European Union. But these projects were located predominantly in England, where Japanese companies in particular combined their preference for English-speaking workers with access to pan-EU markets and highly developed infrastructures that facilitated greater flexibility, subcontracting relations, and just-in-time production methods. Like other TNCs, especially in the 1990s, Japanese firms tended to locate nearby other Japanese firms, so that their location in England had a cumulative effect. Scotland and Wales received a share of foreign investment, but mainly competed with the south of Ireland and other parts of the European periphery.

Although many analysts and Northern politicians have blamed the war for deindustrialisation, other factors were primarily responsible. Even before the 1970s, there was a clear difference between Northern and southern patterns of investment. During 1966–71, for instance, only 10 plants from outside Britain located in the north, compared to 94 in the south (Rowthorn, 1981:9). The most successful single year for attracting new foreign investment was 1961, when 5,811 jobs were promised in new foreign projects (although only about one-third of these actually materialised) (NIEC 1983). Afterwards, the number of jobs promised in new foreign investment began falling rapidly, to less than 150 jobs per year in the mid-1970s. While these numbers probably would not have fallen as far in the absence of conflict, it remains clear that factors other than war were primarily responsible for the north's inability to attract foreign investment. The most important factors were its structural dependence on British investment and its political subservience to British policy makers, which tied the Northern economy to a source of manufacturing investment that was in rapid decline, while keeping it from creating a culture of attracting more expansive foreign firms.

Employment in non-British foreign subsidiaries in the south increased at twice the rate of the north during the 1960s. As American companies began entering the south in large numbers in order to gain duty-free access to the common market, the combination of British disinvestment and insufficient new foreign investment produced the opposite result of rapid industrial decline in the north. The Northern Irish share of inward manufacturing investment into the 'United Kingdom', which was only 4 per cent in the early 1970s, fell below 2 per cent by the 1990s.[16] As a result, manufacturing employment halved between 1955 and 1985, falling yet further in the 1990s. As Figure 2.3 indicates, Northern manufacturing decline cannot simply be attributed to war because it so closely follows the British pattern, although more severely and from a lower employment base.

As a result of their different experiences of inward investment, the Northern and southern industrial economies were distinctively different by 1990, when 629 non-British transnational companies employed 73,800 people in the south compared to just 86 such subsidiaries employing 17,826 people in the north (Hamilton, 1992:39–40). Moreover, just 27 per cent of foreign employment in the south was in the more traditional food, clothing and textiles sectors, while 58 per cent (and rising) was in metals, engineering

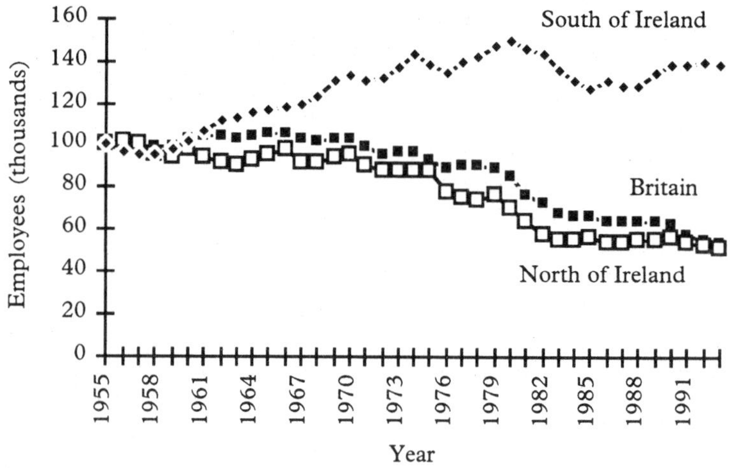

Sources: CSO (Ireland), CSO (London), N. Ireland Annual Abstract.

Figure 2.3 Manufacturing employment in Britain and Ireland, 1955–93

and chemicals. The Northern structure was the opposite: 51 per cent in food, clothing, or textiles and only 34 per cent in metals, engineering or chemicals. Overall, manufacturing fell below one-fifth of Northern employment, while services swelled to three-quarters.

Like the south, the north has chronic unemployment and under-employment – the first partly disguised by a sectarian segmented labour market where Catholic men are consistently unemployed at two and a half times the rates of Protestant men; the second, by the rising proportion of part-time women employees in services. The Northern Irish have been protected from the worst effects of economic decline, however, by British-subsidised social welfare and employment programmes. Some estimates put this fiscal subvention at more than £4 billion per annum (excluding most military costs) in the 1990s, funding half of Northern state expenditure. Under Thatcher, however, British living standards crumbled so rapidly that the southern standard of living began to catch up with and exceed the north in many respects (Goodman 1996:162–5).

The north's dependence on British subsidies, government-sponsored jobs and welfare led one economist to refer to the region as a 'vast workhouse in which most of the inmates are engaged in servicing and controlling each other' (Rowthorn 1987:117–18). Like a workhouse or prison, the gap between revenues and costs is paid by taxing an external population.

Conclusions

Ireland in the 1980s was in a kind of funk. The immediate optimism of EC membership which, at least in the south, brought short-term industrial growth through foreign investment and a transitory rise in income for some farmers, had turned into a nightmare of emigration and unemployment. Much of the blame for this economic despondency lay with a system that favoured foreign over domestic industry, at a time when not enough foreign industry was investing in Ireland to counteract the decline of Irish business. Ireland drew its radical outward strategy from the prevailing ideology that favoured export-orientation and free trade and, as time went on, this ideology seemed to be affirmed by the rise of the export-oriented East Asian tigers and the failure of the state-directed Latin American economies. But the southern Irish state did not adopt the *whole* East Asian model, which (with the partial exception of Singapore) favoured domestic rather than foreign industry as its main exporters and backbone of industrialisation.

The nature of the foreign sector was itself a problem. While it appeared vibrant in some terms, its vibrancy did not spread to the economy in general. The differences between the local developmental effects of foreign and domestic firms in 1990, as Ireland was on the verge of becoming a 'tiger economy', are summarised in Table 2.5. American-owned computer and pharmaceuticals firms accounted for 15.9 per cent of industrial output in the south of Ireland in 1990, but they accounted for only 3 per cent of local material purchases by industrial companies. Likewise, forward linkages from American computer and pharmaceuticals subsidiaries were non-existent. Since they exported more than 98 per cent of their product, their share of Irish industrial exports was 26 per cent, much higher than their share of output (as we shall see in Chapter 3, their export share is inflated by corporate accounting practices). American TNCs as a whole account for more than two-thirds of Ireland's non-food exports, although they produce only a third of industrial output. This kind of disconnected economy was entirely at odds with the kinds of networks that formed the basis of East Asian successes, where industrial and distributing firms were closely linked in networks where the successes of one group of firms reinforced and encouraged the growth of scores of suppliers and buyers.

Table 2.5 Contribution of leading US-owned sectors to Irish industrial categories, 1990

Sector	*% of output*	*% of exports*	*% of profits*	*% of total Irish purchases*	*% of Irish material purchases*	*% of Irish service purchases*	*% of wages paid*
(1) Computers	10.44	16.92	24.17	5.05	1.38	11.71	4.44
(2) Pharmaceuticals	5.47	9.07	19.28	2.23	1.65	3.29	4.52
(1) and (2)	15.91	25.99	43.45	7.28	3.03	15.00	8.96
All US TNCs	33.22	51.83	76.36	18.37	10.06	33.43	25.24

Source: author's calculations from survey data supplied by the IDA.

Another pair of categories is of particular interest. Leading-sector American TNCs in 1990 received 43.5 per cent of the industrial profits accumulated in the south of Ireland – three times their share of output (American TNCs overall received more than three-quarters of industrial profits). Yet they paid only 9 per cent of industrial wages. While these TNCs created little spending on local products through wages, they repatriated their superprofits rather than reinvesting them. Thus, the largest beneficiaries of the efforts of Irish industrial labour were TNC parent companies and regions outside of Ireland.

There has never been much public criticism of the fact that southern Ireland's development strategy has benefited external regions and classes more than the Irish economy. EU membership limits southern Irish policy choices and gives the state little choice of economic strategy and policy instruments, just as the north is severely constrained under the union with Britain – so, from one point of view, there is little point in complaining when it is difficult to develop strategic alternatives that are much better. Any radical departure from a strategy of TNC-dependent industrialisation would arguably involve a break from the EU, which in turn would leave Ireland politically isolated and economically marginalised. Yet neither was there great optimism before the 1990s that Ireland could attain the same level of prosperity as its continental partners in the EU. Spurts of optimism accompanied short-lived periods of rapid inward investment in the early 1960s and the 1970s. But the 1980s – with its high unemployment, stagnation, and rampant public debt – appeared to bring a prospect where the best Ireland could hope for was to attract as many foreign investments as possible, perhaps encourage the odd indigenous industrial venture in some small niche, and rely on European handouts for the foreseeable future. Economic pessimism translated culturally into a kind of national inferiority complex, perhaps most apparent in the widespread guilt-ridden breast-beating that accompanied each action by the IRA in England or the north. Various forms of Irish cultural identity, from traditional and folk music to nationalist literature and history, were often suspect of IRA sympathies. All of this changed practically overnight in the 1990s, with the emergence of an apparently vibrant economy and a confident culture that came to be known as the 'Celtic tiger'.

3 The Most Wonderful Thing about Tiggers: Economic Growth

Something was happening in Ireland in the 1990s. By 1995, this was apparent to most everyone. Record economic growth rates were hitting the headlines. Cranes dotted the skyline of Dublin which, with its own *zona rosa* in the form of a large night-clubbing development in the Temple Bar district, was becoming the biggest short-term holiday destination for young Europeans. In turn, Dublin youth were streaming to towns like Galway and Westport to consume 'alcopops' and Irish traditional culture. Pop stars were buying castles. Somebody was buying luxury cars in record numbers. Multi-ethnic migrants were arriving. Ireland had become the place to be.

More of something was definitely happening. The Irish tiger was 'developing' in ways that no one could have envisaged back in the gloomy 1980s. Yet such 'development' has come under increasing critical scrutiny in recent years. It is commonly associated with the production of more material things, and it is only a secondary question whether it is necessarily a good thing to produce these extra things: who they are produced for?, why?, and at what cost to whom? For many years, critical development theorists worried about whether the extra things would be distributed fairly, either among classes or among regions. Marxist theorists recognised the powerful productive potential of capitalism but condemned it for separating the logic of production from that of consumption – those who worked the hardest often ended up among the most impoverished; more or less of a commodity was produced according to the profit it could bring to the capitalist (exchange value) rather than its usefulness to society or groups within society (use value). We will return to these questions in Chapter 5. At an even deeper level, however, more recent analysts have questioned the very use of the term development, because of the detrimental effects that expanded production has had on our environment, on producing communities in the periphery, and on even consuming communities in the core. Not only do they question the sustainability of our present form of development, many would question whether it is spiritually worth sustaining (see, for example, essays in Sachs 1992).

The prevailing developmental ideologies, however, remain decidedly productionist. More is better. Indeed, although today's version of neoliberalism may be a bit greener, culturally more aware, and more socially conscious than yesterday's *laissez-faire* conservatism, it is probably more hegemonic in society at large. Few people question the common wisdom that market-oriented free enterprise economies are more likely to be successful. And, until the Asian crisis of 1997 raised some eyebrows, few would have questioned the perception that the East Asian economies are 'successful' followers of the century's most spectacular economic success: Japan. The one thing that the four East Asian economies and Japan have had in common – the thing that defines their mutual 'success' – is rapid and sustained economic growth. The one thing that led people to question their seeming economic invulnerability was when these rapid growth rates appeared to be crashing to a halt. Few people outside of limited academic or activist milieu, therefore, actively question the notion that 'success' in economic terms is primarily based on a country's performance in terms of economic growth. Rapid economic growth is still the golden chalice that states seek to ensure their popular legitimacy.

In this chapter, therefore, we deconstruct Ireland's 'successful' economic growth which has earned it the accolade of a 'tiger'. This involves a series of questions. First, how impressive is Irish growth performance, compared to East Asia and to other regional European economies? Is Ireland converging economically with the richer economies of Europe and elsewhere? Second, is Irish economic growth real or illusory – how much does it correspond to a real expansion of material productivity, or how much is it a creation of creative bookkeeping? An associated question is that of the origins of economic growth. In the south of Ireland economic growth has been associated primarily with exports, and secondarily with domestic demand. What does export growth really mean in the Irish context? Is Ireland taking its place as a competitor in global markets, as many would say South Korean and Taiwanese producers have already done? And, finally, is Irish economic growth 'sustainable'? Again, this question is directly associated with the structure of economic growth: the degree to which expansion in one economic sector spreads to other producers and sectors; the effects of expanding foreign activities on domestic sectors; the degree to which mere growth is associated with technological upgrading and true innovation; whether the Irish 'tiger' can sustain itself if – or, more likely, *when* – foreign investment and/or foreign (EU) aid contract.

Southern Irish Economic Growth: how Exceptional is it?

'The Irish economy is the most rapidly-growing economy in the European Union ... .' Thus started the Morgan Stanley report that first asked whether Ireland was a 'Celtic tiger'. After that, things got even better. Each June announcement of the new Irish growth figures was accompanied by similar claims: 'most rapidly growing economy in Europe'; 'most rapid growth in OECD'; 'record growth figures'. Certainly, by Irish standards this century these have been exceptional rates of economic growth. And compared to a Europe in recession they have also been impressive. But 'rapid' growth is a relative concept that depends on what yardstick by which one is measuring it. Since the popular claim, at least implicitly, is that southern Ireland's economic growth rates compare to those of the East Asian tigers, it is worth making the comparison directly.

Table 3.1 contains growth rates for the south of Ireland and the four East Asian tigers. Two things stand out immediately. One is the vast difference between Irish and the East Asian growth rates. Even during its most successful period, the 1990s, Ireland achieved average economic growth rates of just 4.7 per cent, hardly even close to the 8 or 9 per cent growth rates of the East Asian economies. The second is the duration of growth. Even if we accept that Ireland is growing 'rapidly', it has sustained high growth rates for just half a decade. On the other hand, the characteristic that has drawn such awe among observers of East Asia is not simply the rates of growth recorded there, but the *duration* of rapid growth in all four countries. Each has sustained rapid growth rates – the highest in the world – for more than *three* decades. The Singaporean state considered its economy to be in difficulty in the 1980s because it achieved only about 7 per cent annual growth for the decade!

Compared to this kind of performance it is hard to think of the southern Irish economy as a 'tiger'. Yes, it has achieved rates of growth that are historic for Ireland, but its two- to three-year spurts of 6–7 or even 8 per cent growth are hardly the stuff tigers are made of. Indeed, many economies in the north and south – Brazil, Mexico, even Botswana – have achieved several-year spurts of growth that exceed Ireland's. A realistic observer, familiar with the actual performance of the East Asian economies, would say let us wait a few years before jumping to the conclusion that the Irish economy has hooked on to something exceptional.

Table 3.1 Irish, East Asian and EU real GDP growth rates, 1960–95

Years	*Ireland*	*S. Korea*	*Taiwan*	*Singapore*	*Hong Kong*	*EU*	*Thailand*
1960–70	3.9	8.5	9.2	8.8	10.0	4.7	7.7
1970–80	4.2	8.7	9.7	9.0	9.5	2.9	6.7
1980–90	3.2	9.2	9.0	6.9	8.9	2.2	7.6
1990–95	4.7	6.6	n.a.	8.3	5.7	1.9	8.2
1960–95	3.9	8.5	9.3*	8.2	8.9	3.1	7.4

*Refers to 1960–90.
Sources: CSO, Chowdhury and Islam (1993:8,14,17), World Bank, World Development Report (various years).

It is not Ireland's similarity to East Asia, then, that has earned it the accolade of being a 'tiger'. Rather, Irish growth is exceptional compared to the rest of the European Union. It is strange to recall, but less than a decade ago Europe was seen by some analysts as the most vibrant economic region on the globe. In his influential work, *Head to Head*, the US political economist Lester Thurow (1992) even went so far as to predict that Europe was the most likely winner of a three-way struggle with the US and Japan for world economic domination. Similarly important works of the late 1980s, such as Michael Porter's work on competitive advantage, singled out Europe for its ability to adapt Japanese-style flexibility to Western conditions (Porter 1990). This was quite a turnaround from the Europe of the late 1970s and early 1980s, which earned the term 'Eurosclerosis' for its less than impressive economic performance. But by the early 1990s, it seemed, Europe returned to its sluggish economic self. Germany, paying a heavy price for its reunification, could no longer lead Europe as it had in the 1980s. Other major European countries, too, were in recession while the future of many of the booming corporations of the 1980s, like the Italian Olivetti, no longer looked so promising.

In this context, Ireland stood out as the only economy in the EU to dramatically improve its economic performance. During 1990–95, while the EU economy as a whole was growing at a rate of about 2 per cent, accounting for inflation, the south of Ireland grew at 4.7 per cent. Yet even here we should qualify Ireland's exceptionalism. As Figure 3.1 shows, Irish growth rates during the 1980s (as before) have tended to cycle around the overall EU rates of growth, sometimes higher for a time, then lower for a time. Ireland had been a laggard during most of the 1980s. Its per capita GDP declined in some years and grew by less than 1 per cent in others. Until 1988, Ireland's economic growth performance was below the EU average. Its sudden turnaround toward the end of the 1980s was impressive. During 1988–90 it achieved two years of greater than 6 per cent growth. Then, after three mediocre years, it again achieved three years of 6 per cent plus growth during 1993–96. This time around, economists predicted that the southern Irish economy would maintain growth rates of 4 per cent and above until the year 2000 and beyond. Only time would tell whether this was optimism or realism.

There is another basic issue about growth that is worth considering at this point, because it comes up time and time again in the Irish case. Ireland is unique in Europe to the degree that its GDP exceeds its GNP. The reason is simply a direct result of Irish dependence on foreign investment and, to a lesser extent, on foreign debt. Unlike GDP, GNP does not include profits, dividends and interest that are removed from a country. In a sense, then, it is a better measure than GDP of the degree to which economic growth benefits a country as a whole, because it measures the resources that remain in a country as a result of its economic efforts. In other words, if GDP measures effort expended in the economic activities of a nation, GNP is a better measure of the returns these activities bring to the nation.

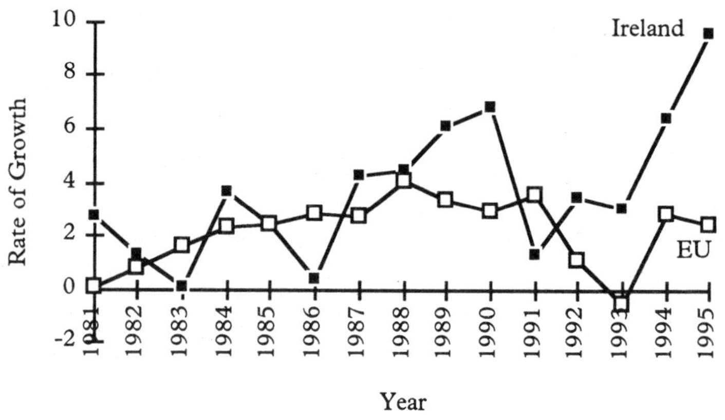

Sources: Irish CSO, Eurostat.

Figure 3.1 Rates of growth of real GDP in Ireland and the EU, 1981–95

As we have already seen in Chapter 2, TNCs came to dominate Irish manufacturing in the 1970s and 1980s, in terms of investment, employment, output and, especially, exports. By the 1980s, TNCs were a large enough sector that their behaviour was strongly affecting the Irish economic structure. Most importantly, the amounts of profits received by foreign corporations in the south of Ireland and subsequently removed through repatriations, became larger and larger. By the 1990s, foreign profit repatriations approached 15 per cent of GDP. At the same time, the state had incurred a very large foreign debt – one of the largest in the world relative to national income. As the net amount of profit incomes leaving Ireland grew, the gap between GDP and GNP widened. In other words, Ireland's GNP grew at a slower rate than its GDP.

The degree of this difference is shown in Figure 3.2. In 1980, southern Irish GNP and GDP were practically equal. Since that time, however, the two began to diverge substantially as more foreign profits were repatriated so that GDP grew at a more rapid rate than GNP. By 1996, southern Irish GNP was more than 13 per cent lower than GDP (the large degree to which foreign profits account for GDP growth will be analysed shortly). In simple language, this meant that GDP overstated, by more than an eighth, how much material wealth was created for Ireland by the economic activities of its people. Less and less of the fruits of Irish labour remained in the country and more flowed abroad. If we compare Ireland's *GNP* growth with East Asia's, then, the disparity between the two is even greater than when economic growth is measured by GDP. And, as we shall see, if we compare Irish GNP with that

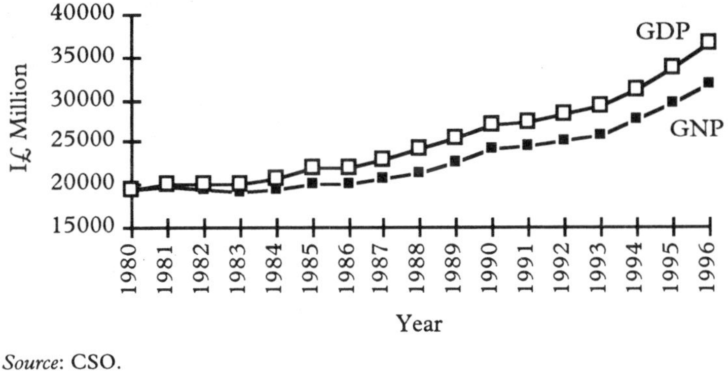

Source: CSO.

Figure 3.2 Southern Irish GDP and GNP, 1980–96 (current values)

of other European states, its recent economic performance is not as impressive as it is when GDP is used as the basic measure of the economy.

In strict terms of economic growth, which are the very least criteria for judging economic success, we now have the bare data to answer the question, '*is* Ireland a tiger?' Compared to the East Asian economies, it is clearly not. Compared to Europe, the rather clear answer is, 'not yet'.

Is Ireland Really Converging Economically with Europe?

'We are no longer a poor country!' The headlines blared from Irish newspapers after EU statistics showed that Ireland had for the first time exceeded 80 per cent of the average European GDP per capita. If Irish economic growth rates do not compare to those of the East Asian economies – or even some Southeast Asian newly industrialising economies like Malaysia or Thailand – they certainly appear to be rapid enough to achieve a major goal of the Irish state: to take its place as a fully-fledged 'European' among some of the richest nations in the world.

Up to now, Ireland participated in the European project as a poor relation. It was always *peripheral*. This meant that Ireland was eligible for significant amounts of EU aid, some of which went to subsidise farmers and some of which was used to upgrade the country's ancient transport and communications infrastructures. But peripherality also gave Ireland a sort of inferiority complex. Despite the state's attempts to promote Ireland in vibrant terms – a famous advertisement by the IDA proclaimed, 'we're the young Europeans' – the country pretty much had to take orders from its continental big brothers while its leaders went cap in hand to Brussels. The government, for example, justified its nearly sycophantic support for the Maastricht Treaty on the ground that failure to join would leave Ireland out in the cold and rob it of critical aid funds. Since many Irish had originally hoped that EEC membership would help the country escape from taking orders from its other 'mainland big brother', as it had been forced to do for centuries, this was a sometimes galling (no pun intended) state of affairs.

Thus, one can imagine the excitement when the European dream finally seemed to be becoming a reality, and the Irish economy converged with the European average in terms of the basic indicator of GDP per capita. It was icing on the cake that this coincided with

Ireland's half-year presidency of the EU, giving the country a real sense of pride. As one of Ireland's leading social commentators wrote, in a year-end review that spoke of 1996 as the 'triumphant culmination' of the new independent Ireland, 'we found ourselves approaching the destination that we used to dream of – that of the Irish as average Europeans, standard citizens of the rich North, driving along our splendid new EU-financed motorways from our American computer plants to our British shopping centres ... ' (O'Toole 1996).

Irish pride increased as others expressed a desire to emulate Ireland. In 1996, the Scottish National Party created good publicity for Ireland (and embarrassment for the British government) when it elicited research from the House of Commons Library in London showing that Ireland would 'become more prosperous than the UK and Scotland by the year 2000' (SNP 1996). According to a press release by the SNP leader, Alex Salmond, Ireland showed how a small country with practically no natural resources could '[use] their imagination and human resources in order to drive their economy forward'. If Ireland could do it, Salmond argued, how much more could an independent Scotland do with its much greater energy reserves and human resources.

According to official EU statistics, this convergence was no joke. In the 1970s, the southern Irish economy had produced only half as much per capita as the UK, its former colonial ruler. By 1996, not only had it succeeded in outstripping the British levels of output, it had also exceeded the EU average! Moreover, the Euro-statisticians predicted that, by 1998, Ireland's southern economy would be more than 6 per cent above the EU average.

At this point, the careful reader might be confused. One group of economic commentators was telling us in 1996 that Ireland had surpassed the crucial level of 75 per cent of the EU average level of per capita GDP. This is why they worried that the country would lose much of its annual gift of EU aid, totalling up to 6 per cent of GNP. But another group of commentators was telling us that Ireland had just *surpassed* the EU average. One group was claiming that GDP was essentially a third higher than the other group. What was going on – just more lies, damned lies and statistics?

Ireland's position relative to the rest of Europe depends on which measuring rod we choose to use. Like major corporations, the EU keeps two sets of books (although, unlike corporations, both EU sets are published and are open to public scrutiny). The two sets of books are based on two sets of logic. One logic says that a country's income compared to another is equal to the amount it could buy *in the other country's currency*. Or, to compare the income of all countries in the EU, each country's GDP is converted into a common monetary unit: the European Currency Unit (ECU). This represents the common 'market worth' of each country's income. By this measure, Ireland's GDP was about 82 per cent of the EU average in 1995.

The other logic says that price levels are different in each country, and that each country's income should be equalised according to how much it could buy *at the price level of that country*, not at international exchange rates. Poorer countries generally have much lower price levels than richer countries, partly because their wage rates that go into making products or providing services are considerably lower. A hairdresser in Ireland makes considerably less than one in Germany, so the cost of a hairstyle is less in Ireland. Thus, although Irish GDP is only 82 per cent of EU GDP in money terms, it could buy more than 82 per cent as many hairdos. By this logic, the *purchasing power* of Ireland's GDP is more than 82 per cent of the EU average.

The Euro-statisticians have a method to account for these different price levels, which they call *purchasing power parities* (PPS). If they translate each country's GDP into PPS, rather than foreign exchange rates, they come up with different results. Generally, poorer countries' PPS rates are higher than their foreign exchange rates, so the use of this accounting mechanism makes it appear as though income distribution is much more equal throughout the EU. Ireland appears to be about 16 per cent 'richer' according to the PPS accounts than it is according to its foreign exchange levels. It receives not 80 per cent of the EU average income, but nearly 100 per cent. In a similar manner, Greece seems 36 per cent 'richer' according to the PPS system, Spain 22 per cent, Portugal 55 per cent (Germany, on the other hand, appears to be about 14 per cent 'poorer'). Moreover, since the disparities between foreign exchange rates and PPS are increasing for the poorer EU countries, the PPS accounting system creates the appearance that they are converging on the EU average GDP much more rapidly than their relative economic growth rates would suggest.[1]

But, as I have already shown, a *third* measure of convergence – GNP – reflects a country's average standard of living relative to other countries more accurately than GDP. This is especially true in Ireland's case, where an increasing proportion of GDP consists of TNC profits that are removed from Ireland. GDP, therefore, is at best a measure of how much value is created in Ireland through production and rendering of services, but it seriously overstates the contribution of economic activity to Ireland's material well-being. Therefore, it is misleading to assume that the convergence of national GDPs reflects a convergence of material well-being.

Comparing the different estimates of material well-being calls into question Ireland's supposed convergence to average European income levels through rapid economic growth. Different measures of convergence, as Figure 3.3 shows, clearly have different outcomes. When GDP is expressed in purchasing power units (PPS), the southern Irish economy appears to converge dramatically with the EU average income after 1988, reaching practical parity in 1995. But this is mainly because of rapidly changing PPS rates, which create the illusion of convergence, rather than rapid Irish economic growth. If we take Irish and EU-average GDP for 1988 and hold PPS constant, we can apply actual rates of GDP growth to see how much of this measured convergence was due to higher Irish economic growth rates as opposed to shifting PPS rates. This exercise shows that Irish economic growth rates alone would have

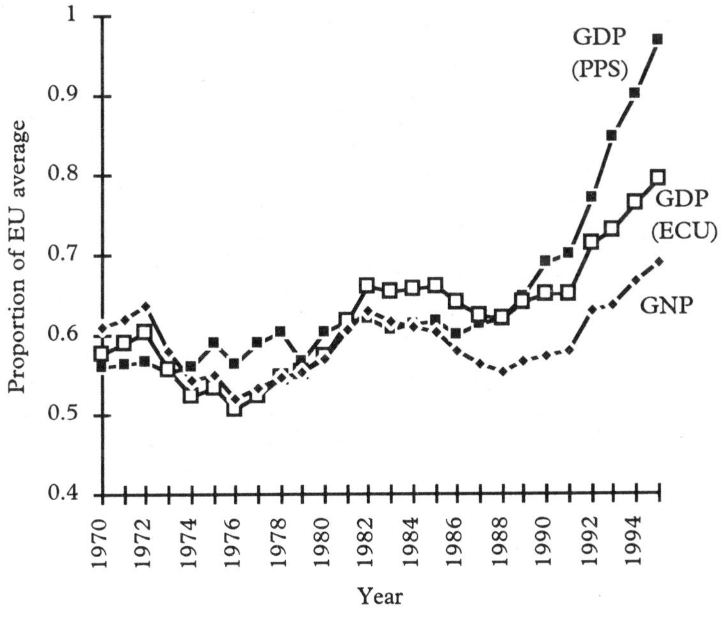

Sources: Irish CSO, Eurostat.

Figure 3.3 Different measures of Irish convergence to EU average per capita income levels, 1970–95

only brought its GDP to 75 per cent of the EU average in 1995 (from 62 per cent in 1988). In other words, higher economic growth is responsible only for convergence of 13 per cent, while changing PPS rates are responsible for 21 per cent (nearly two-thirds) of Ireland's convergence with the EU.

Thus, when GDP is expressed in ECUs (at the prevailing foreign exchange rates) instead of PPS, convergence is much less dramatic. Expressed this way, Irish GDP reached only 80 per cent of the EU average in 1995. Moreover, the pattern of convergence is a cyclical one, where Irish GDP levels rise and fall relative to the EU average, with the trend rising slowly over time.

But when GNP – a much better measure of national economic well-being – is used, the cyclical pattern becomes even more apparent and convergence practically disappears. Since 1970, Irish GNP cycled between about 55 and 65 per cent of the EU average. Only in 1994 and 1995 did it rise above the upper limit of that cycle, to about 70 per cent of the EU average. It is still too early to tell whether the southern Irish economy has finally moved into a pattern of convergence with other EU economies, has moved to a slightly higher cycle of relative GNP (perhaps, between 65 and 75 per cent), or has simply had a few years of exceptional growth relative to the rest of Europe and will settle back into the previous cycle.

This gets at the heart of the question of sustainability. In the rush to proclaim Irish economic 'success', which is of course in the interest of state actors and governing politicians, most commentators have simply assumed that the new higher growth rates are here to stay. Few, however, have asked whether the structure of growth – its underlying causes – is likely to remain viable in the long run. Since Irish growth, as we shall see, has been so dependent on the activities of TNC subsidiaries, there are two immediate threats to sustainability. One is the question of whether Irish economic growth is 'real' or 'phantom'. The other is its dependence on external decisions about the location of production, which is in turn driven by global changes that may not always be as favourable for Ireland. In order to predict whether Ireland will actually graduate into 'tigerhood', therefore, it is necessary to examine the sources of Irish economic growth.

Intel Inside: Tigerhood and Industrial Agglomeration

The received wisdom in Ireland in the mid-1990s was that prosperity had come to stay. Nearly all of the major economic prognosticators, from the Central Bank and the Dublin-based Economic and Social Research Institute to the European Commission and the OECD, predicted that high growth rates would persist into the twenty-first century. The official Irish development plan forecast annual economic growth of 4 per cent during 1994–99, while the European Commission projected annual growth of 5 per cent during the same period. We have seen that these are hardly 'tiger' growth rates from the East Asian point of view, but they are rapid in the European context.

Some of the optimism was based on the ideological argument that growth was the result of macroeconomic stability, which itself came from measures for fiscal restraint and low inflation which began in Ireland in the late 1980s. We saw in Chapter 1, in the case of the East Asian economies, that on ideological grounds the World Bank preferred 'getting the prices right' to state intervention as an explanation of economic success. In a similar way, orthodox economists in Ireland, the European Commission, and the OECD noted the coexistence of Irish austerity programmes and rapid growth and asserted that one caused the other.

Bradley et al. (1997), for example, argue that recent Irish growth is the result of a series of mainly domestic factors including the accumulation of human capital, outward economic orientation, tight fiscal policy, restrictive pay agreements, strong currency policy, a stable macroeconomic environment, and demand growth by Ireland's major trading partners. In fairness, the report argues that these domestic factors interacted with global changes to create a positive outcome, but it still gives local factors primacy over global ones. Likewise, a European Commission report credits Irish success to fiscal consolidation, exchange rate stability and a restrictive pay agreement (European Commission 1996).

From a more critical point of view, however, macroeconomic stability only indirectly contributed to growth. The structural story of southern Ireland's economic recovery in the late 1980s and 1990s was a fairly straightforward one: it captured a crucial segment of foreign investment into Europe during a time when such investment was agglomerating in fewer locations following the global restructuring of the 1980s. Foreign corporations were attracted to the south of Ireland primarily by its low tax rates, which essentially qualify it as a tax haven. The attraction was magnified by restrained wages for Ireland's well-educated labour force and by government incentives, both of which supplement the profits on which TNCs pay little tax. Ireland was structurally able to attract the new wave of TNCs (1) because southern governments had invested heavily in educating Irish engineers in the 1980s, and these were in surplus because the previous wave of foreign investment did not require them; and (2) because EU aid, supplemented by state spending, was used to create much improved transport and communications infrastructures which are crucial for the new investors. 'Macroeconomic stability' was icing on the cake.

We have already seen that Ireland was in the 1970s and 1980s one of the economies most dependent on foreign investment. If anything, it became even more dependent in the 1990s. The foreign share of fixed capital investment rose from about 60 per cent in 1988 to 75–80 per cent in the 1990s. Dependence on US investment became particularly acute. Such investment made up only 40–50 per cent of foreign investment during the mid-1980s, admittedly a period of large-scale American disinvestment. By the mid-1990s unpublished IDA data showed that American corporations were making more than 75 per cent of foreign direct investment and 60 per cent of fixed investment in manufacturing overall.

The computer industry is the main story in this regard. In the 1970s, the IDA decided to target electronics companies and successfully attracted a small but important group of minicomputer companies on the basis of its zero tax rate and generous grants to foreign investors. This sector, however, was unable to sustain growth, and the restructuring of the computer industry during the mid-1980s led to disinvestment and relocations that hit Ireland extremely hard. Many of the major companies in the 1970s electronics 'boom' in the south of Ireland, such as Digital, relocated at a great cost to the economy.

The global restructuring that led one group of investors to contract, however, eventually provided opportunities to attract new foreign investors. In the new world of flexible specialisation, a fresh wave of foreign investors was emerging, this time agglomerating their production facilities close to one another in order to reduce transactions costs and establish networks with other firms that could respond more quickly and flexibly to rapidly changing markets. Ireland benefited in the 1990s because it became one of the few locations of agglomerated foreign investment in computers and its surrounding industries, like software and computer services. The main reason was astonishingly simple: Intel. In 1990, at a historically high cost to the IDA and the Irish state, Intel chose a location near Dublin as its European site for the production of computer chips.

Intel moved into Ireland in two stages – in 1991 and 1995 – investing I£1 billion in the first stage, of which nearly I£70 million was paid directly by grants from the Irish government. Moreover, the company financed its investment through tax loopholes that cost the state an additional I£140 million by the end of 1996. The cost per job was huge: some I£75,000. Keeping Intel in Ireland for its second stage proved even more costly, with the IDA agreeing to pay I£100 million of a I£750 million investment. Assuming similar tax-driven loan packages in the new investment, the cost to the state could rise to nearly I£140,000 per job. To put this cost into perspective, the IDA claims that its average cost of attracting foreign jobs in the 1990s has been about I£12,000 (close to the average annual wage of the jobs it attracted).

But the IDA was not just buying jobs. In spending so much to attract Intel, it bought rapid growth for the 1990s. *It bought tigerhood.*

Nearly every major player in the computer industry followed Intel to Ireland. Within a few years, the TNC sector in Ireland was a practical who's who in computers. PCs: Gateway, Dell, AST, Apple, Hewlett-Packard, Siemens-Nixdorff. Integrated Circuits: Intel, Fujitsu, Xilinx, Analog Devices. Disk drives: Seagate and Quantum. Software: Microsoft, Lotus, Oracle. Telemarketing and technical advice: Dell, Gateway, IBM, Digital.[2] These leading firms are only the tip of an iceberg that includes less well-known makers not just of these products but also of boards, power supplies, cables, connectors, data storage, printers, networking – in short, everything that goes into or around computers, and many services that use computers.

The rapidity of this change was astounding. In the midst of it I wrote – following the work of people like Amin (1992) and Perrons (1992) – of the changes in investment patterns world-wide, and how they were becoming more agglomerated (O'Hearn 1993a). I argued that this agglomeration could have grave consequences for the European periphery because more and more countries were competing for a limited number of foreign investments. The degree of competition was heightened in the post-Soviet era by the fact that the EU was expanding, so that low-cost Eastern European locations like Hungary had begun to compete for and win many of the investments that would have earlier gone to Ireland, Portugal or Spain. Most importantly, there could only be a couple of 'winners' in this competition, because companies were locating close to each other, to take advantage of the flexibility and economies provided by their proximity to networks of suppliers and consumers.

For the European periphery as a whole, the facts bore this assessment out. As inward investment agglomerated in places like Britain and France, many regions found themselves unable in the

1990s to attract the share of inward investment they had gained in the 1970s. What I underestimated, and perhaps could not have known at the time, was that Ireland was becoming one of the few 'winners' in terms of its ability to attract a huge network of foreign companies in computers, computer peripherals, software, and computer-related internationally traded services. Since 1988, according to the IDA, Ireland attracted 40 per cent of American electronics investment in Europe. This, together with a similar but smaller agglomeration of foreign chemical (pharmaceutical) companies, turned Ireland into a 'tiger economy' practically overnight.

The inflow of foreign manufacturers in the 1990s corresponded to a large share of TNCs in the growth of exports and output, indicators which are usually invoked to proclaim Ireland as a 'tiger economy'. As Table 3.2 shows, TNC value-added was growing considerably faster than GDP during the 1990s. Therefore, whereas TNCs were *directly* responsible for 15 per cent of GDP in 1990, they were responsible for 24 per cent in 1995. Moreover, TNCs spent additional amounts on (or the Irish state bought for them) Irish construction, materials, and services, which indirectly added to GDP.

Table 3.2 Share of TNC value-added in southern Irish GDP, 1990–95

Year	*(1) TNC profits*	*(2) TNC wages*	*(3) TNC value-added*	*(4) GDP*	*(3)/(4)*
1990	2,664	1,428	4,092	27,190	.150
1991	2,662	1,520	4,182	28,224	.148
1992	3,334	1,964	5,298	29,980	.177
1993	3,680	1,939	5,619	32,218	.174
1994	4,153	2,243	6,396	34,844	.184
1995	5,962	3,219	9,181	38,638	.238

Source: Irish national income accounts.

Perhaps the most startling thing about increased dependence, however, is not the share of TNCs in GDP, but their domination of economic *growth*. During 1990–95, Irish GDP grew by I£11,448 million. At the same time, TNC value-added in the south of Ireland grew by I£5,098 million. In other words, TNCs were directly responsible for 45 per cent of Irish economic growth during the

1990s, and were indirectly responsible for an unknown additional amount of growth.

Within this rising dependence, the importance of American-owned firms is indicated by the share in economic growth of three manufacturing sectors that are dominated by US firms: chemicals, computers, and electrical engineering.[3] These three manufacturing sectors have dominated Irish economic growth in the 1990s, accounting for more than 50 per cent of GDP growth in three of the six years during 1990–96. Over that whole period, these three sectors – predominantly American corporations – accounted for nearly 40 per cent of Irish economic growth! Clearly, rapidly rising dependence on foreign investment is the most salient feature of Irish tigerhood. It is barely an exaggeration, then, to say that the Irish tiger economy boils down to a few American corporations in computers and pharmaceuticals.

Antoin Murphy (1994:2) summarises the structure of TNC domination concisely. According to his estimates for 1994, TNCs accounted for nearly three-quarters of net manufacturing output ('value-added') in Ireland. Within this, three sectors – computers, chemicals and cola concentrates – produced two-thirds of total net manufacturing output by TNCs. Within these three sectors, the ten top companies accounted for nearly two-thirds of net output. From there, the arithmetic is simple: ten large TNCs accounted for about a third of value-added in southern Irish manufacturing in 1994.[4] By now, this concentration is even greater because of the further expansion of the computer giant Intel and the growth of output by such companies as Dell and Microsoft.

A handful of experts, including a strange mixture of conservative economists and radical academics, have been more agnostic than the mainstream about the sustainability and even the reality of such extremely foreign-centred economic growth (Mangan 1994, Murphy 1994, 1995, Shirlow 1995, O'Hearn 1995b). The conservatives concentrate on showing that Irish output and economic growth have been overestimated because TNCs inflate their value-added, as I will explain below. But radical critics are concerned additionally about the negative consequences that depending on TNCs has for the sustainability of Irish development. They have argued that the removal of such great amounts of resources by TNCs threatens sustainability; that TNCs fail to link up with domestic economic sectors; that they create few jobs; and that the neoliberal policies that were necessary to attract foreign investors have been detrimental to domestic sectors and contributed to increasing poverty and inequality (O'Hearn 1989, Mjøset 1993, Munck 1994, Kirby 1997).

Perhaps the most immediate problem with foreign domination, however, is that overconcentrating on TNCs in a few key sectors leaves the Irish economy vulnerable to changes in the world economy, without economic diversity to pick up the pieces if these leading TNCs disinvest. Closure or contraction by just a few key TNCs in electronics and pharmaceuticals could severely affect Ireland's economic growth rates. This already happened in the 1980s. In the 1990s, the pattern of investment agglomeration made the southern Irish economy even more dependent on TNCs from a few sectors where, if one or two key firms leave, whole agglomerations may follow. Moreover, since foreign companies are *still* not deeply linked into the Irish economy (see Chapter 2), except through their purchases of services, the growth they create is practically limited to their own activities. If they disinvest, they do not even leave behind many local companies that might stick during times of global restructuring. This is an important difference from the East Asian tigers, where growth has created diverse groups of strong indigenous manufacturers.

These TNC sectors will inevitably face another downturn, a shakeout, and another cycle of restructuring. The upward swing of the investment cycle of the 1990s has created more Irish growth than that of the 1970s – partly because this round of inward investment was not accompanied by large-scale closures of indigenous firms, as happened in Ireland after it joined the EEC; and partly because such a large group of associated firms moved into Ireland along with Intel. Because inward investment was so agglomerated, any coming downturn could be all the more devastating.

Software and Tigerhood: a Real Home-grown Niche?

In all of the hubbub surrounding Irish economic tigerhood, there does appear to be one major exception to previous patterns of Irish industrialisation. In the 1970s and 1980s, as we saw in Chapter 2, there were few linkages from TNCs to other sectors, nor were there any substantial spin-offs. US electronics TNCs, for example, were fully offshore export-platform operations, which imported practically all of their components from other corporate subsidiaries and exported all of their product. Frustrated engineers from these companies, or those who could not get work, tended to emigrate from Ireland rather than set up their own companies. Despite a lot of talk about industrial niches (O'Malley 1992), and calls for upgrading *indigenous* industries by two major consultant groups (the so-called Telesis and Culliton reports of 1982 and 1992), hardly anything seemed to happen.

But with tigerhood came something new. When Intel moved into Ireland with all its associated hardware clients, software companies came as well. Software was already a significant and growing sector by 1994. By 1996 it was being heralded as a real success story of the Irish economic 'miracle', the place where 'the new breed of entrepreneur – the Celtic Tiger' was most well-represented (Lucey 1996). There were two reasons for this optimism. First, Ireland was emerging as a top site for world software production by TNCs. But, more importantly, there was a significant *domestic* software industry. Whereas TNCs had maintained a 90 per cent share in the Irish electronics sector since its emergence in the 1980s (and more than a 95 per cent share of output), observers noted that *half* of software employment in Ireland was in *domestic* firms. Truly, it seemed, we were finally witnessing the emergence of a transnational sector that encouraged Irish participation. Moreover, this vindicated decades of state policies to educate engineers because, finally, all of the excess engineers were working in or even starting Irish firms rather than emigrating.

The growth of the Irish software sector was truly impressive. In the two years from 1993 to 1995, software exports from the south of Ireland rose by nearly 60 per cent, from I£1.8 billion to I£2.8 billion (from $2.8 billion to $4.4 billion). Total output grew by 50 per cent to I£3 billion. And software employment grew from 9,000 to 11,784. The country had become one of the top five software producers in the world.

Most important to the Irish regime was that nearly half of the employees were in domestic firms (5,773 versus 6,011 in TNCs). Nor were the 400 indigenous firms just local subcontractors to the big TNCs. Nearly 80 per cent of them were involved in exports to some degree, and nearly half exported most of their product (Forbairt 1996). To some, this indicated that Ireland was developing its own indigenous world-class players in a high-tech sector, just as the East Asian tigers had done before. One commentator asked whether Ireland was beginning to compete 'in the premier division' (Lucey 1996).

On closer examination, however, Ireland's emerging software sector looks less exceptional. First, the industry is dominated by TNCs in every respect except employment. In 1995, TNCs accounted for 87 per cent of Irish software sales and 92 per cent of software exports from Ireland. Moreover, the TNC sector is highly concentrated, with Microsoft alone accounting for at least 40 per cent of exports and Lotus taking an additional substantial share (Forbairt 1996). The Irish side of the industry, on the other hand, mainly consists of very small firms. In 1995, more than 250 of Ireland's 390 indigenous software companies employed fewer than ten people (the average indigenous firm employed less than fifteen). Of course, smallness in itself is not necessarily a bad thing, either economically or in terms of the conditions faced by workers in small firms as opposed to big ones. But it indicates that the Irish software sector like the rest of the economy is essentially dualistic – highly developed transnational giants alongside a scattering of very small domestic firms.

Yet there is a twist in the tail of software dualism, which has been the basis of local optimism. Unlike other sectors where indigenous firms have some presence, Irish software firms appear to do much more technically sophisticated things than their TNC counterparts. Once again, it is worth emphasising that 'high-tech' sectors like software are not monolithic but consist of quite differentiated subsectors and nodes of commodity chains. Like other high-tech sectors, we should distinguish between high-end software development and low-end software production and adaptation.

Observers of the Irish software industry distinguish two segments: logistics and localisation, which is dominated by American TNCs, and product development, which is dominated by small- to medium-sized Irish companies. Software TNCs in Ireland primarily perform what are known as localisation activities: the adaptation of software which was already developed in the United States to local languages and cultural and technical formats so that they can be sold in those markets. Ó'Riain (1997:9) notes that Ireland is the 'undisputed premier location in Europe' for software localisation. On the other hand, TNC managers told him that their parent corporations keep practically all of their product development in the US – 'it's like the crown jewels,' said one, 'they won't let them go' (p.16). Thus, Ireland's situation is similar to that which Peter Evans describes in India, another 'world leader' in this sector, where American TNCs 'generat[e] "software exports" by directing their local software engineers to routine tasks that US software people would like to avoid, like debugging existing software, extending the life of old operating systems, or porting existing applications to different platforms' (Evans 1995:195). While such activities require substantial training of engineers in computer programming and language skills, the actual work involved is more in the nature of repetitive semi-skilled assembly-line work. Indeed, both Lotus and Microsoft were attracted to Ireland because they required a European hub for localisation and distribution as the 1992 single market approached, and Ireland provided among the lowest costs in the EU with a friendly political environment (Ó'Riain 1997:10).

If the TNC software sector is rather typical in terms of the routine nature of its economic activities, the indigenous software industry is different. While some domestic 'software' companies supply routine services for TNCs – printing manuals, providing translations, subcontracting routine programming – a fairly distinct and apparently growing local sector does small-scale software development independently of the major TNCs. Many of these firms began by developing software services for firms in Ireland (including TNCs) that were adopting computer systems, but they gradually developed their software applications into products which they sold in international niche markets. These companies, like small software companies elsewhere, survive because they provide products whose turnover is too small to attract the major companies. Many began by supplying customised products to businesses and then developing them into products.

One should not overestimate the long-term local developmental effect of this sector, however, for two reasons. First, it is far too small to sustain the emergence of a real indigenous high-tech economy on the lines of the East Asian tigers. Much was made of the growth of indigenous software up to 1995, yet its output is still only 13 per cent of the whole Irish software sector. Its firms account for less than 3 per cent of industrial employment in the south of Ireland. Second, as indigenous companies expand and attempt to go global, they tend to be transformed in ways that reduce their positive developmental effects on the indigenous economy. Successful Irish software firms are typically bought out by American TNCs. Others join in joint ventures or go public on the American stock market. Once this happens, development usually shifts to the US to satisfy new parent companies or investors. As Ó'Riain notes, the more an Irish company succeeds the more it expands globally, the more it expands globally the less it is embedded in the Irish economy. The company may become more profitable, but it brings less benefit to the Irish economy (1997:22). Building structures to reverse this trend of disembedding would be a difficult thing, especially for such a neo-liberal 'hands-off' state such as Ireland. The withdrawal of development functions to the US reinforces an already existing tendency for low rates of research and development in the indigenous software sector. Survey research shows that expenditures on R&D make up about 12.7 per cent of output, a level which one expert calls 'worrying' for companies in such a high-tech sector (Lucey 1996). Moreover, expenditure on training fell during 1993–95 from 3.1 to 2.4 per cent of revenues.

Software, then, in many ways appears to be a new departure from the older and more dominant export-platform system in the south of Ireland. Networks of local supply have been built up around TNCs who rely on local firms, especially for services rather than products. And the educational policies and communications infrastructures that were built to accommodate TNCs have had positive externalities, as Irish engineers and businessmen were induced to set up and develop Irish software companies. This differs from previous waves of inward investment, where most of the externalities were negative – institutions that attracted foreign investments such as free trade also decimated local industries. Yet the positive example of domestic Irish software, so far, is too limited to counterbalance Ireland's rapidly increased dependence on a small concentration of foreign investors in electronics and pharmaceuticals.

The Irish software sector, as Ó'Riain puts it, 'cannot bear the burden of the huge expectations which have been placed on [it]' (1997:24). Some companies are still highly dependent on a few TNCs and, in the case of manual printers, are inevitably doomed once new technologies move documentation into electronic media (Jacobson and O'Sullivan 1994). Perhaps more importantly, home-grown companies that do real software development tend to become victims of their own success, and are internationalised by buyouts, partnerships, stock launches and other processes. This often involves the stripping of the most technically advanced and profitable development processes, which are relocated to the US. And finally, of course, the indigenous software industry is notable mainly because it is unique – it is the first truly indigenous sector that has worked its way into an important export niche. It is still very small, and it is hard to locate other significant niche sectors that will follow its example. In many ways, software is the 'exception that proves the rule'.

'Elvis Lives in Irish Trade Data': Reality and Illusion in Economic Growth

Beyond questions of the sustainability of foreign-dominated growth, both conservative and radical critics are concerned that a large part of recorded southern Irish economic growth may actually be 'phantom' growth. While part of economic growth undoubtedly reflects a real expansion of productive activity, another unknown proportion is a result of creative bookkeeping by corporations that wish to shift their profits to Ireland to take advantage of low tax rates.

Conservative concerns about whether growth rates are inflated are part of an ideological argument that Irish economic policy is still too dominated by government and trade unions. Despite government austerity programmes and national pay agreements since the late 1980s, they argue, southern Irish economic policy has not become *neoliberal enough*. If output levels are inflated, public expenditure and taxes are underestimated relative to GDP or GNP and therefore government spending should be cut back even further than it was under post-1987 austerity policies (Murphy 1994:3). Moreover, inflated output statistics also inflate the measured rate of growth of labour productivity, encouraging trade unions to seek 'excessively high' wage increases (Murphy 1995:28). Despite the extreme wage restraint that Ireland has experienced during a decade of national wage agreements, it appears that these economists would like to restrain workers even further. A rather strange variation of this conservative scepticism has come from some right-wing unionist economists in the north of Ireland, who argue that the south is still economically backward, and is therefore unable to 'afford' an all-island economy (Roche and Birnie n.d.).

Some radical critics are also suspicious of TNC bookkeeping practices. A long-standing theme in the development literature holds that TNCs often manipulate the prices at which their subsidiaries sell things to each other, so that their *paper* profits are shifted to tax havens. Not only does this enable corporations to evade taxes in the places where they really produce things, including low-wage peripheral countries, it also creates a false sense of economic growth and well-being in low-tax zones where false *paper production* is shifted. In Ireland, these questions raise additional concerns about the sustainability of economic growth compared to the East Asian tigers because economic growth has not been matched by investment. Related concerns also need to be addressed about the low technology base of Irish growth (despite its concentration in high-tech sectors), and its failure to introduce and develop new technologies or to encourage skill formation among Irish workers and experts.

Among the first major public doubts about the reliability of Irish economic growth figures were reports by economists working for two Dublin stockbrokers, Davy and Money Markets International

(Mangan 1994, Murphy 1994). The reports, which questioned whether the southern Irish economy was, in Antoin Murphy's words, a 'Celtic tiger' or a 'tortoise', focused on Irish export data. They contended that official export data were significantly inflated by corporate transfer prices, a theme that was captured by a Reuters news service headline, 'Elvis lives in Irish trade data'.

The transfer pricing argument is an old one in the literature on TNCs (for a review of the literature, see Emmanuel and Mehafdi 1994:55–88). According to many studies, TNCs regularly distort the internal prices at which their subsidiaries sell materials and components to each other so that they can shift large proportions of their profits to countries with the lowest taxes. Subsidiaries in low-tax countries like Ireland import components at artificially cheap prices, assemble them, and sell them on at inflated prices, recording artificially high profit rates. Such practices are especially prevalent in sectors where components have no clear 'open-market prices', like electronic components or patented preparations for pharmaceuticals and soft drinks. Since taxing authorities find it difficult to impute a 'fair' or 'arm's length' price for such products, as even the American Internal Revenue Service (IRS) admits, TNCs can sell them among their subsidiaries at vastly distorted prices (Wheeler 1990).

A soft drinks company could, for example, sell the ingredients and secret formula to mix its patented concentrate to a subsidiary at an artificially low price, and this branch could sell the concentrate on to the company's bottlers at a much higher price, thus artificially increasing the share of company profits that go to the distributing subsidiary. If the distributor is in a tax haven like Ireland, where profits taxes for manufacturers are just 10 per cent compared to the more standard rate of 30–40 per cent, the parent TNC will pay lower taxes overall and increase its retained profits.

Research indicates that transfer pricing has large and increasing economic effects. Dunning and Pearce (1985), for example, found that more than 50 per cent of European 'exports' in computers, pharmaceuticals, and motor vehicles were intra-company transfers (the proportion is substantially higher for exports originating in American-owned firms). Data quoted by Jenkins (1987:115–16) indicates that one-third to one-half of American and Western European foreign trade consists of transfers between subsidiaries of a single parent firm. A number of studies have found that many of these internal transactions are carried out at distorted prices. Borkowski (1992), for example, found that two-thirds of his sample of 79 American TNCs kept two sets of books, suggesting that one set was for tax purposes and the other for evaluation of performance by subsidiaries.[5]

If such transfer pricing manipulation is as widespread as the literature suggests, it could have a dramatic effect on the host country where the TNC aggregates its profits. Because it sells the intermediate good at a lower price, imports in the country appear to be lower than they 'should' be. Because it sells on the good at a higher price, exports in the country appear to be higher than they 'should' be. Value added is inflated because import costs are recorded as profits and, therefore, GDP is inflated. In years when such foreign activities are increasing dramatically, the economic growth rate may appear to be quite high, although much of it is just a phantom of accounting. Thus, if they engage in significant profit shifting, much of the activity created by TNCs amounts to the economic equivalent of smoke and mirrors. One result of this accounting behaviour is real, however: the taxes paid by TNCs to the local exchequer. Whether this makes the state a 'winner' from TNC transfer pricing activities, as one Irish economist claims (Durkan 1995), depends on the amounts of investment attracted by low-tax policies, the costs of attracting them, and the effects of policies to attract foreign investors on the viability of domestic firms and other economic actors.[6]

Unfortunately, since TNCs keep their profit shifting activities tightly secret from tax authorities, it is very difficult if not impossible to uncover concrete evidence of such behaviour. But there are strong macroeconomic indicators of significant transfer pricing behaviour. Particularly high TNC profit rates in the sectors most prone to profit shifting is an immediate clue that such behaviour is going on. But there are additional indicators of profit-shifting. Normally, in order to increase output substantially, firms must invest in capital equipment. There should, therefore, be a strong increase in fixed investment before and during such a period of expanded production. Employment should also increase – perhaps not at the same rate as output, but still substantially – on the basis that higher output requires some greater amount of labour input. Therefore, important indicators of significant transfer pricing are (1) rapid increases of output without associated capital investment, and (2) rapid rises of labour productivity that cannot be explained by other factors such as the use of higher technique or discernible improvements in skill-formation. Finally, it may be possible to uncover specific examples of profit shifting in individual corporations, for example, as a result of investigations by tax authorities. If these are common among foreign corporations in specific sectors of a given economy, then one can infer that additional uncovered activities are common.

Stewart (1988) uses many of these indicators in his study of transfer pricing in Ireland. Although he did not have access to profit data, he used such indicators as value-added per employee and comparative import–export prices to build a case that TNCs in Ireland were engaged in significant profit-shifting. In addition, he assembled a series of American company reports that referred to Ireland as an important site for tax reduction.[7] In a number of cases, companies reported that tax claims were made against them by the American IRS on the basis that they underpaid taxes on their Irish operations (pp.52–3).

Since Stewart's study, however, more systematic information on profit rates has become available from unpublished Forfás (previously IDA) annual surveys of Irish economy expenditures. These show some rather stunning facts. American pharmaceutical companies regularly maintain profit rates (profits as a percentage of sales) of 50 per cent. American computer companies maintain profit rates of about 35 per cent. American soft drinks companies in Ireland can make profits up to 70 per cent! Overall, American companies have profit rates of around 30 per cent in the south of Ireland, receiving more than three-quarters of manufacturing profits there.[8]

To give an idea of how exceptional such profit rates are in Ireland, non-US computer firms have profit rates of around 10 per cent. Irish chemical companies generally get negative or zero profits. Irish companies overall average 3–5 per cent profit rates. Admittedly, American firms use more modern technologies and produce more profitable products than their Irish counterparts. Yet these factors alone are not enough to explain such astonishing profit rates.

A more conclusive indicator of the exceptionalism of profit rates received by American TNCs in Ireland is the fact that they are so much higher than the same companies' profit rates elsewhere. According to the US Department of Commerce's *Survey of Current Business*, American TNCs have maintained profit rates (net income as a percentage of sales) of about 25 per cent in Ireland during the 1990s, some *five times greater than the 5 per cent profit rates they receive elsewhere*. This distinction has been recognised for some time, but has substantially increased. In the early 1970s, the IDA's main publicity campaign emphasised that American companies' profit rates in Ireland were two and a half times higher than in the US. This hardly drew comment at the time, even though Ireland was a tax-free zone for US investors who exported their product,[9] but it indicates that significant tax shifting into Ireland has probably been going on since the 1970s. It was only in the 1980s that its degree became great enough to potentially distort Irish economic statistics. And it was only in the 1990s that Ireland had high enough relative growth rates to raise the suspicions of some economists about the profit-shifting issue.

Perhaps the most telling indication that TNCs artificially inflate their output levels, thus inflating Irish growth rates, are their low rates of investment. Foreign companies have expanded their output at historically rapid rates in the 1990s without expanding their investment. In real terms, the rate of growth of TNC investment has fallen since the early 1980s. According to IDA data, in the first half of the 1990s TNCs invested at less than two-thirds the rate they invested in the first half of the 1980s, even though their output was growing at a historic rate and driving Irish tigerhood.

Overall, fixed capital formation in the south of Ireland fell throughout the first half of the 1990s, only reaching its 1990 level again in 1995. As a result of the decline in capital investment, capital stock fell as a proportion of Irish GDP by 15 per cent between 1960 and 1996, whereas it rose as a proportion of GDP in every other EU country (European Commission 1996). Private investment drove the recent downturn, falling by more than a third between 1990 and 1994, while state investment rose slightly.[10] The fall of private investment was especially large in manufacturing, where capital invested in 1993 was only 60 per cent of the 1990 level, mainly due to a rapid decline of investment in machinery and equipment. The share of manufacturing investment in total capital investment fell from nearly 20 per cent in 1990 to 16 per cent in 1996. This is somewhat surprising given the fact that industry accounted for 60 per cent of GDP growth during that period.

Moreover, the fall-off of investment in electronics and chemicals – the sectors that were growing by far the most rapidly – was greater than the average for manufacturing as a whole. Together, these two sectors accounted for about 55 per cent of fixed investments in manufacturing in the 1990s, although they accounted for nearly two-thirds of growth of manufactured output. It appears that the most rapidly growing sectors in terms of output grew *least* in terms of investment. This is consistent with the suspicion that a large percentage of growth in manufacturing, and therefore of overall economic growth, was a phantom of accounting, since there is little indication that growth was based on investment.

These low rates of foreign investment contribute to perhaps the greatest anomaly of Celtic tigerhood: rapid growth *without* investment. Where commentators referred to the growth of Irish manufacturing output in the 1980s and early 1990s as 'growth without employment' (O'Hearn 1995b), experts in the mid-1990s began to refer to 'investmentless growth' (Bradley et al. 1997).

By contrast, the East Asian tigers are all noted for maintaining the highest investment rates in the world. They rapidly built up their real productive capabilities over the past thirty years. In Chapter 1, it was noted that one of the key characteristics of the 'tiger' economies of East Asia was their association between high growth rates and high investment rates. Indeed, high investment was the key to rapid export growth, which was in turn seen to be the key to economic growth. The nature of investment differed from country to country. All of them invested heavily in infrastructure and education. Some of them – South Korea and Taiwan and, more recently Singapore – invested heavily in the development of new technologies. And in the crucial case of Singapore, whose economic structure appears to be closest to Ireland's because of its high dependence on foreign investment, the country achieved the world's highest investment rates. Not only have foreign companies invested heavily in Singapore, but the state has heavily invested in infrastructure, state companies, and its own foreign portfolio. In all of these cases, high rates of investment seem to be a crucial prerequisite of high growth rates.

But what of Ireland? Far from being another Singapore, the southern Irish economy has had the *lowest investment rates in Europe* during the 1990s, a fact that was virtually ignored until after 1996.[11] Figure 3.4 compares Irish investment rates with the EU average. Although Irish investment ratios were relatively high before 1985, after that they fall well below the average EU ratios. By the early 1990s, they had fallen below 15 per cent and were the lowest in the EU. Compared to the East Asian countries, these investment rates are stunningly low. Singapore maintained an investment ratio of 41.3 per cent during 1980–92, a ratio that has been rising consistently since the 1960s (Huff 1995:1422). Overall, the four East Asian tigers increased their average investment ratios from around 20 per cent in 1965 to more than 35 per cent in 1990 (Page 1994:617).

Many mainstream economists are not very concerned about the anomaly of Ireland having Europe's most rapid economic growth rates and its least rapid investment growth rates. They argue that TNC profits rates are not extraordinary, since TNCs produce leading-edge products like computers and pharmaceuticals. Moreover, they say, TNCs bring the latest technologies to Ireland,

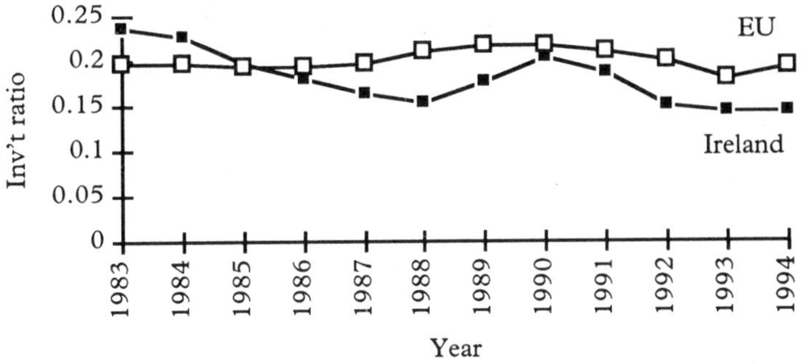

Source: Eurostat.

Figure 3.4 Irish and EU investment ratios, 1983–94*

* Investment ratio is Gross Capital Formation divided by GDP.

so it is no wonder they can produce more with less investment. The authors of a 1996 report for the European Commission try to explain the Irish anomaly in terms of rapid growth of productivity, proclaiming that Irish 'capital productivity' is the highest in Europe, if not the world. Rather than trying to explain why Ireland has the lowest capital stock in Europe relative to GDP, these economists try to explain the apparent inverse: why Irish 'capital productivity' is the highest in Europe. Using a technique developed by the economist Robert Solow, they find that Irish economic growth is not a result of capital accumulation (because there has been so little investment) nor of extra labour (because growth has taken place largely without commensurate new employment). This leaves just one other factor – a rise in 'total factor productivity' – to explain rapid economic growth. 'The role of total factor productivity,' claim the authors, 'has clearly dominated the Irish growth process in all periods since 1960' save for 1978–81, when growth was driven by fiscal spending (European Commission 1996:68). In the rest of Europe, they find, a rise of total factor productivity accounts for only a third to half of economic growth. Yet it accounts for over two-thirds of Irish growth. The difference, they speculate, may be the result of a much more rapid increase in education and skill levels among Irish workers, along with the high-tech nature of incoming foreign firms, leading to a particularly rapid rise in productivity.

What the European Commission economists entirely fail to consider is whether a large part of Irish growth, dependent as it is on foreign investment in a few sectors, is an artefact of corporate accounting. Thus, an alternative (or at least complementary) explanation of the rapid rise in 'productivity' that underlies rapid economic growth is corporate profit shifting to Ireland. If it is true that output figures are inflated by foreign companies to the extent that they shift profits into Ireland, then a significant amount of the recorded rise in 'total factor productivity' due to foreign operations is also a phantom.

Mainstream arguments like those of the European Commission are quite unconvincing because they fail to distinguish between investment from within high-tech sectors and high-tech investment. Many nodes of a high-tech commodity chain, even within a given company, are relatively low-tech in terms of their skill requirements and technologies of production. But economists and business journalists largely ignore distinctions between different nodes of commodity chains, simply assuming that foreign projects in high-tech sectors like computers or pharmaceuticals are doing high-tech things. In Ireland, however, most US TNCs still do quite a lot of relatively low-skill, low-tech assembly operations, even though they are assembling high-tech products. This is reflected in the growing proportion of part-time and contract jobs in TNCs, as will be discussed in Chapter 4. While foreign investment is predominantly by American high-tech companies, the nodes that are located in Ireland are relatively routine.

Even if they were relatively high-tech, however, it could not explain the vast differences in profit and productivity levels between their subsidiaries in Ireland and elsewhere. Experts commonly accept that the highest-profit activities are research and development and product design. American companies still do the vast proportion of these high-profit activities at home, while they send lower profitability operations to places like Ireland. Yet their *recorded* profit rates are much higher in Ireland than in the US. The most likely explanation is 'creative' corporate accounting.

As much as it may hurt to admit it, it is simply absurd to argue that Irish industry is the most productive in the world, as its recorded statistics of output per worker or output per invested capital would indicate. Irish productivity has risen as more of manufacturing is taken over by large American companies. But its recorded rise, like Irish economic growth in general, is vastly inflated by corporate bookkeepers.

On the other hand, *even if* recorded Irish economic growth is vastly inflated, it could continue for some years as long as foreign activity and related domestic activities continue to expand at a rapid enough rate. While many critical students of development are sceptical of the likelihood that late industrialisers – especially those that depend heavily on TNC investment – can grow rapidly for long periods of time, they would have to admit that cases of *dependent development* have occurred. One social scientist used a biblical phrase to summarise East Asia's economic successes within a sea of Third World developmental failures: 'many are called, few are chosen' (Cumings 1984). The question whether Ireland, like South Korea, has been truly 'chosen' is a question of the sustainability of recent Irish economic growth.

Conclusions: the Sustainability of Growth

One reason why so many Irish people are proud of recent economic developments is the feeling that they are finally part of a modern nation, no longer dependent on more powerful countries and, especially, fully equal to Britain. The southern Irish economy had been quite welfare-oriented in the 1970s and 1980s, depending on EU transfers in the form of agricultural subsidies (under the Common Agricultural Policy (CAP)) and structural funds for EU peripheral regions. Yet it invested these funds well, upgrading its transport and communications infrastructures. And it trained numerous engineers and other professionals. Now, the country was reaping its reward. Irish people could be proud of making their own dynamic contributions to world culture and world economy. But their still lingering doubts were captured in a headline: 'Can Ireland survive after EU aid?'

Once Ireland's recorded per capita GDP reached 80 per cent of the EU average – regardless of whether this was inflated by transfer pricing – it stood to lose EU transfers. Some politicians argued that Ireland should keep these transfers, either on the basis that GNP was a more accurate reflection of the country's actual well-being or by dividing the country into unequal regions, with Dublin losing its transfers but the other poorer regions retaining theirs. With the EU about to enlarge to the East after the year 2002, however, it became clear that Ireland would begin to be weaned off of its transfers after 1999 to make them available for poorer new entrants.

Of themselves, the losses of EU transfers may no longer be such a disaster for the expanded Irish economy. But taken together with increased Irish dependence on TNCs, the possibility of structural problems looms as the biggest economic risk to Ireland's new-found tiger status. In 1995, EU transfers amounted to about 6 per cent of southern Irish GDP, CAP accounting for 3.5 per cent and structural funds accounting for the rest. But TNCs were *directly* responsible for a quarter of GDP and, through their local expenditures, for perhaps 5–10 per cent more. Thus, something between 35 and 40 per cent of southern Irish GDP directly depends on foreign economic activities (including transfer pricing).

But this is just a static account. In terms of economic dynamics, the foreign sector is even more important. The increase of value-added by TNCs in the 1990s accounted for nearly half of southern Ireland's economic growth. In 1995, the record year when GDP growth reached 10 per cent (at current market prices), *value added in TNCs accounted for 73 per cent of economic growth*!

Can an economy sustain rapid growth on the basis of such extreme foreign dependence? The overwhelming experience of semi-peripheral economies is that they cannot, at least without developing strong indigenous sectors to counteract their foreign dependency. This has been true, for example, of NICs such as Thailand, whose dependence on TNCs in electronics and other sectors appeared to be creating rapid growth comparable to the East Asian tigers. Yet a downturn in the electronics sector in 1997 sent the Thai economy into a tailspin, from which many experts wonder whether it can recover. In a similar manner, Ireland itself experienced one of its most severe recessions ever in the 1980s when American electronics TNCs and other TNCs disinvested heavily.

An exception, it may appear, is Singapore. Perhaps Ireland can take hope from Singapore that foreign dependency can be combined with stable long-term growth. Perhaps, but there are characteristics of recent Singaporean economic change that call into question its significance as an exemplar for Ireland. A most obvious difference is Singapore's size. It may be much easier for a city-state to maintain high growth rates by attracting foreign investments. Singapore may compare more to Dublin than to Ireland, insofar as foreign investments may have been adequate to create tiger-level rates of growth in the Irish capital, at the cost of increasing regional inequality on the island as a whole (we shall return to this theme in Chapter 5).

Yet there are other worrying aspects of the Singapore–Ireland comparison. As we have seen, Singapore has perhaps the highest investment rate in the world. Ireland, despite its rates of growth (or perhaps *because of* the way they are structured in the foreign sector), has the lowest investment rates in Europe. Singapore's developmental state has combined its own dynamic programmes of foreign investment with a state-led policy of building high-tech infrastructural companies that not only build industrial complexes at home but also export them throughout Asia and further afield. This outward flow of investment capital has been balanced by a rapid inward flow of foreign investment which, so far, has proved to be more recession-proof than any other export-platform in the world. This stability was reinforced by Singapore's success at becoming the Asian centre for investment banking, a role perhaps equal in Europe to London and Frankfurt combined.

Ireland, unfortunately, can make no such claims. While its dependence on TNCs in electronics and pharmaceuticals has been complemented to some degree by its emergence as a centre for international financial services, this is tiny compared to Singapore's success as a financial centre. Even its emerging domestic software sector, while encouraging, has yet to show that it can become significant in terms of output and exports, or that its more successful companies can avoid the tendency toward American corporate takeovers and stripping of product development to the US.

I began this chapter by noting that something has happened in Ireland in the 1990s. The popular view has been that the southern Irish economy has become a 'tiger', the most dynamic economy in Europe and even in the OECD. While the figures show that Ireland is no tiger economy in the East Asian sense, one has to admit that its record of economic growth in the 1990s, especially since 1993, has been impressive. Most experts expect this dynamism to continue well into the next century. But few have looked closely at the structure of growth, and especially at the drastic levels of increasing dependence Ireland has had to encourage to achieve its rates of growth. Recent economic history raises the question about whether such dependent growth can be maintained in the long run, at least without the kinds of networked structures that have allowed domestic companies in the East Asian economies to emerge and upgrade. And even in East Asia there are limits to growth, including the 'glass ceilings' on technology upgrading that appear to keep the highest-tech product development in the US and Japan, or the chronic problems of maintaining levels of skill-formation that match the needs of an expanding economy. Significantly for Ireland, some of the most difficult limitations have been faced by Singapore which, among the four original tiger economies, had the hardest time maintaining its growth rates during the 1980s.

It is the economic growth aspects of tigerhood that have drawn most admiration from observers of Ireland in the 1990s. I have tried to show that Irish growth may face structural limitations, especially if global downswings bite at the foreign-led sectors in which this growth is so concentrated. Surely, the recent Asian experience tells us that no country, even the fabled Asian tiger economies, can depend on rapid growth *all* the time. But it is not just growth, or even primarily growth, that raises questions about Ireland as a tiger economy. Even in its most successful phases – the years from 1993 onward – there have been nagging questions about whether Ireland, even with its high growth rates, can provide adequate work for its people or distribute the fruits of economic growth in an equitable way. It is to these problems that we now turn.

4 Work and Employment

On 17 January 1996 Intel announced that it had achieved record turnover and profits for its Irish operations in the previous year. As a result of this 'surge' in sales and profits, the company paid each of its 2,800 employees I£1,475 in bonuses, nearly equivalent to one month's pay.

On 29 January, less than two weeks later, Intel announced that it was laying off half of its 500 fixed-contract employees due to 'weaker than expected' demand for its computer components world-wide. A spokesman for the company said that there were 'no guarantees' for the remaining fixed-contract jobs.

Such drastically mixed signals were a far cry from the previous wave of TNC electronics investments in Ireland in the 1980s. At that time, Digital Electronics Company (DEC) broke trade union organisation of the transnational sector in Ireland by refusing to accept the IDA's standard arrangement whereby incoming firms agreed to a union shop under a no-strike 'sweetheart' arrangement with Ireland's largest trade union. In return for non-recognition of the union, DEC guaranteed that as a 'good employer' (these were the days of the 'soulful corporation') it would never lay off a single worker. DEC kept its promise for some years until it restructured in the 1990s and moved its Irish operation to Scotland.

The US companies that came to Ireland in the 1990s, on the other hand, were part of a new wave of *globalisation*, where flexibility was key. Ireland was finally attracting the big magnet TNCs that would bring others with them into a Celtic 'Silicon Valley', creating jobs in the process. But the nature of employment was changing, and not always for the better.

Changing Globalisation, Changing Work

Many experts who studied the world economy during the 1980s and 1990s argue that certain of its features had changed dramatically compared to the 1960s and 1970s. Most analysts perceive a sort of 'Japanization' of the world economy, where many of the features of the Japanese-led regional economy in the Pacific have been copied in other regions throughout the world. Under the new *globalisation* regime of the past decade, not only have US and European companies attempted to copy Japanese flexible production and distribution strategies within their home countries, they have also deployed similar strategies in their operations world-wide. TNCs have invested in new, often smaller, foreign subsidiaries which often produced smaller runs of components that could be increased or slowed as world demand warranted, or modified to suit rapidly changing product designs. Wherever practical, they have also engaged in subcontracting for many of their products and components, so that they can pass on the costs of adapting to market changes.

But Japanese-style flexible accumulation was not imposed wholesale by Western TNCs. They had their own corporate structures, production technologies and marketing strategies that could not simply be changed overnight to adapt to a new 'Japanese plan'. Thus, the restructured global economy of the 1980s and 1990s incorporated a combination of the old and the new, mass production *and* flexible production together (McMichael 1996:105–8). Many semi-peripheral regions that had hosted foreign investors in the 1970s were especially suited for the new combination; they already had 'flexible' labour forces due to rapid urbanisation and surplus labour, relatively weak trade unions, and workers who were used to moving in and out of formal employment, alternating it with informal work and even subsistence agriculture. New flexible agglomerations of foreign investment projects – like the *maquiladoras* along the Mexican–US border or export production zones in Malaysia – combined assembly-line production of components for cars and electronic equipment with more flexible work arrangements that included more part-time work, zero-hour contracts, and even home working. Flexible specialisation in the periphery often became a nightmare of unprotected low-wage casual work.

A common pattern in the 1990s was the agglomeration of associated firms in key zones like Malaysia, Thailand, or Ireland. TNCs at different points of commodity chains could maintain close relations with each other, suppliers and buyers, making them more able to adapt flexibly to changes in international markets. In some cases, like East Asia, TNCs were associated with whole networks of local subcontractors and suppliers, creating a powerful if sometimes unstable source of economic activity and employment throughout a local economy. In other cases, a regional agglomeration was set up primarily to gain access to important markets nearby.

The power of flexible accumulation to create jobs was shown by the experience of the East Asian tiger economies. Rapid economic growth in South Korea, Taiwan, and Singapore was associated with very rapid growth of manufacturing employment. Manufacturing employment in South Korea and Taiwan increased annually by 10.4 and 10.6 per cent, respectively, during 1970–85. In Singapore, it increased by 8.3 per cent annually during the same period. This compares to overall annual rates of employment growth ranging from 3.7 per cent in South Korea to 5.4 per cent in Singapore. These figures indicate two important structural features of East Asian economic growth. First, that it induced especially high rates of employment growth in manufacturing; and, second, that employment growth was concentrated in manufacturing rather than in other economic sectors such as services.

Such rapid employment growth was the result, at least initially, of the high labour-intensity of East Asian export industries. Unlike the recent Irish experience, economic growth in East Asia was mostly a result of unusually rapid growth in the use of both labour and capital, rather than a particularly rapid rise in labour productivity. East Asian industry demanded large quantities of workers, from highly skilled engineers to factory operatives. Even as thousands of workers moved from rural agriculture to urban industry, they were absorbed rapidly in the larger firms at the heights of industry as well as in the vast networks of subcontractors that supplied them. As a result, unemployment rates fell in each country, leading to upward pressures on wages (Haggard 1990: 228).

Taiwan reached full employment by the late 1960s and chronic labour shortages became a problem thereafter. Between 1976 and 1980, wages doubled due to these pressures (Gold 1986:98). Singapore reached full employment by the early 1970s, despite the fact that its labour force was growing by more than 4 per cent each year. Unlike Taiwan, its government avoided wage inflation by strictly controlling labour demands and wage levels, even in TNCs. Yet the Singaporean state was still concerned that labour shortage would stifle economic growth. By 1988, as labour shortages threatened the expansion of many of Singapore's industries, the state responded with massive training programmes and other measures to encourage industrial upgrading and raise labour productivity (Huff 1995, Soon and Stoever 1996:329). Similar patterns occurred in South Korea (Amsden 1989).

In addition to industrial upgrading, each of the East Asian tiger economies imported low-wage migrant workers from Southeast Asia to increase their labour supply. They also exported industrial investments back to Southeast Asia and China. Since the 1980s, East Asian companies have been among the most active foreign investors, especially in Asia but also in such far-off places as the north of Ireland.

Full employment, however, also made it possible for the East Asian states to pursue relatively liberal labour-market policies. Unlike in Latin America, companies could flexibly hire and fire workers without the social consequence of high unemployment. This liberalism helped suppress labour costs, including costs of severance, counteracting the upward wage pressures of excess demand for labour (So and Chiu 1995:6–7). Labour demands were also controlled by state repression of trade unions and, in Singapore, by corporatist arrangements of labour control. These corporatist agreements among the 'social partners' of state, private industry, and labour are not entirely unlike the national agreements that have prevailed in the south of Ireland, to keep wage costs from rising beyond a competitive level and to help insure labour peace. It is not surprising that Singapore, the East Asian country that is most like Ireland in this respect, is also the East Asian country that depends most heavily on direct TNC investments.

Market flexibility and labour control are enhanced in all of the East Asian countries by the widespread use of vulnerable workers such as young women. By the mid-1960s in Taiwan, for example, one-third of the workforce consisted of young women who moved in and out of the workforce according to their marital and child-bearing status (Gold 1986:89). Yet high rates of economic growth and labour shortages in East Asia limited some of the negative social consequences of flexibility that are more common elsewhere. Large South Korean firms, like larger Japanese firms, have been able to offer more stable terms of employment, although flexible conditions like home work and zero-hour contracts are more common among the smaller subcontractors. Overall, the East Asian economies have not been as marked by trends of labour casualisation which have been so rampant in the newly industrialising Southeast Asian countries and in flexible-production zones like the Mexican *maquiladoras*.

There appears, then, to be two models of 'flexible accumulation' in late industrialising countries. One set of countries, most notably the East Asian tigers, has maintained rates of economic growth that are rapid enough to ensure full employment. Upgrading has reduced the restrictive impact of labour shortages on economic growth, but as a response to growth the substitution of machines and higher-skilled labour for semi-skilled labour has not created serious unemployment or casualisation of labour. While there may be a degree of 'duality' in East Asia, in terms of a labour market that is segmented between highly skilled technical workers and semi-skilled assembly workers (many of whom are migrants), the latter group still find themselves relatively secure with respect to their ability to find full-time work.

Other countries have not been able to maintain rates of growth that are sufficient to achieve full employment. Core and peripheral countries alike have experienced increasing labour surpluses. In the core especially, the labour surplus has been increased because rising labour productivity has not been matched by a reduction in working time. In the periphery, the surplus has been exacerbated by the rapid migration of labour from the countryside to urban centres. This migration has been especially rapid since the Second World War, as great areas of peripheral land have been brought into production for the global market. Migrants have created pools of cheap labour for globally oriented production. While TNCs have not transferred enough production to these regions to absorb surplus workers in the periphery – except, as noted, in the tiger economies – they have none the less moved enough industry to the former Second and Third Worlds to aggravate the labour surplus and unemployment in their home countries.

As McMichael (1996:179–89) notes, these circular processes have created structural unemployment throughout the global economy in the 1980s and 1990s. Core economies, including even Japan, have been 'hollowed out' of their industries, which have been moved offshore to places like Southeast Asia or Mexico. In return, these core economies have become more concentrated in the production of services and information-based industries. Many of the service jobs that replaced their lost industrial jobs since the 1980s have been 'pink collar' jobs: low paying and insecure. Moreover, jobs that were once considered high-tech – data processing, insurance and credit processing – have increasingly been moved offshore. Software programming jobs are no longer concentrated in California or Boston, but in Israel, India and Ireland.

As some core regions like Britain declined, they too increasingly competed with semi-peripheral countries for offshore TNC investments. Indeed, some scholars have noted that Third World-style sweatshops are as likely to appear in core regions as in peripheral ones. Increasingly, both core and peripheral economies find that a growing proportion of their jobs are part-time and/or temporary. As McMichael (1996:186) notes, competition in the new global economy 'compels firms not only to go global, but also to keep their sourcing flexible and, therefore, their suppliers – and their workers – guessing'. The resulting casualisation of work spans a continuum from clothing retailers like Liz Claiborne who have no manufacturing facilities or even any long-term contracts with their suppliers, to global TNCs like Intel who build flexibility into their subsidiaries by creating many part-time and fixed-term contract jobs while maintaining sub-supply relationships with networks of other firms who sustain similar flexible work regimes.[1]

Both core and peripheral regions have been marked by a rising proportion of low-paying, part-time, and temporary jobs. Yet it would be a mistake to take from this that the two kinds of regions are 'converging' in a sort of undifferentiated 'post-industrial' global economy. The most high-tech research and product design activities are still concentrated in a few of the richest countries, where they are tightly controlled in corporations and research institutions. Vast amounts of wealth still concentrate in these regions, and they still consume an increasing proportion of the world's resources. And workers in the north still earn more than workers who do the same jobs in the south or in the northern peripheries. Yet the social contract that gave the majority of citizens in these core countries the right to a secure job and a rising family wage has broken down, replaced by higher unemployment and inferior employment.

Still, the situation for citizens of peripheral regions is worse. Their economies sometimes experience booms, but they also experience busts. Bereft of the high-tech high-profit activities that remain in the core, they depend on foreign firms and associated local firms – often subcontractors – to create work. The result is usually unemployment rates that still exceed the core; jobs that are more often part-time or temporary; and more families that must engage in informal economic activities as well as formal jobs in order to survive.

Employment and Unemployment in Ireland

As we saw in Chapter 2, a major complaint about Ireland's dependent development in the 1980s was that foreign investors could not create enough jobs to compensate for the indigenous jobs that were lost under free trade and agricultural restructuring. By some measures, unemployment rose above 20 per cent during the mid-1980s, for the first time since the creation of the Irish Free State. Not even during the depression of the 1930s had unemployment risen so high. Even as Ireland recovered in the late 1980s and early

1990s, the low rate of job creation led some commentators to refer to *'jobless growth'*. The numbers employed in full-time jobs in the south of Ireland, for instance, remained stagnant at just over one million through the early 1990s, until 1994. The numbers working in manufacturing, where most economic growth was concentrated, also stagnated at about 225,000. The numbers employed in all of industry actually declined. A pair of academics coined the phrase 'Irish disease' to describe a situation where the inflow of TNCs crowds out employment in indigenous firms (Barry and Hannan 1995).[2]

Employment stagnation, along with liberalised regulations that allowed more people to claim unemployment benefit, caused the numbers of registered unemployed to swell from 225,000 in 1990 to 294,000 in 1993, even as Ireland emerged as a 'tiger economy'. On the basis of the unemployment register, the unemployment rate rose even higher than it was in the bad years of the mid-1980s.

As the decade wore on, however, the firms that followed Intel into Ireland, and others that expanded along with Intel, finally began to create more new jobs. The IDA announced record figures for job creation in manufacturing in 1994 and again in 1995. Even domestic manufacturers created record levels of new jobs, although indigenous sectors remained unstable and lost nearly as many jobs through closures and cutbacks as were gained through expansions. Thus, *net* job growth in manufacturing was concentrated almost entirely in foreign companies. In 1994, for example, employment by foreign companies in manufacturing and international services rose by 5,324 while employment in domestic manufacturers rose by only 146 (Forfás 1995). But at least employment in domestic industry was not declining steeply, as it had in the first two decades after Ireland joined the EEC, so the expansion of jobs in the foreign sector had an overall positive effect on industrial employment in the mid-1990s.

Despite its high media profile, however, new manufacturing employment has been minuscule compared to services, where the largest expansion of employment took place (the distribution of employment changes during the 1990s is shown in Figure 4.1). Service employment stagnated nearly as much as industrial employment at the beginning of the 1990s, but after 1991 the numbers of service jobs rose by about 4 per cent annually. Overall in the 1990s, the rise in the numbers employed in services accounted for 102 per cent of total employment expansion in the south of Ireland (LFS 1996:24)!

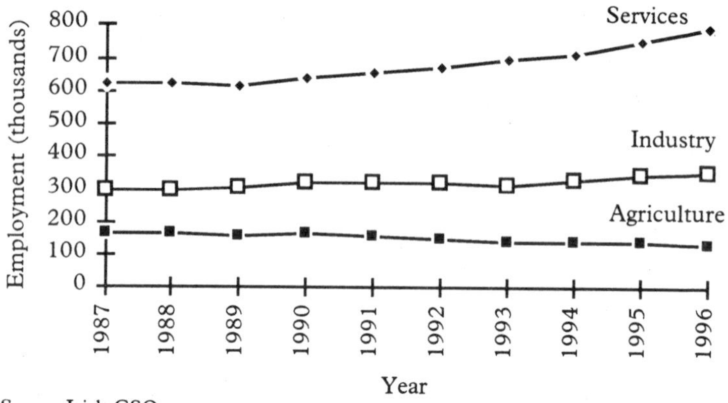

Source: Irish CSO.

Figure 4.1 Sectoral increases in employment, the south of Ireland, 1987–96

But, of course, 'service' employment includes a wide spread of occupations, from clerks and hairdressers to accountants and managers. Its expansion in some countries has been seen to denote a maturation of economies, of the sort referred to by Bell (1974) as 'post-industrial' (although, even in core countries recent services expansion has involved the spread of clerks and janitors as much as the spread of 'knowledge-based' technicians and experts). More optimistic observers of Ireland might imply that this has also been the case of recent expansions there, since economic growth has been so concentrated in high-tech industrial sectors. Certainly, the Irish media has portrayed an image of high-tech service employment in the 1990s, as is embodied in highly publicised projects such as the International Financial Services Centre in Dublin's docklands. In more peripheral countries, on the other hand, one would expect the expansion of services to include a higher proportion of low-paid employees like clerical workers and shop assistants. More recently, such semi-peripheral services would also include a series of activities that were previously concentrated in the richer countries, such as the processing of financial and insurance transactions or software programming. Among these jobs, one would expect a large proportion of women.

It is this second, more peripheral pattern that still appears to predominate in the south of Ireland. The increase of employment in Ireland's 'tiger economy' of the 1990s – 150,000 workers in all – has been heavily concentrated among low-wage, often part-time service occupations that are dominated by women. Half of new employment was routine clerical workers, shop assistants and miscellaneous service workers. Another third was classified as 'professional and technical workers', but even these jobs were mostly low-paid semi-skilled work. And more than a tenth of the new jobs were in the booming tourism sector, where employment is notoriously unstable and low paid. Overall, women have dominated the employment rise of the 1990s, accounting for 70 per cent of new jobs. Only two sectors experienced significant employment increases that were mostly men: 'administrative, executive and managerial workers' (10 per cent of the total employment increase) and, in manufacturing, 'electrical and electronic workers' (6 per cent).

The expansion of service occupations is directly and indirectly connected to the rise of the Celtic tiger economy since the late 1980s. As we saw in Chapter 3, economic growth and exports have been concentrated in the 'big three' transnational sectors: computers, chemicals and cola concentrates. A large proportion of this growth makes its way into the accounts of TNCs in the form of corporate profits, most of which are repatriated. Yet this rapid expansion has created surprisingly little direct employment growth, even in the highly publicised electronics and engineering sector, because TNCs spend such a small proportion of their total costs on labour. But the expansion of TNCs, especially computer firms, has created the indirect 'linkage' of a demand for local services – accountants and solicitors at the 'high' end, telemarketing and teleservice operators for computer and insurance companies at the low end – and this has had a major impact on employment in Ireland.

Surveys of corporate expenditures show that foreign firms still buy the vast majority of their material inputs abroad. The proportion of their material inputs that they purchased in Ireland increased during the 1990s. Foreign computer firms, for instance, only bought 10 per cent of their material inputs in Ireland during the mid-1980s, and they now buy nearly 20 per cent in Ireland (Forfás 1996). But this rise mainly reflects the agglomerated nature of recent investments: Gateway or Dell, for example, buy their computer processing units from Intel *in Ireland* instead of importing them from Intel abroad, as they would previously have done. The same is true of a range of inputs, from Seagate's hard drives to Microsoft's operating systems. With respect to employment, however, even to the degree that these companies buy material inputs in Ireland, they buy them from other foreign firms who employ very little labour in production, so TNC purchasing practices have a limited effect on manufacturing employment.

On the other hand, TNCs have continually increased their Irish purchases of services, both in absolute amounts and as a proportion of their overall service purchases. Since services are very labour-intensive, this has had a greater affect on Irish employment than their materials purchases. Accountants, software-system installers, telemarket operators and even custodial services or tea-room assistants add directly to the numbers employed in the Irish economy. Augmented numbers of Irish teachers, administrators, and other providers of public or semi-public services is indirectly linked to TNC-led economic growth, as the Irish state has extended programmes that are intended to encourage the further expansion of the tiger economy. Finally, the increase of economic activity itself has encouraged spending and speculation by higher-paid workers and professionals, which has encouraged the creation of jobs in areas such as clerical work and tourism.

This high-end spending and speculation spree has been supplemented by Ireland's widespread cultural popularity as a place for Europeans to visit and to buy property. Famous musicians, film stars and sports figures are often seen to outbid each other for the most expensive Irish castles and estates. In one recent case, locals were kept guessing for months about whether a luxurious castle was about to be bought by the famous German Grand Prix racing driver Michael Schumacher or his brother Ralf, only to read in the papers that it was bought by the Irish singer-songwriter Enya. All of this luxury spending boom feeds into the expanding service economy.

To emphasise the rise of service employment, especially in occupations where women predominate, is not to say that the expansion of Irish employment in the 1990s has only been in low-paid services. Indeed, many professionals such as accountants, highly trained technicians, and managers have been included among the new employees. In terms of material prosperity, the rise of highly-paid professionals and managers has been a major legacy of the 'Celtic tiger'. Yet, as discussed in Chapter 3, most 'professional and technical workers' do rather routine tasks such as software localisation and teleservice work. Even highly trained engineers working in leading electronics TNCs often find themselves doing quite routine work. As a result, a dualistic expansion of highly paid professionals, on the one hand, and low-paid service workers, on the other, has had mixed social effects, particularly in the form of increased social inequality, which will be examined in the next chapter.

Casualisation of Work versus Unemployment?

The net results of this expansion on southern Irish employment and unemployment depend on which set of figures one chooses to believe. As Figure 4.2 shows, there was a growing disparity since 1985 between the register of unemployed and employment surveys in terms of the numbers of people they found to be unemployed. According to the unemployment register, the numbers of unemployed rose, in spite of rapid economic expansion, from 225,000 in 1990 to nearly 300,000 in 1993, then stabilising at about 280,000 and at an unemployment rate around 20 per cent. On the other hand, employment surveys showed a starkly different story with unemployment peaking at 232,000 in 1987 and then falling to 190,000 by 1996. Thus, some 90,000 fewer were counted as unemployed in the Labour Force Surveys (LFS) than were on the unemployed register.

By one measure, unemployment was rising to record levels even as economic growth recorded historic highs; by the other measure, economic growth was slowly driving unemployment down toward more acceptable levels. Since much of the public relations aspects

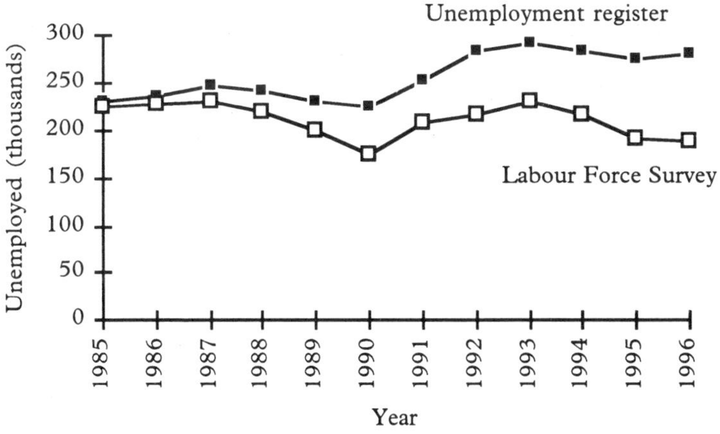

Source: Irish CSO.

Figure 4.2 Estimates of unemployment, the south of Ireland, 1985–96

of government economic policies revolved around job creation and reducing unemployment, it was important to distinguish which measure was more 'accurate'. For Irish governments, it was important to establish credible claims that their policies were creating economic growth and, as a result, were *also* creating jobs and reducing unemployment. In other words, this rising tide was lifting *more* Irish boats, if not all of them.

With this in mind, some orthodox economists and government politicians launched a major press assault against the use of the unemployment register to calculate unemployment rates, arguing that there was a clear-cut case for using unemployment surveys in their place. Statisticians from the Central Statistics Office argued that many of those who registered as unemployed were not really unemployed according to the definitions used by the International Labour Office (ILO). Some right-wing commentators claimed that the unemployment register was bloated by an army of welfare frauds who were working full-time while they received their unemployment benefits. A leading academic economist claimed that a 'severe health warning' should be attached to the unemployment register figures (*Irish Times*, 11 December 1996).

A major critic of the unemployed register, the former Taoiseach Garret FitzGerald, forcefully put the case for using employment surveys in a series of articles in the *Irish Times* (20 July 1996; 15 June 1996). His explanation clearly reveals why the two rates are so different, but it ironically tells as much about the inadequacy of using surveyed unemployment rates to measure public welfare as it does about the shortcomings of the unemployment register to measure unemployment. According to FitzGerald's calculations, the difference of nearly 100,000 between the numbers on the unemployment register and those found to be unemployed by surveys could be easily explained. 30,000 were part-time workers who claim unemployment for times they are not working. 17,000 were single women working at home, who are entitled to 'credits' in lieu of actively seeking paid employment. 13,800 were wives who prefer to sign on independently of their partners instead of being treated as adult dependants. Most of the rest have been unemployed for so long that they have given up actively seeking work, although they may formally be defined as students, retirees, on home duties, or sick or disabled. The disparity between measures grew over time because liberalised regulations allowed more part-time workers and non-working partners to register as unemployed, while more long-term unemployed became discouraged and stopped actively seeking work.

Now, none of these categories are considered unemployed by the standard ILO definition, thus they do not show up on unemployment surveys. Yet there are strong arguments for considering many of them to be unemployed, or part-time unemployed, especially as more Irish workers find that they are employed on increasingly flexible terms, or economically marginalised altogether. To put it another way, to the degree that the categories of people mentioned above are swept off our definitions of 'unemployed', and therefore not considered to be socially problematic, perhaps we should seriously question our conceptions of what it means to be 'unemployed'.

Irish work has undoubtedly become more casual and less secure since 1985. In industry and services alike, more and more employees have flexible status like part-time, temporary and fixed-contract work. This is partly a result of newly created jobs that are on flexible terms. But it is also the result of large numbers of employees who have been shifted from full-time permanent status to more flexible terms.

Although flexibilisation of labour is a global phenomenon, it has happened differently in Ireland than either in the East Asian or the Western core economies. In the south of Ireland, as Jacobson (1996) outlines, management has tended to use a 'cherry-picking approach' to new forms of productive organisation. Industry in Ireland has never taken on the networked 'world-class manufacturing' character that many experts would claim is found in Japan and East Asia but, rather, introduces just those aspects of flexibilisation that suit employers. In general, this has meant the introduction of practices that weaken trade union power and increase management's ability to hire and fire or manipulate working hours.

One way this has been done is by creating a dual employee structure in a single firm, where *core workers* – with relatively good conditions, performance-based pay, and share ownership – work alongside a 'buffer' of part-time, temporary, and contract workers. This is the model indicated by the contradictory practices of Intel, noted at the beginning of this chapter. According to Roche (1995), this model prevails in the new American electronics firms that exemplify the 'Celtic tiger' image, although it has also become common in banking and finance. Yet a more common approach is that which predominates the broader service sector, where flexible part-time or contract work has simply encroached on a higher proportion of employment, where employers have simply begun hiring more and more atypical workers in place of full-time permanent employees.

Sadly, although flexibility is a global phenomenon, part of the responsibility for the degree of loss of worker status lies with initiatives of the Irish trade unions themselves. During the 1990s, Irish unions have been among the most receptive to changes associated with flexibility, even though these changes create huge risks for Irish workers (Gill et al. 1993, ICTU 1993 and 1994, Jacobson 1996). In the late 1980s, Irish trade unions pressured the southern state to reintroduce corporatist tripartite national agreements such as the Programme for National Recovery (PNR) (1987), the Programme for Economic and Social Progress (PESP) (1990), and the Programme for Competitiveness and Work (PCW) (1996). Under the PESP, especially, national-level agreements were used primarily to moderate wage rises.[3] But a special clause allowed employers to give extra wage rises of up to 3 per cent of basic pay on the basis of local negotiations. These local agreements became quite common, and were successfully concluded in 77 per cent of enterprises monitored in one government study. Most importantly, in the overwhelming proportion of these local agreements employees gave trade-offs in return for the 3 per cent pay rise. The most common trade-offs for higher pay were acquiescence to more part-time work, more temporary work, more fixed-term contracts, more subcontracting and new technologies (Taylor 1996:269–71).

Thus, as a result of management and union practices together, the new Irish employment of the 1990s became more flexible at a rate that exceeded the core regions of the EU. Employers introduced these new forms of work, of course, because they were more profitable. Trade unions and the southern Irish state went along largely because the Irish economy – despite its dynamism and its new-found 'tiger' status – is more dependent than ever on foreign corporations, who have led the way in their introduction. As Wickham (1993) notes, if the choice is between atypical work and no work, the decision is obvious.

Part-time workers

One of the least studied but most important aspects of Irish employment expansions during the 1990s is the rapidly changing nature of work. More and more Irish employees are so-called 'atypical workers', who are employed part-time or on fixed-term contracts. Because of the expansion of part-time and fixed-contract labour, Irish workers who find work are in more unstable positions than in previous times. Of course, this is an aspect of flexible accumulation around the world, even in the most economically 'developed' countries. But the degree of part-time and contract jobs among new jobs in Ireland is worrying. One study found that Ireland already had the second-fastest growth rate in the EU in numbers of part-time employees during 1987–90, at 5.5 per cent per year (ICTU 1996:11). Yet even this rapid rate nearly *doubled* during 1990–95 as the number of part-time employees increased by 10.2 per cent per year (LFS 1995, Table 28).

The rise of new forms of work is apparent both in industry (where economic growth has been concentrated) and in services (where new employment has been concentrated). In the economy as whole, the number of part-time workers rose by 66 per cent during 1990–95 while their share of total employment grew from 7.9 to 12 per cent. Moreover, 10 per cent of southern Irish employees were on fixed-term contracts in 1995. Thus, between a fifth and a quarter of Irish employees had become 'atypical' workers who had neither a full-time job or the relative security of job tenure.

The proportion of part-time and contract jobs rose especially rapidly in TNCs. In 1986, only 2 per cent of TNC employees in the south of Ireland worked on a contract or part-time basis. This proportion then rose steadily, reaching 6 per cent in 1993. Thereafter, 'flexible' workers made up a disproportionate share of the 'record numbers' of new manufacturing jobs in foreign companies. In 1994, 40 per cent of the employment increase in TNCs consisted of part-time and temporary/contract workers. In 1995, 28 per cent of the TNC employment increase was in these 'flexible' categories. Thus, whereas TNCs provided one of every five new jobs, they accounted for a quarter of the new *part-time* jobs (IDA 1995). As a result, the proportion of part-time and temporary jobs in total TNC employment rose to 11.2 per cent in 1995. This is still a low percentage compared to the service sector, but its rate of growth is significant.

Therefore, the behaviour of Intel in 1996, noted at the beginning of this chapter, provides a new threat to rising numbers of Irish workers in foreign companies. In the past, their main concern was TNC flight – that foreign companies, who were mainly interested in grants and tax-free periods, would 'take the money and run' when these incentives ran down (as happened in several famous cases in both the south and the north during the 1980s). Today, there is still a danger that global collapse could cause wide-scale restructuring of TNC production. This could cause Intel and the electronics companies agglomerated around it to leave Ireland altogether, causing severe unemployment. Moreover, regional trade disputes could cause massive damage, as was threatened when Brussels decided to block imports of American pharmaceuticals into the EU in late 1997 because American firms refused to follow anti-BSE measures and remove cattle brains and spinal cords from their chemical preparations. But the more immediate threat, which causes ongoing worry to large groups of workers, is that periodic downturns will cause layoffs on a smaller scale. Such layoffs are easier to implement because of the rise in flexible terms of employment.

Of course, such casualisation of work has been a feature of service sectors, where women and youths are concentrated, for some time. Services have been the fastest growing sectors in Ireland in terms of employment for decades, not least during the 1990s. Much of recent employment growth has been in service occupations where casual labour is most concentrated. The most rapidly expanding occupations in terms of employment in the 1990s have been 'professional and technical workers' (63 per cent of new jobs filled by women, 40 per cent of whom work less than 30 hours per week), 'service workers' (74 per cent women, 31 per cent working part-time), clerical workers (89 per cent women, 28 per cent working part-time) and 'commerce, insurance, and finance workers' (99.5 per cent women, 19 per cent part-time). Together, these highly casualised sectors alone have accounted for 80 per cent of the employment expansion of the Irish tiger economy of the 1990s (LFS, 1990 and 1996).

Certain economic sectors have been especially prone to casualisation in the 1990s. In the retail sector, the numbers of part-time jobs grew by more than 50 per cent between 1991 and 1995 while the number of full-time jobs fell. As a result, the proportion of part-time jobs in that sector grew from 13 to 20 per cent (LFS, various years). A report by the Irish Congress of Trade Unions predicted that this proportion would grow to 46 per cent by the year 2000 (ICTU 1996). Thus, while the 'Celtic tiger' finally appears to be creating more jobs than it is destroying, a very high proportion of them are casual. Worker insecurity is highlighted by reports that less than half of Irish workers are in occupational pension schemes (*Irish Times*, 30 April 1997).

Figure 4.3 shows the overall importance of part-time work in recent employment expansion. While the numbers of full-time jobs fell consistently from 1990 to 1994, the expansion of employment was entirely due to new part-time jobs. Full-time employment expanded more rapidly in 1995 and 1996, yet part-time employment still accounted for a substantial proportion of the employment increase. The concentrations of new employment in services and, especially part-time service work, goes directly against the common public perceptions of the main employment effects of Irish tigerhood. This public image is overwhelmingly one of new opportunities for high-tech engineering graduates and skilled professionals.

Indeed, experts and IDA administrators began to worry in 1997 that the numbers of highly skilled engineers was running out, and that if something was not done to quickly train new engineers, Irish economic success would be threatened by the turn of the century both by the unavailability of such skilled labour and, consequently by their high cost (see, for example, *Sunday Tribune*, 14 September 1997). This scenario is reminiscent of labour-shortage problems that beset the East Asian economies after years of economic growth, and which ultimately became one the major rationales for moving South Korean and Taiwanese production into Southeast Asia. And there is certainly truth to the concern that TNCs would be less likely to invest major projects in Ireland if they perceived a threat of skilled-labour shortages or a significant upward wage-push. Yet concerns about these highly publicised jobs are numerically but a tiny part of the employment expansion that is really going on in the Irish 'economic miracle'.

The rising proportion of part-time workers is an important consideration with respect to recent arguments about unemployment in Ireland. The tendency, which is encouraged by Irish governments, has been to emphasise Labour Survey statistics because they give much lower rates of unemployment and higher rates of employment. Yet the Labour Surveys significantly overestimate the true numbers

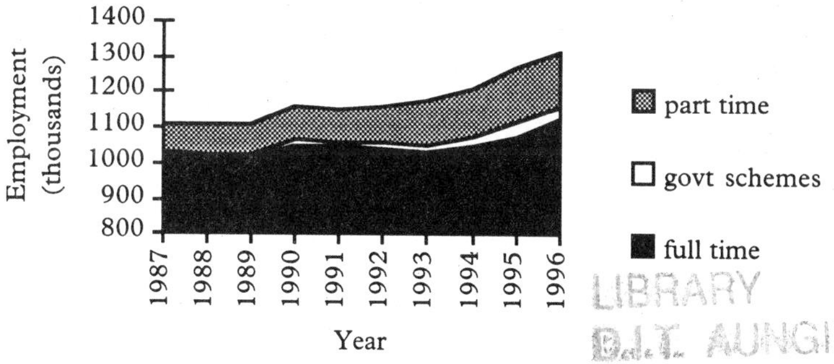

Source: Irish CSO.

Figure 4.3 Components of increase in employment, the south of Ireland, 1987–96

employed because they count part-timers and those on government schemes as 'employed', the same as full-time employees. According to ILO definitions, even someone who works one hour in a given week is 'employed'. Thus, governments are all too keen to recognise part-time employment, but they have no conception of *part-time unemployment*. This practice inflates the denominator of unemployment rates, thus reducing them even during times when the numbers of unemployed are actually rising. The emphasis on employment statistics ignores questions about the quality of employment, and all indications are that the new era of flexible accumulation is creating work that is of lower quality, in terms of hours worked, conditions of employment, and stability of employment.

Long-term unemployment and discouraged workers

Perhaps the greatest problem of unemployment in Ireland, south *and* north, has been the rapid rise of long-term unemployment. During the 1980s southern Irish unemployment changed from primarily short-term to primarily long-term. According to the OECD, Ireland had one of the lowest ratios of long-term unemployed in Europe in 1983, when just 37 per cent of unemployed had been out of work for more than a year. But by 1990 Ireland had the highest ratio of long-term to short-term unemployed in the EU, at 67 per cent (OECD 1992a). Moreover, Ireland's long-term unemployment rate of 9.4 per cent was the highest in the OECD. Only Spain (7.8 per cent) came anywhere close to Ireland, while the other OECD countries had long-term unemployment rates that ranged from Sweden's 0.1 per cent to Belgium's 4.3 per cent (NESF 1994:6). Indeed, Ireland's long-term unemployment rate was (and remains) greater than the *total* unemployment rate of most OECD countries.

The recent trend of long-term unemployment in the south of Ireland is shocking. The proportion of unemployed persons who had been out of work for more than a year rose in just two years from about a third in 1983 to nearly two-thirds in 1985. This was perhaps Ireland's worst period of economic recession since partition – certainly so in terms of unemployment. The overall unemployment rate sky-rocketed between 1981 and 1985. There were so few new jobs being created that those who lost their jobs during that time found it especially hard to find new work. Thus, long-term unemployment followed overall unemployment in its rapid rise. When the unemployment rate finally began to come down in 1987, however, many of these long-term unemployed remained out of work. Thus, while the proportion of long-term unemployed went up with overall unemployment, it did not come back down when the unemployment rate began to fall.

Indeed, the problem became worse in absolute terms during the 1990s, as job openings went overwhelmingly to already employed persons, the short-term unemployed and new labour-market entrants fresh from education. A survey of private sector companies in 1991 found that only 6 per cent of their recruits were long-term unemployed (NESF 1994:22). By 1996, according to the Irish Labour Minister, 72 per cent of the unemployed in the south had been out of work for at least a year. The numbers of long-term unemployed on the unemployment register stood at 136,394, the highest figure ever recorded, more than half of whom had been out of work for more than three years (NESF 1996). Long-term unemployment is particularly high among men, although it has risen more rapidly among women than among men. Surprisingly, it hardly varies by age – it is a problem of youth as much as it is a problem of older workers.

A similar structural problem has affected the north of Ireland, where half of the unemployed are long-term, with an additional sectarian bias against the Catholic population that is particularly worrying (Borooah 1993:6,15, O'Dowd 1995, Sheehan and Tomlinson 1996). The problem in the north, however, is even worse than the official estimates would indicate, because such a large number of unemployed men were encouraged to go on sickness benefits throughout the 1980s. And, whereas southern unemployment benefits were liberalised somewhat in the 1980s and early 1990s (although there were indications of a backlash in the mid-1990s), the Northern welfare regime became much harsher in 1997 when the British Tory government introduced the 'Job-Seeker's allowance', whereby the unemployed are forced to go through rigorous testing of their intentions to find work despite the fact that little work exists.

Yet, just as many unemployed people in the north were disregarded by reclassifying them as 'sick', many long-term unemployed people in the south are not officially considered to be unemployed according to the definitions of the LFS. In 1996, for instance, the survey only found 102,300 to be unemployed for more than a year, more than 30,000 less than appear on the unemployment register. Most of these 30,000 are people who have become discouraged by their inability to find work and have simply stopped trying. They sign on for welfare benefits but admit to the surveyors that they are no longer actively searching for work. According to

LFS definitions, this makes them 'non-active' rather than 'unemployed'. By considering these people *not* to be unemployed, many experts are sweeping a giant social problem – equivalent to one-fifth of the unemployed – under the rug. People who are severely marginalised and who represent one of Ireland's most serious social failures, are officially reclassified in other categories. The numbers of male 'students', 'early retirees', and 'sick' climbed steadily in the 1990s beyond what would have been demographically projected – in all, the number of males not in the labour force swelled from 367,000 in 1990 to 419,000 in 1996.

Such rampant long-term unemployment is a severe indictment of Irish social and economic policy. Despite many economic and sociological arguments that full employment is a thing of the past, it is clear that Ireland has been far less able to approach it than any other country in the EU, with the exception of Spain. To be fair, the Irish state has attempted to address long-term unemployment with a series of job schemes that are designed, in theory, to reintegrate workers back into employment. But these programmes have suffered from a variety of problems, including a failure to successfully target the long-term unemployed for the job schemes and an extremely low success rate in keeping participants in employment after the schemes end. Studies have shown that the overwhelming number of places on the schemes have gone to short-term rather than long-term unemployed, while less than a fifth of participants in the main scheme for reintegrating the long-term unemployed into work still had a jobs one year after the scheme ended (NESF 1994:46, see also *Irish Times*, 27 December 1996).

Overall, it appears that the state lacks real dedication to tackle the problem of long-term unemployment. There is a strong suspicion that employment schemes are not seriously meant to solve the problem of long-term unemployment, but are instead motivated by a desire to artificially reduce official unemployment rates and have often been funded because EU money is there and earmarked for that purpose. The numbers of people on temporary state-sponsored employment schemes, most of which are mandatory for those who wish to receive unemployment benefits, rose rapidly in the 1990s, from 13,000 in 1990 to 41,000 in 1995 (LFS 1996). This accounts for 27 per cent of the employment rise in the south of Ireland during that period! It artificially reduces the measured unemployment rate by about 2.5 per cent, and is therefore a useful social policy in terms of public relations. On the broader scale, however, it is clear that a problem such as long-term unemployment will not and cannot be solved simply by introducing such schemes. This is because long-term unemployment is a structural consequence of Ireland's liberal development strategy, which depends so intensively on attracting TNCs and counting on 'the market' to create work, little of which has benefited the neediest workers.

Changing Gender Balance of Work

The expansion of employment in the 1990s, then, has not so much 'put people back to work' as it has created a new set of jobs for a new set of workers. The most striking consequence of this process has been a shift in the gender balance of employment. This shift consists of two elements: a rising number of women participating in paid employment, and an increasing number of men who do not actively seek work.

The rise of Irish women at work has not been confined to the expansionary period of the 1990s. As Figure 4.4 indicates, women have been working in greater numbers since the 1970s. This is not surprising, as new jobs in industry and services were created throughout that time and the vast majority of them went to women. In the crucial decade of the 1980s, the restructuring of Irish work was not simply a matter of employment stagnation. There was also a basic shift in the gender balance of work, as the numbers of women in paid work rose by some 57,000 while the numbers of working men fell by more than 61,000. Yet the rise of women in paid

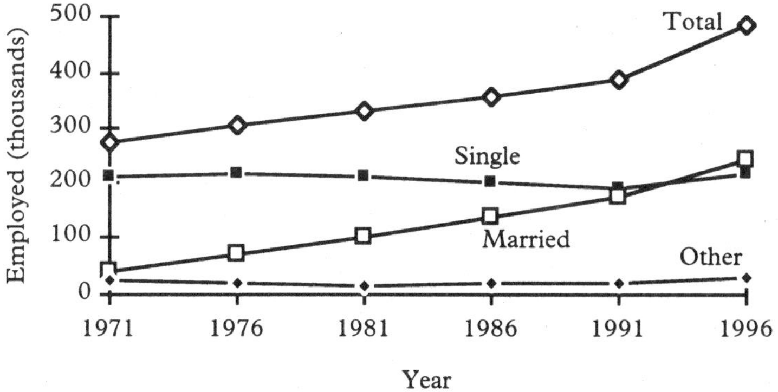

Source: CSO.

Figure 4.4 Women in paid employment, the south of Ireland, 1971–96

employment intensified during expansion of the 1990s. While the numbers of women in employment rose by 1.8 per cent annually during the 1970s and by 1.6 per cent annually during the 1980s, they rose by 4.7 per cent per year during the 1990s.

This expansion of employed women is almost entirely due to married women, whose labour-force participation rates had been low by European standards, entering the labour force. The numbers of single, widowed and divorced women who were in paid employment in 1996 was barely more than in 1971. Yet the numbers of married women who were employed grew during that time by a factor of six. In the 1990s, the numbers of married women in employment rose annually by a remarkable rate of 6.6 per cent, driving the upward surge of formally working women.

As we have already seen, however, questions arise about the nature of this new, largely female employment. The most common concerns are that the new jobs that are being created for women are, as they have been in most places around the globe, inferior jobs. They are inferior in the sense that they are largely quite routine service jobs, they are low-paying and they lack job security. Unfortunately, this appears to be an outstanding feature of the new women's work in Ireland. Of the rise of women's employment in the Celtic tiger of the 1990s, 90 per cent were in services (as we have seen, largely tourism, clerical workers and shop assistants). Half were part-time jobs. This means that many women working in the home, who could not or would not work full-time, have access to employment. Yet flexibility cuts both ways. It is also clearly true that employers in Ireland are increasingly taking advantage of married women's structural disadvantages on the labour market to fill more of their labour needs with people who will work on casual terms for less pay. In 1996, the average woman worker received hourly pay that was 74 per cent of average male hourly pay, and weekly pay that was just 65 per cent of the male average.

If the Irish economic 'miracle' has created inferior work for many women, it has simply passed by many Irish men who have been marginalised from the economy. Problems such as long-term unemployment and hidden unemployment (worker discouragement) are concentrated among men of all ages. This problem has received little public attention in Ireland, despite the fact that the proportion of southern Irish males aged 15 and over who were employed fell from 71 to 59 per cent between 1975 and 1995, while the numbers of these men who were outside the labour force more than doubled. As Murphy and Walsh (1996:474) show in their study of the 1993 Labour Force Survey, this rapid fall in the proportion of men who work has been caused in about equal measure by rising male unemployment and a drop in male labour force participation. Falling male participation is almost entirely due to discouragement rather than to young people staying on longer in school. Almost all of the increase in male non-participation is due to labour force drop-outs: either middle-aged men taking early retirement or men of all ages registering as invalids or permanently disabled.

Again, Murphy and Walsh's analysis of the 1993 Labour Force Survey sheds light on this issue. I have already mentioned that the ILO definition of unemployment is very restricted. A fifth of males who say that their 'usual situation' is unemployed are not counted as such in official statistics, because they do not meet the ILO definition. This is overwhelmingly because they are not 'actively seeking work' according to the ILO's strict definition. Many are discouraged. Others are passively seeking work. Still others are not able to start work within the two weeks subsequent to the survey.

Murphy and Walsh refer to the large numbers of Irish men who 'regard themselves as in some sense "unemployed" but have ceased any form of job search and no longer express an interest in a job'. An increasing number of these men, those who cannot take early retirement or get reclassified as disabled, say they are not looking for work and do not want a job. These tend to be middle-aged or older unskilled men (1996:486). The fact that there have been no jobs available for them in Ireland for more than ten years, and that the new jobs created by the Celtic tiger are so clearly not for them, is one of the most bitter and unjust legacies of Ireland's dependent development strategy. If these discouraged men alone – not even counting the excess early retirees and disabled – were added to the unemployment rate, it would rise by nearly 2 per cent.

Tigers, Growth, Jobs and Work

At the outset of this chapter, I noted several patterns of change in the recent world economy. The East Asian tigers, with which the Irish economy has recently been compared, have experienced rapid economic growth with chronic labour shortages. Their growth was initially concentrated in labour-intensive activities, which used up more unskilled and semi-skilled labour than was being supplied by rural–urban migration and rising female participation in paid work. Moreover, growth in these countries was rapid enough that the demand for skilled labour also outstripped the supply coming from their educational and training systems. Even as the East Asian countries improved their training and education and became involved in higher-skill activities, they continually experienced labour shortages of both skilled and unskilled workers. Their excess demand for labour was eased by encouraging immigration of unskilled labour from other parts of Asia and by exporting investments to labour-surplus regions. Thus, although Japanese-style production systems in East Asia involved new forms of flexible labour, this was not associated with severe unemployment or underemployment.

The experience of other regions was very different. Industrial core regions of North America and Europe experienced 'industrial hollowing,' as many lower-value activities were exported to the periphery, leaving behind a larger share of 'McDonaldised' services to employ their populations (Ritzer 1996). The jobs in these places tended to be less stable, lower paying and carry less attractive terms like part-time work and zero-hour contracts. As the organisation of work in these societies became more 'flexible', more people began to experience both long-term structural unemployment and temporary periods of employment between one job and another. As unemployment became more common, experts and politicians began to develop a new ideology about how full employment was a 'thing of the past', so that today's citizens should no longer expect a guarantee of work or a life-time job (with respect to Europe, see the essays in Compston 1997).

Late-industrialising regions like Ireland have had a different experience. Rising inward investments gave the promise of industrial jobs to some, but very few places experienced enough job creation to provide paid work for the large numbers of migrants who arrive in industrial regions looking for work. In many cases, vast numbers of people either find themselves unemployed and impoverished, or working in low-wage service jobs, from informal retail work to telemarketing and software programming. Those regions which have experienced significant employment from inward investment and associated subcontracting networks find their jobs under constant threat from changes in global markets and niche markets. As Thailand and Malaysia experienced in 1997, periods of boom and employment creation can rapidly turn around into periods of decline and unemployment. Because these regions are so dependent on outside forces for their economic activities, they have little control over these booms and busts.

Where does the 'Celtic tiger' fit into these three broad scenarios? Perhaps surprisingly, it fits least with the East Asian 'tigers', not just because of its chronically high experience of unemployment and long-term unemployment, but also because job creation in the tigers has been so concentrated in manufacturing while, as we have seen, services have accounted for more than 100 per cent of the net job increase in Ireland during the 1990s. While both economies have created large numbers of jobs for women, many of which pay low wages, these are more often industrial assembly jobs in East Asia while they are typically casual (part-time and temporary) service jobs in Ireland.

There are, however, some interesting similarities between Ireland and the East Asian economies with respect to work. Like East Asia, there has been much publicity in Ireland about the upgrading of some work, and the demand for professionals such as engineers. Where this much-publicised upgrading in countries like South Korea masks the degree to which the bulk of new work is routine assembly-line work, the publicity about engineers in Ireland masks the much greater expansion of routine service work. Moreover, even the usual perception of 'engineers' in both regions is stretched in the public imagination, covering a reality of work which is much more routine. The South Koreans, for example, find that their most demanding engineering work even in giant corporations like Samsung still has to be sited in the United States; the Singaporeans and Irish find that TNCs jealously keep their highest level engineering work in their home countries, while local experts often perform very routine tasks including software localisation or even teleservicing.

Ireland's recent experience of employment and work is more like that of less dynamic economies than the East Asian tigers, with which it has been compared. Like late industrialisers of the former Third World, it has faced flexibilisation and casualisation of employment *along with* rising labour surplus. Like a few other late industrialisers, Ireland has become a key site for an agglomeration of foreign investments in key expanding sectors like electronics and pharmaceuticals. Yet, despite the rapid rates of economic growth these investors cause, they create few jobs. The much-touted excess demand for Irish engineers is but a thin veneer on the real employment changes in the Irish economy: a fundamental shift from full-time work to part-time and temporary work; from mixed growth in industrial and service employment to an overwhelming concentration in basic services; and from a mixed-gender, even slightly male-dominated expansion to female domination of new work. Moreover, the shift towards casualisation does not just affect new jobs. There has also been a fundamental restructuring of existing work toward the new flexible conditions that have come to prevail in Ireland as in so many other places across the globe.

The 'winners' in this process are the large foreign corporations which have made such profits out of the Irish expansion, and a small but growing group of Irish entrepreneurs and professionals who have made significant sums by their ability to service the Celtic tiger. Women workers, especially married women, are 'winners' insofar as they have found access to work in numbers that would have been unthinkable less than a generation ago. But the new conditions of work make women, like many male workers, the 'losers' in a vast economic restructuring that has eroded their rights and economic security, often forcing them to work in order to provide an acceptable family wage. The undoubted 'losers', the unpublicised downside to the Irish 'success story' of the 1990s, are the many marginalised people, mostly former unskilled workers, who have fallen into long-term unemployment and poverty in the country's urban estates, smaller towns and rural landscapes. Putting the Celtic tiger experience in such terms raises a crucial question of overriding public concern: has the undoubted economic revival of the 1990s created general prosperity, improving the material standards of life of the Irish people as a whole; or, have the fruits of growth been unequally distributed, creating conditions of 'poverty amid plenty'?[4]

5 Poverty and Inequality: Is the Tiger Neglecting her Cubs?[1]

> Consumer spending: shop till you drop. And we did, we did. Retail floor space in Dublin rose by 25 per cent and sales of 3-series BMWs rocketed 22 per cent ... 1996 was a year of excess for the Irish consumer.
>
> The waiting list for the ultra sporty Mercedes SLK is growing. Prospective owners of the stylish twoseater, launched in this country in November, will have to wait up to 12 months for their flash new motor.
>
> Large swathes of Dublin ... became out of reach for many of the people who grew up in them ... Investors were particularly active in the residential market making it more difficult for couples to buy both new houses and second-hand homes.
>
> Another reason for the air of disaffection that was so palpable in 1996 was that the new money has not been spread evenly ... the poverty gap is getting bigger because, while a senior company executive has received a salary increase of 133 per cent since 1987, the social welfare payment to an unemployed person with four children has risen by just 62 per cent.[2]

1996 was a very good year in Ireland. On the political front, the country could claim to be a world-class player for the first time in its history, as it hosted the presidency of the European Union. Ireland's cultural revival throughout the Western world and beyond was evidenced in the popularity of the musical *Riverdance*, the new Irish pubs that opened in practically every major city around the world, and the rise of Dublin and its Temple Bar night-club district as the most popular short-term holiday destination in Europe. Economically, the south followed its record GDP growth rate of 1995 with another year of growth that was nearly as high. The term 'feel-good factor' was on the tip of every journalist's pen as they wrote their annual year-end reviews, such as those quoted above from the *Irish Times*. But how deep did the feel-good factor reach? Certainly, it was the talk of the town in the upper middle-class districts of Dublin's south-east region. But did the residents of the impoverished estates of north or south-west Dublin 'feel good' about the Celtic tiger? And what of the towns and countryside of rural Ireland?

While the economic growth rate rose by some reckonings to about 10 per cent in 1995, the rate of growth of consumption actually *fell* to 4 per cent. Again in 1996, economic growth exceeded consumption. Thus, there was a large discrepancy in the rate at which the economy was growing and the rate at which people actually experienced an improvement in their material standards of living. Still, some people had very real reasons to feel good about the feel-good factor. Despite the fact that overall consumption was not rising to record levels, the evidence of luxury car sales, property speculation, and expansion of retail space all show that *someone* was increasing their material consumption at a rapid rate. This evident discrepancy between luxury consumption and overall consumption raises the concern that Irish tigerhood has been associated with increasing inequality, unlike some East Asian experiences where inequality actually decreased along with economic growth.

Economic Growth, Class, Income and Poverty

Until East Asia, orthodox economists thought they had a pretty good handle on the relationship between economic development and income distribution. Simon Kuznets introduced his famous inverted 'U' curve in 1955, and it soon became gospel in economic thought. Kuznets observed that incomes in 'traditional' societies were relatively equal, if low; that income inequality tended to rise as countries went through their early stages of economic growth; and, then, that they again equalised as countries finally became developed industrial nations and were able to spread more of the fruits of their wealth (see also Adelman and Morris 1973, Paukert 1973). This fit well with the version of the so-called Protestant ethic which held that whole societies, like modernising persons, should forgo current pleasure for future gain. In the hands of institutions like the World Bank, it was the basis of an ideology which told Third World states to postpone social welfare programmes until they were modern enough to afford them; and to forgo progressive income redistribution policies because they would interfere with economic growth, which by its nature created inequality for a time. In the 1980s and 1990s such economic orthodoxy was still the basis of neoliberal prescriptions that less wealthy countries should dismantle state programmes because they were 'living beyond their means'.

Radical political economists proposed a different version of the relationship between 'development' and income inequality. Following analysts like Andre Gunder Frank (1969), they generally held that societies became more unequal as they were integrated into the world economy. Their productive structures were increasingly oriented to core needs, as in the case of mono-cropping export agriculture. This outward orientation of production was commonly enforced by violent and highly unequal social structures, where alliances of local elites and large foreign companies amassed more and more of the countries' wealth. Even populist revolutionary regimes such as Mexico's were eventually consigned to give way to authoritarian states where corruption and the imperatives of economic growth led to the reassertion of social inequality (Hamilton 1982).

But some experts claimed that East Asia was different. In Singapore, a benevolent authoritarian state provided housing and a living wage for its citizens, even encouraging them to amass private wealth through programmes of enforced saving. South Korean growth depended to a large degree on encouraging domestic consumption, which was achieved by controlling income inequality, introducing land reforms, and setting a floor on rural incomes.

Taiwan was most often quoted as the 'deviant case' to both orthodox and radical expectations. There, rapid economic growth appeared to go hand in hand with the *equalisation* of incomes and wealth (Barrett and Whyte 1982). Where the South Korean and Singaporean development models were based on growth and stability, one expert argues, Taiwan's 'shared growth' strategy gave equal priority to growth, stability, *and* equality (Jeon 1995). Indeed, the statistics seem to bear out this assessment. Taiwan's Gini coefficient, the standard economist's measure of income inequality, fell from 0.36 in the 1960s to 0.30 in the 1980s, a remarkable achievement by international standards. The ratio of incomes of the top fifth of households to the bottom fifth fell during the same period, from 5.3 to 4.2. This ranked it along with Japan and the Netherlands as one of the most equal income distributions in the world, outside of the communist blocs (Greenhalgh 1988:73).

Several explanations have been advanced for this apparent relationship between rapid growth and equalisation of incomes in Taiwan. Most follow on the first popular academic work that emphasised the Taiwanese anomaly, the aptly named *Growth with Equity: the Taiwan Case* (Fei et al. 1979). Their largely internal explanation focuses on how the Taiwanese state created a new capitalist class while enforcing comprehensive land reforms. The state broke up large estates into small farms, which were granted to peasants, thus significantly equalising incomes and wealth. At the same time, it gave the dispossessed landlords shares in its new industrial companies, transforming them into a class of medium-sized capitalists in a relatively decentralised industrial structure. In addition, as we have seen, Taiwan like the other East Asian countries engaged in quite labour-intensive industrial activities, which rapidly absorbed surplus labour and put upward pressure on wages. High levels of literacy and education reinforced the pattern of equitable growth.

While most observers of Taiwan agree with the essential elements of this explanation, some put greater emphasis on how the Guomindang regime's global position enabled it to achieve autonomy from indigenous classes, particularly the landlords. Taiwan's heavily armed mainland Chinese government was supported and advised by the US in their policies to destroy the economic base of the indigenous Taiwanese landlords and to garner support from the masses of peasants. Land reform was such a strongly equalising process that the 'developmental' Taiwanese state could even moderately suppress wages to keep them competitive without increasing inequality (Deyo 1987, Evans 1987, Koo 1987). Later, in the 1970s and 1980s, state-fostered export-oriented industrialisation encouraged multiple-waged families while public education and housing programmes reduced poverty (Deyo 1987, Greenhalgh 1988).

Many of these characteristics are also present in the other East Asian tigers. The South Korean state, for example, has engaged in widespread education, housing, and social welfare programmes despite its decidedly (often violently) authoritarian character. For the Irish comparison, however, the example of Singapore is more important, since it is the one tiger economy which has depended on foreign investment to anything like the same extent as Ireland. Like the other tigers, the Singaporean state has had some success in increasing the standard of living of many of its people, despite – or even because of – its authoritarian state. Its programmes to improve the well-being of its population have been mainly in areas that are connected to its strategy of economic growth, and especially to its attempts to attract TNC investments. Singapore has instituted major education programmes since the 1970s – including measures to quickly expand its technical higher education and the establishment of national research centres and institutions – but these are directly connected to the government's perception that it must increase the numbers of technically skilled workers in order to upgrade the kinds of inward investment it can attract, since it can no longer compete with low-wage Asian regions for labour-intensive investments (Tang and Yeo 1995). It has also imposed a consistent policy of providing housing for all of its citizens, acquiring land at low cost through compulsory purchases and then building housing on a massive scale. The proportion of Singapore's population living in public housing rose from 8.8 per cent when the national government took power in 1959, to nearly 90 per cent in the 1990s. But, as Ramesh (1995:255) shows, the housing programme is primarily aimed at strategic economic goals rather than social welfare. Cheapening the cost of housing allowed the state to suppress wages further, increasing the country's attractiveness to foreign investors. Moreover, the housing programme was tied to a scheme of compulsory savings, which not only subsidised it but also increased the general rate of savings and investment in the country (which, as we have seen, is the highest in the world).

On the negative side, however, the drive to attract foreign investments has ultimately caused increasing inequality and strict limits on social welfare in Singapore. The regime has from its inception been hostile toward statutory income maintenance programmes, partly because the experience of Western states shows that such expenditures tend to rise over time and also because social security reduces worker insecurity, making them less flexible and pliant, which would be a definite disincentive to foreign investors. The only social security programme promoted by the government is a compulsory savings scheme for retirement, which not only replaces a state-sponsored scheme and involves no public expenditure, but which also provides no protection for part-time and self-employed workers or the chronically unemployed. Health care, too, is largely financed through a programme of compulsory saving. Public assistance for marginalised groups such as the disabled are extremely stringent and provide a level of payment that is significantly lower than the government's own definition of the minimum subsistence income. As a result of these anti-welfare attitudes, state spending on social security has declined from 8.3 per cent of public expenditure in 1972 to 6.8 per cent in 1989 (Ramesh 1995:255).

Wages policy, too, has been primarily aimed at attracting foreign investors. Until the late 1970s wages were strictly suppressed. In 1979, in response to the perception that labour shortages were emerging, the state introduced a 'wage correction' policy which increased wages in order to attract higher-tech investment and to induce existing industries to automate (this was part of the regime's strategy to target foreign electronics companies in particular). But the major shift with respect to wages and inequality has been the attraction of more women into the labour force. Keng Mun Lee directly relates the drive to attract foreign investment to the 'feminisation' of the Singaporean workforce. In the 1960s, women made up less than a third of the workforce in manufacturing, but by the mid-1970s they made up half of those working in manufacturing in Singapore and today they probably account for at least 55 per cent of manufacturing employees. Three-quarters of women are found in low status and low-paying jobs, especially assembly-line jobs with repetitive tasks (Lee 1997:65). According to one expert, 'Singapore's economic miracle has been made possible ... by overworking and underpaying the female half of its working population' (Pettman 1992:55).

Overall, Singapore's TNC-dependent model of development created conditions that led to increased inequality. Initially, between the mid-1960s and mid-1970s, income inequality declined as new job opportunities became available for thousands of workers who had not been in formal employment or had been in inferior jobs. In the 1980s and 1990s, however, income inequality increased substantially (the Gini coefficient, which measures inequality, jumped drastically from 0.42 in 1980 to 0.49 in 1983). A dual economy emerged, between higher-paid skilled workers and low-paid women and migrant workers. Foreign investment, despite its high-tech appearance, increased the economy's requirements for low-paid workers, and many foreign firms (with the encouragement of the Singaporean government) began to fill both their unskilled jobs and many of their most skilled jobs with immigrant workers, who comprised a quarter of manufacturing workers and one-tenth of total workers in the 1990s (Lee 1997:66). Immigrants provided maximum flexibility: a practically unlimited number of unskilled workers who were willing to work at low pay and in poor conditions and who, as we have seen during the crisis of 1997–98, can be fired and expelled from the country at will without seriously destabilising the local political situation.

With the rise of competing low-wage regions in Southeast Asia, however, Singapore has recognised that it will have difficulty attracting its former share of investment, not to mention the fact that other Southeast Asian state corporations have begun to undercut its dominance of regional infrastructural projects. Singapore weathered the early stages of the 1990s Asian economic crisis (discussed at some length in Chapter 6) much better than the other 'tigers'. But the effects of Asian restructuring, with vastly cheaper labour as one of its major features, on Singaporean economic performance in general and social welfare, in particular, are yet to be seen. Meanwhile, the Southeast Asian 'tiger cubs' have experienced rising inequality with growth rather than the East Asian patterns of falling or stable inequality.

Growing Irish National Income: for People or for Profits?

If Ireland's economy has been growing rapidly, like some Asian economies, has this growth been associated with decreasing inequality and poverty, as in Taiwan, or increased inequality, as in the other TNC-dependent 'tigers' of Southeast Asia? One way to interpret Irish economic growth is to say that the national product is growing. In other words, Irish labour is producing greater amounts of goods and services each year. As we saw in Chapter 3, the production of goods and services in the south of Ireland, as measured by gross domestic product, rose in real terms by about a third between 1990 and 1996. Some of this measured growth was surely inflated by corporate accounting, but none the less the economy grew rapidly. When one views economic growth in this way, by expanded production, one obvious question is 'what was produced'? Much of the analysis in Chapter 3 analysed this question. But another basic question is, 'who benefits from this vastly increased production'?

If a country did not trade, and simply consumed what it produced, then the connection between production and consumption would be automatic. If the country produced more food, the people got more food to eat. If the country produced more luxury cars or diamond jewellery, those who could afford them engaged in more conspicuous consumption. But Ireland is an open economy. It has always exported agricultural products like beef, and continues to do so today. Yet its economic growth depends on computers, drugs, and cola concentrates. This does not make the Irish people 'rich' in computers, drugs and cola concentrates because practically all of these products are exported to England and the European continent.

In order to determine how Irish people have benefited materially from economic growth, therefore, we must interpret economic growth in another way: as the incomes that are received for this vastly increased production of goods and services. It is important, therefore, to examine the degree to which increased production of goods and services translates into increased income for different sectors of a population, including foreign corporations and investors.

Social scientists usually do this by measuring income distribution. They usually begin with individual income distribution and ask how much incomes change over time for people at different income levels, on a continuous scale from poorest to richest. If the rich receive a greater share of total incomes from one year to the next, and the poor a smaller share, then we conclude that society is becoming more unequal.

While this is one legitimate way to conceive of inequality, it does not accurately reflect some important underlying causes of social inequality, particularly the effects of economic change on different social classes. If one considers social class to be the underlying form of social inequality, from whence individual inequalities (or social 'strata') emerge, then one might first want to analyse how economic change affects class inequality. One way to do this at a general level is to analyse changes in 'factor incomes': wages and salaries (the returns to labourers for the work they perform) and profits (the returns to capital for providing investments and means of production). In line with some recent neo-Marxist and neo-Weberian approaches to classes, one might additionally ask whether unequal access to education and training, particularly in terms of entrance to certain professions, affects the income differentials between poorer workers and richer workers.[3] In the case of dependent economies, it also is important to measure the degree to which profits are divided among indigenous and foreign capital, because this has strong influences on future economic change and on within-country inequality.[4] Finally, marginalised classes (sometimes referred to as an *underclass*) have drawn increasing attention in recent years, and a crucial component of inequality is how the numbers and position of the unemployed and other marginal people have changed. We have already seen in the case of Singapore that immigrants, one of the most commonly marginalised sectors of populations, can be particularly important to economies that depend on foreign investment.

Beginning at the broadest level of class, Figure 5.1 shows how factor income shares have changed in the south of Ireland since 1985. Until 1987, they changed very little.[5] But as the rate of economic growth began to rise, these income shares began to shift quite rapidly. The share of wages in non-agricultural incomes began to fall, initially from 69 per cent in 1987 to about 63 per cent in 1991, around where it remained until 1994. Then, as very rapid growth began again in 1994 the wage share again dropped rapidly to 59 per cent. Conversely, the profit share of incomes rose from 37 to 41 per cent. Overall, during the decade since 1987 which many people refer to as Ireland's 'economic miracle', the wage share of non-agricultural incomes fell by about 10 per cent and the profit share grew by the same amount. This shows conclusively that the overwhelming 'winners' from economic growth are capitalists, who have enjoyed a rapid rise in their profit incomes – not just absolutely, but also relative to wages.

It is significant that the class distribution of incomes rapidly became more unequal in favour of capital since 1987. But it is also important to determine how this affected the distribution of incomes among groups of the population. The old Irish adage of a 'rising tide that lifts all boats' is largely based on the conservative conception that higher profit rates are good for the population as a whole, because they will be reinvested in the economy, creating self-sustaining growth that will eventually raise wage incomes as well. From this perspective, wages may rise more slowly than profits, but rapidly rising profits will pull them up more rapidly than they could have risen in the absence of high profits and reinvestment.

We saw in Chapter 3, however, that this common fantasy of a 'Protestant ethic', where enterprising men indefinitely forgo their present pleasure by investing their proceeds for future gain, does not really fit the Celtic tiger. One of the most striking features of the southern Irish economy in the 1990s has been its historically *low* rates of investment – the lowest, in fact, in the European Union. That profits are not being rapidly reinvested *in Ireland* is obvious from the changing disposition of incomes, again a striking change that is directly associated with the most recent period of economic expansion.

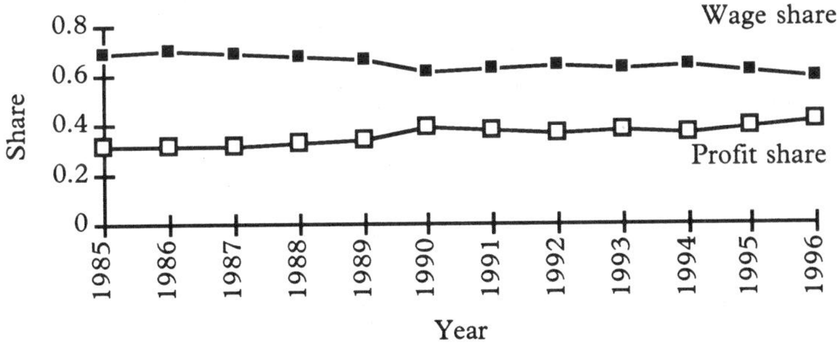

Source: CSO, *National Income and Expenditure.*

Figure 5.1 Changing factor shares of Irish income, 1985–96

The national income accounts include tables on 'expenditure on gross national product'. These tables divide incomes among their different uses, or forms of 'expenditure': personal consumption, public consumption, investment, and the trade balance of goods and services.[6] The importance of the first three categories is apparent: the public well-being is obviously affected (although not always in obvious ways) by the degree to which incomes are spent or reinvested. The last component of incomes, the excess of export earnings over import costs, may also be important to the degree that it consists of transnational corporate profits that are removed from the country.

If the incomes from economic growth give immediate material benefit to a population (ignoring, for a moment, how it is distributed among that population), then the two forms of consumption should rise relatively quickly. If profits are rising rapidly, but are being ploughed back into the economy to further increase economic growth, then investment should rise relatively quickly. But if profits are rising rapidly and being retained by corporations, then the excess of export earnings will rise especially quickly – if these profits are concentrating in the hands of foreign corporations or nationals, then the rise of repatriated profits will be closely related to the rise of excess export earnings. By decomposing the economic growth in this way, it is possible to broadly outline the extent to which it has benefited consumers,[7] national capitalists, or foreign corporations. Table 5.1 shows how the shares of GDP have changed since 1985.

Table 5.1 Changing shares of GDP expenditures, 1985–96

Year	*(a) Private consumption*	*(b) State consumption*	*(c) Total consumption*	*(d) Investment*	*(e) Export surplus*
1985	59.6	18.6	78.2	20.0	1.9
1986	59.9	18.8	78.7	18.7	2.6
1987	59.3	17.7	77.0	16.5	6.5
1988	58.9	16.3	75.2	15.8	9.0
1989	56.9	15.2	72.1	18.5	9.4
1990	58.8	15.0	73.8	21.5	4.7
1991	59.6	15.9	75.5	19.6	4.9
1992	59.9	16.2	76.1	16.3	7.6
1993	58.1	16.2	74.3	15.0	10.7
1994	58.5	16.0	74.5	15.6	9.8
1995	56.1	15.4	71.5	16.9	11.6
1996	55.4	14.8	70.2	18.8	11.0

Source: CSO, *National Income and Expenditure*.

The most obvious and significant change in the disposition of incomes is a rapid fall in the consumption and investment shares, and a rise in the share of surplus exports. The share of personal consumption in GDP fell from about 60 per cent in the mid-1980s to about 55 per cent in 1996. Taking personal and public consumption together, the overall consumption share fell during that period from 78 per cent to 70 per cent. The investment share is more cyclical, but it too has fallen on average from a high of about 20 per cent in the mid-1980s to around 16 per cent in the mid-1990s. This means that neither consumption *nor* investment have been pushed significantly upward by Ireland's rapid economic growth. The tide does not appear to be lifting all boats at a very rapid pace, but that may be partly because the *investment* part of the tide has not risen with (or before) economic growth, as it would in a normal economy (and, indeed, as it has in all of the East Asian tiger economies). Instead, the return from exports has accounted for the largest share of economic growth, about twice as much as consumption during most of the 1990s.

What does this mean? A rise in consumption or a rise in investment is easily comprehensible to most people. The first means that people are buying more goods and services, whether they be cars, houses, food, clothing, public transport or haircuts. The second means that capitalists are investing more in the economy, which would hopefully increase economic growth and eventually increase people's consumption. But a rising share of exports has no obvious meaning. To understand what is happening we should go back to the discussion in Chapter 3, where it was shown that the overwhelming proportion of economic growth in the south of Ireland was from the production of exports, and this was dominated by computers and pharmaceuticals, which was in turn dominated by TNCs like Intel. This indicates that a large part of the rising share of 'export surplus' in GDP probably represents profits for TNCs. And the predominant share of those profits, as we have seen, are taken out of Ireland rather than reinvested.

If this is the case, then, the main recipients of the fruits of economic growth in Ireland are a *foreign* capitalist class rather than a domestic one. Figure 5.2 charts the growth of the export surplus and repatriated profits in the 1990s. The two follow a remarkably similar path, confirming suspicions that the export surplus is mainly TNC profits. Therefore, it is largely correct to say that the recent period of growth has been associated with a rapid rise in profits that accrue to foreign capital, at the expense of the consumption of Irish people *and* even at the expense of reinvestment. Ireland in the 1990s is essentially in the same structural position as it was in the 1970s – dependent almost entirely on new incoming foreign activities for its economic growth without the kinds of self-sustaining relationships between investment, growth and increased consumption that have been so remarkable in an economy like Singapore's. It has sustained a high growth rate simply because foreign activities have expanded so rapidly.

In terms of the distribution of the fruits of economic growth, this form of dependent development contributes to international inequality because it produces such high returns for a foreign class. The removal of such large profit incomes does not necessarily mean that Ireland is being impoverished relative to richer regions. I argued in Chapter 3 that Ireland's convergence on the wealthier regions of Europe has been exaggerated, not just because of the difference between GDP and GNP but also because of the way international income comparisons are calculated. Yet Ireland's national income has undoubtedly converged some on the European average, so one could hardly argue that it has been impoverished. Rather, the agglomeration of global investments in places like Ireland not only concentrates TNC profits in such places, to be removed according to the companies' global strategies; they also create a degree of dependent economic growth which raises average incomes in those regions *as long as TNC production continues to expand at a rapid rate*. Foreign capital is the main beneficiary of such dependent growth, but host countries like Ireland benefit somewhat less

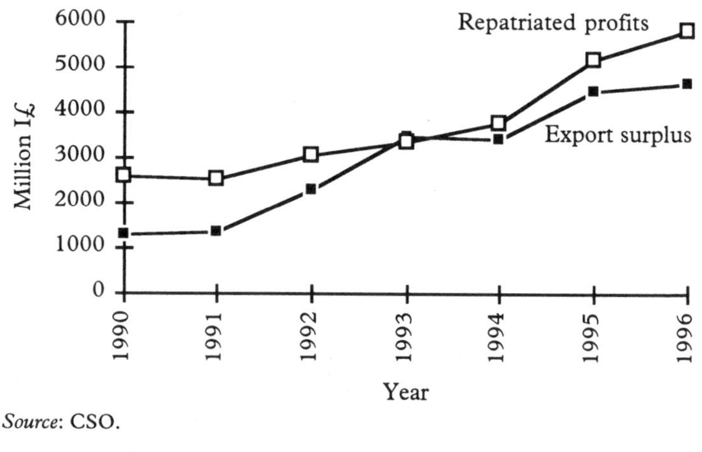

Source: CSO.

Figure 5.2 The relationship between the export surplus and repatriated profits, 1990–96

(speaking purely in terms of average incomes). The real *global* losers in the medium term are regions which lose foreign investment and become marginalised within global commodity chains. In terms of long-run growth, however, regions like the south of Ireland are still seriously endangered by sectoral overspecialisation and geographical overdependence on a small range of foreign investors.

Economic Growth and Personal Income Distribution

The question remains of how rapid growth has affected inequality *within* Ireland. In the past, ironically, the removal of such vast amounts of wealth tended to reduce social inequality because the class that received most incomes from economic growth was *foreign* capital – of course, they do not show up in the Irish income distribution. Within Ireland, the main class benefactors from dependent growth have been the professional classes who service the foreign sector and some indigenous capitalists in finance and construction who benefit most from general prosperity. This certainly was the scenario in the 1970s and early 1980s, when individual incomes became slightly less unequal. During that time, income equalisation was also helped by the decimation of the protected Irish capitalist class, which reduced unearned incomes at the top end of the scale, and by the secular movement of farmers into higher-paying industrial or service jobs (O'Hearn 1989). In the 1990s, on the other hand, these trends may have weakened since there are fewer indigenous capitalists left to go out of business and because most of the transfer of labour from farming to waged employment has already taken place.

Other trends may have tended to increase income inequality, including the changing nature of work during the late 1980s and 1990s (see Chapter 4) and the rise of long-term unemployment. It would appear that the Irish labour market has become more segmented during the 1990s, with a clear distinction between core and peripheral jobs. Peripheral jobs, more often filled by women in services who often work part-time or on a fixed contract, are relatively low paying. Core jobs and especially professional positions, more often filled by highly educated men, are higher paying. In addition, some of the industrial jobs for higher-qualified engineers reportedly pay relatively high wages. Long-term unemployment, both disguised and recorded, would also be expected to increase income inequality. Not only has the total number of long-term unemployed increased markedly since the 1980s – it stood at just

67,000 in 1983 but rose above 100,000 in 1985 and has never dropped below since then (O'Connell 1997) – but the numbers of household heads classified as 'disabled', 'retired' or on 'home duties' has also expanded rapidly during that period.

As this labour market segmentation has become more pronounced it is likely that measured individual income distributions will have become more unequal. In terms of disposable incomes, whether the bottom 10 per cent of income receivers have fallen behind higher-income groups would depend on whether pensions and social welfare payments kept pace with wage increases, since the retired and unemployed make up the vast proportion people with the lowest incomes. The peripheralisation of work, if it has affected incomes, would more likely show up in a reduced income share for the next 20 or 30 per cent of workers and their households, since so many of the new jobs associated with the Celtic tiger are of a peripheral service character. On the other hand, one might expect that the incomes of the best-paid core workers will have risen more rapidly than others, since recent economic growth appears to have favoured them much more than poorer Irish people.[8]

The available data show that both wages and personal incomes have rapidly become more unequal during the period of rapid economic growth since 1987. Data on wage and income distributions are available from two sources: large-scale household surveys on 'living in Ireland' that were carried out by the Dublin-based Economic and Social Research Institute (ESRI) in 1987 and 1994, and large-scale household budget surveys carried out by the Irish Central Statistics Office (CSO) in 1987 and 1994–95. The ESRI surveys sampled 3,294 and 4,048 households respectively, while CSO surveys sampled about 8,000 households mainly for the purpose of updating the consumer price index. The first survey gives detailed data on wages, incomes, and living standards (access to basic consumption and leisure items) while the second gives detailed data on incomes and spending patterns. Both surveys measure the proportions of total incomes received by each decile of the population, and their comparison across time shows how rapidly average incomes have risen or fallen for each decile of the population. Since each of the surveys took place in 1987 (as Ireland emerged into its period of rapid growth) and 1994–95 (as economic growth reached its apex), they give us a good indication of how prosperity has affected income distribution to date.

Figure 5.3, based on data from the CSO surveys, shows the average annual rates of income growth for each decile of the southern Irish population between 1987 and 1996. First, it is worth repeating that the economy (GDP) grew at a real rate of about 4.8 per cent during that time, yet consumption was growing much slower, with real annual growth of disposable income ranging from 0.8 to 2 per cent. This reflects our earlier point that growth has had a vastly unequal impact on classes because profits grew much more rapidly than incomes – although, again, most of these profits accrued to foreign capital. But we are now more interested in the question of whether economic growth has made *Ireland* a more equal or a more unequal society, and the household expenditure survey measures incomes of Irish people, whether they be wages, state benefits, or unearned incomes from wealth.

The data in Figure 5.3 clearly indicate that in relative terms the rich have become richer, and the poor poorer, under Celtic tigerhood. In terms of direct incomes, the lowest decile actually received less in 1995 than in 1987, although this was partly compensated by state transfers such as social welfare and pensions, so that their real disposable incomes grew annually by 1.33 per cent. But the most striking feature of income distribution after nearly a decade of rapid economic growth is that the incomes of the second, third and fourth poorest deciles of the population grew so slowly, at less than 1 per cent annually. The disposable incomes of the top 40 per cent of households, on the other hand, grew *twice as quickly*

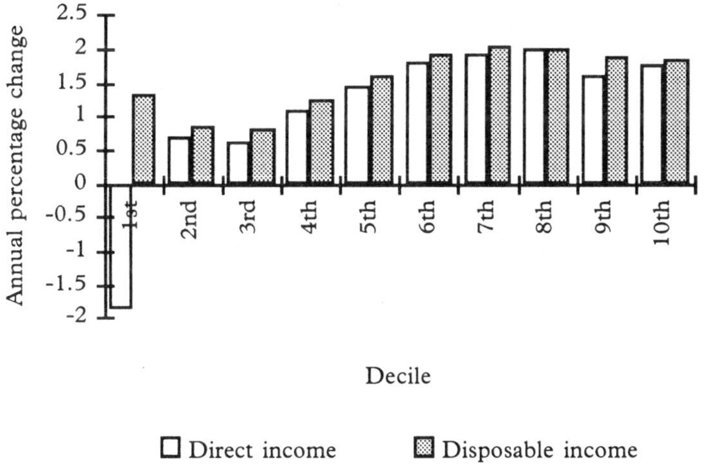

Source: Household Budget Surveys, 1987 and 1995.

Figure 5.3 Annual rates of household income growth 1987–95, by deciles

as those of the bottom 40 per cent. This clear pattern of rising inequality accords with the anecdotal evidence about rising consumption of luxury goods like cars and expensive houses.

Rising income inequality may result from two sources: rising wage inequality and/or greater numbers of economically non-active people who receive no wages (the unemployed, sick and disabled, retired, students, and housekeepers). It is therefore important to disaggregate Ireland's rising inequality to determine which of these factors is responsible for rising inequality.

The ESRI surveys are especially useful for measuring the distribution of wages and salaries in the south of Ireland. Like incomes in general, there was no rise in earnings inequality before 1987. But since then, wages and salaries (like incomes) have rapidly become more unequal. Nolan and Hughes (1997:4) find that 'from 1987 to 1994 there was a consistent widening in dispersion for both weekly and hourly earnings, particularly at the top of the distribution'. In terms of hourly earnings, the average wages of the bottom quarter fell from 73 per cent of the median income in 1987 to 67 per cent in 1994. Average earnings for the top decile, on the other hand, rose from 196 per cent of the median income in 1987 to 226 per cent in 1994, a rather astounding increase in a period of just seven years (thus, all the new BMWs)! The same pattern emerges in terms of weekly earnings. Here the bottom quartile fell from 72 to 68 per cent of the median income, while the top 10 per cent rose from 184 to 198 per cent (Nolan and Hughes 1997:5).

Nor is this widening inequality of wages and salaries due simply to changing numbers of male (more often core) versus female (more often peripheral) workers, or older versus younger workers. Nolan and Hughes find that earnings became more unequal both for men and women, and for both younger and older employees. In fact, the fall in hourly wages was especially large for the bottom 10 per cent of male workers, whose average wage fell from 53 to 45 per cent of the median (1997:6).

An examination of the occupational structure of low-paid workers, and of the occupations that are most at risk of low pay, shows that the problem is directly connected to Ireland's recent structure of economic growth. We have already seen in Chapters 3 and 4 that the Celtic tiger is based on two forms of expansion: rapid growth of exports by a narrowly defined group of foreign companies and rapid employment growth in service occupations. Thus, 'tigerhood' is associated mostly with some skilled and semi-skilled operatives in manufacturing, and with many clerical workers, service workers, and workers in commerce, insurance and finance. This coincides precisely with the occupational structure of low pay. Workers in commerce/insurance/finance, service workers and skilled and semi-skilled workers have high risk of low pay, while managers and professionals have very low risk. Nearly half of service and commerce workers are low-paid. Moreover, three-quarters of low pay in the south of Ireland is accounted for by skilled and semi-skilled workers in manufacturing, clerical workers, service workers and employees in commerce, insurance and finance (Nolan and Hughes 1997:10). Without doubt, the Celtic tiger is neglecting its workers.

This becomes crystal clear when some international comparisons are made. The supposed 'affluence' associated with Celtic tiger status, and its supposed economic convergence with the rest of the EU, is not reflected in wages or incomes. According to OECD definitions,[9] the proportion of southern Irish employees on low pay rose substantially between 1987 and 1994, from 20 to 24 per cent of workers – or, from a fifth to a quarter (Nolan and Hughes 1997:7). This places Ireland in a unique position in the EU. Just 12–13 per cent of workers receive low pay in nearly all continental EU countries except in Scandinavia. There, just 5–6 per cent of workers are on low pay. Thus, Irish workers experience about twice as much low pay as the rest of the EU and more than four times as much as Scandinavia. Among European OECD countries, only Britain comes close to Irish levels, with nearly 20 per cent of its workers experiencing low pay. This is consistent with recent analyses of a 'two-track' structure of European economic development, where core countries such as Germany compete on the basis of higher *and* more equal wages, while peripheral countries like Ireland and, increasingly, Britain compete for foreign investment on the basis of low wages.

Moreover, Irish wages are often lower even than East Asian wages – workers in Daewoo's plant in the North of Ireland, for example, earn average wages that are lower than the average wage paid to Daewoo workers in South Korea (Foster-Carter 1997). And Ireland's income distribution also compares unfavourably with the other 'tigers' like Taiwan, where income distribution became significantly more equal during its most rapid period of economic growth in the 1960s and 1970s. The ratio of incomes of the top fifth of households to the bottom fifth fell from 5.3 in the mid-1960s to 4.2 in 1980. This ratio has gone in the opposite direction during the period of rapid economic growth in the south of Ireland, rising significantly from 6.80 in 1987 to 7.24 in 1995. In this respect, Ireland has performed more like the TNC-dependent economies of Southeast Asia, including Singapore.

Conspicuous Consumption, Inconspicuous Poverty

Incomes and wages have become significantly more unequal in the south of Ireland during its period of 'Celtic tigerhood'. As we have seen, low pay also increased substantially according to OECD definitions. But the OECD defines low pay relative to median incomes rather than by any absolute standard, so its increase *could* be due more to rising median incomes than to an increase in the numbers of people on low pay by any absolute standard. Thus, inequality is related to, but not necessarily the same thing as poverty – it remains to explain whether poverty is increasing in Ireland and, furthermore, whether and how changes in poverty are related to recent increases in inequality.

A commonly emerging perception is that Ireland, despite its new-found 'prosperity', has hardly made any inroads into the problem of poverty. Indeed, some analysts argue that the problem of poverty has become *worse* during the 1990s. According to the leading critical religious group, the Conference of Religious in Ireland (CORI), despite the fact that 'the national cake was expanding at a faster rate than was the case for years and the economy and the economy was in a very healthy state' by the mid-1990s, the Irish state had 'presided over a poverty gap ... [where] poverty was the core reality of a great many people's lives'. The economy would continue to grow, CORI continued, 'but a major proportion of the growth will go to the already better-off' (quoted in Pollak 1996).

It is harder than one might think to judge these claims empirically. One obvious reason is that hard evidence about the degree of poverty and its changes is sparse. But a more basic problem is disagreement about how to define poverty. Should poverty lines be set relative to some social average (relative poverty) or absolutely, according to whether one has access to a certain set of basic goods and services? Either definition can be problematical. If one uses a relative definition of poverty – such as the OECD definition that people are impoverished if they receive less than a certain percentage of median income (say, 60 per cent) – then it is possible for people to fall into poverty *if* the median income rises (as might happen during a period of economic 'boom') even though their absolute standards of living have not fallen. On the other hand, attempts to set some absolute standard of poverty are usually biased because experts and officials define which goods and services are 'necessary' or 'redundant'. Government officials and conservative experts tend to set the poverty line low to justify the withdrawal or drastic reduction of state welfare once the poor achieve this line (Townsend

1993). Experts also tend to define 'necessary' items in ways that are biased, for example, against women. Moreover, absolute conceptions of poverty are almost always based on some notion of subsistence rather than on one's ability to afford 'equal participation' in society (Lynch 1997). The ability to participate equally in society and its good things can only be defined in relation to what a given society has to offer to its citizens. Thus, if a country such as Ireland has rapidly rising resources to enable the consumption of leisure goods, then people who are unable to participate in these increasing opportunities of wealth are impoverished. Radical conceptions of poverty and the policies necessary to eradicate it, therefore, would find relative measures of poverty to be more appropriate than absolute ones. They might also insist, however, that poverty is not just a matter of income inequality, but also has qualitative characteristics such as non-material forms of political and social exclusion (Curtin et al. 1996:8).

Recent surveys show that, in terms of relative incomes, poverty has been increasing in Ireland since it joined the EU. As Table 5.2 shows, the proportion of the population receiving less than 50 per cent of the average income rose from 15 to 21 per cent during 1973–94, while those receiving less than 60 per cent rose from a quarter of the population to more than a third. At the 60 per cent level, the rise in poverty has been especially high during Ireland's recent high-growth period, rising by 4 per cent during 1987–94. The proportion of *households* in poverty increased even more than that of individuals over the same period, from 28.5 to 34.6 per cent (Callan et al. 1996). This is quite an indictment of the southern Irish economy, because the 1980–87 period was one of the most economically repressed in the history of the state, with massive rises in unemployment and, especially, long-term unemployment. One would have expected a rapidly growing economy such as that of the 1990s to have slowed the increase in poverty, if not reversed it. But this was not the case. Clearly, an increasing number of people and households are excluded from participating in the fruits of the Celtic tiger.

On the other hand, the depth of poverty has not increased. The proportion of individuals receiving less than 40 per cent of the mean income stayed the same between 1987 and 1994, at 7 per cent. Moreover, *absolute* poverty has not increased according to an index of twenty 'deprivation indicators' assembled by ESRI in Dublin. This index includes such indicators as inadequate heating, arrears on mortgage or public utility payments, and lack of a warm winter coat (Callan et al. 1996). Once this index is added to relative income, the proportion of households experiencing *both* low incomes and enforced 'basic deprivation' stayed about the same between 1987 and 1994, at 15–16 per cent (Combat Poverty Agency 1997a:6).[10] This might lead conservative commentators and public officials to contend that the south of Ireland is 'holding the line' on poverty. Yet, even ignoring for the moment whether such absolute measures of poverty are appropriate, one could expect a state with such rapid growth and budgetary surpluses as Ireland has experienced to make significant inroads into widespread poverty instead of simply holding the line.

Table 5.2 Proportion of individuals in poverty, defined by incomes relative to average income, 1973–94 (%)

	1973	*1980*	*1987*	*1994*
40% line	8	8	7	7
50% line	15	16	19	21
60% line	25	27	30	34

Source: Combat Poverty Agency (1997b).

Who are the Poor?

At a general level, most research points to increasing levels of poverty in the south of Ireland during the 1990s, even while some sections of the population have become fabulously wealthy as a result of the opportunities created by rapid growth. But who are the poor and socially excluded? How does rising poverty relate to rising inequality and low pay in the 1990s? Are the increasing numbers who are low paid also those who have been identified as impoverished? The answers to these questions are more complex than one might imagine. They show how deeply rooted poverty actually is in Ireland, but also how the incidence of social exclusion has changed.

A common pattern among late industrialising countries of the Third World has been that industrialisation has encouraged large-scale movement of populations from the countryside to the city, often in pursuit of the employment opportunities that are popularly associated with industrial growth (although, as in Ireland, most of the actual employment growth is invariably in services rather than industry). Thus, poverty changes from being predominantly rural to predominantly urban. Those who stay on the land often remain in poverty – indeed, their poverty may even deepen – but their numbers relative to the urban poor tend to decrease as people swell into the cities. One of the significant things about the East Asian tigers is that they have largely avoided this pattern. In Taiwan, rural as well as urban incomes have increased on the whole and become more equal. Singapore and South Korea (the latter at least until the crisis of the mid-1990s) have avoided widespread poverty among their citizens through high employment and public housing programmes, although at the cost of severe political repression.

Ireland has followed a more Third World pattern of poverty, albeit in much milder form. Social exclusion has become more predominantly an urban phenomenon, although rural poverty has risen and possibly even deepened in relation to the size of the population (Curtin et al. 1996). This has been a particularly important trend during the 1990s. While farm households consistently made up a quarter of the impoverished households in the south of Ireland during the 1970s and 1980s, they fell to a mere 9 per cent of impoverished households in 1994 (Table 5.3). The unemployed, who account for the largest proportion of households in poverty, sky-rocketed in importance in the recession of the 1980s, rising from 15 per cent of impoverished heads of household in 1980 to 37 per cent in 1987. But the trend of the 1990s has been a rapid rise in poverty among households whose head is either retired or working at 'home duties' – these groups rose from 15 per cent of impoverished households in 1987 to 35 per cent in 1994. As we noted in Chapter 4, however, many 'retirees' and 'house workers' are actually discouraged workers who have stopped actively looking for work, as well as single mothers who cannot afford to work. Rapid growth, then, has not brought about a significant reduction in poverty for the unemployed. As Larry Bond (1997) writes, the rapid increase of unemployment in the 1980s led to a dramatic increase in poverty, but the fall in unemployment in the 1990s has not brought a fall in poverty, partly because such a large proportion of new jobs are going to new job market entrants instead of the unemployed. To a degree, this is a result of a failure of state employment and training programmes to target those who most need jobs and training. In addition, many jobs are so low paying that they do not have a major impact on household earnings.

In Chapter 4, I noted the degree to which the new jobs in the south of Ireland, despite the 'high-tech' manufacturing concentration of new output, were low paying service jobs, often with inferior terms of employment. This raises another interesting difference between the older and newer patterns of Irish poverty. Despite low wages, the risk of poverty for employed workers has actually fallen. In other words, while more workers are working for low wages, fewer of them end up in poverty because of it. A major reason for this apparent discrepancy is that many of the people who have taken up marginal employment are second earners in their households – usually, women and youths. It is not only possible, but quite common, that the collective wages in households made up of two or three people in marginal, low-paying work will be 'above the poverty line'. Most of those who are considered impoverished in Ireland today do not have even marginal work.

Table 5.3 Composition of impoverished households in the south of Ireland, 1973–94, by labour force status of household head (%)

Labour force status of household head	*1973*	*1980*	*1987*	*1994*
Farmer	26	26	24	9
Employee	9	10	8	6
Self-employed	4	3	5	7
Unemployed	10	15	37	33
Ill/disabled	10	9	11	9
Retired	17	19	8	10
Home Duties	25	17	7	25
Total	101	99	100	99

Source: Combat Poverty Agency (1997b:41).

Thus, many people who are socially excluded in the sense that they have marginal jobs are *not* in poverty by the standard definitions. While there has been a recent tendency in the EU to replace the conception of 'poverty' with that of 'social exclusion', therefore, this shows that the two are not the same concept. It is quite possible to be socially excluded in terms of one's position in the labour market without being 'in poverty' by most accepted definitions (or, if one defines social exclusion by access to work, low-paid workers could be in poverty without being 'excluded'). The historic shift in Irish poverty, then, has been from farmers and low-paid workers to unemployed and discouraged workers. In this sense, Irish poverty – although it has not deepened in income terms because of improving social welfare provisions – has truly become *deep social exclusion*.

The poor, by and large, cannot even work. They are shunted into housing estates. They are hidden in flats, homes, and caravans.

Perhaps the gravest consequence of this social exclusion is that so many of the Irish poor are children. Households with children are nearly twice as likely to be in poverty as households without them. The risk of poverty among children has risen in the 1990s to a point where 29 per cent of children were in poverty in 1994 (measured by the 50 per cent threshold of average income) as opposed to 18 per cent of adults (Walsh 1997:19). Overall, the Celtic tiger has increased the disadvantages of the most socially and economically excluded groups of the population. The risk of poverty rose between 1987 and 1994 for the unemployed (up from 57.2 to 59.4 per cent), the ill or disabled (up from 33.7 to 44.5 per cent), and the home worker (up from 9.8 to 34.9 per cent). The rise in the risk of poverty was especially high for households containing children and a single adult. Part of this rise was avoidable, as the Irish state allowed a relative decline in child income support and welfare payments for lone parents and the elderly.[11]

There are also important geographic components to poverty. Highly uneven development between the east and south of the island, on the one hand, and the north and west, has been chronic. Since the state depends on attracting TNCs for growth, and it has made Ireland attractive largely by placing as few conditions as possible on potential investors, it is difficult to induce many companies to locate in the less developed rural areas of the north and west. Some of the difficulty can be overcome by incentives, but where flexibility is concerned the island simply does not have an advanced enough infrastructure to induce island-wide industrial development. A report by the National Economic and Social Council at the end of 1997 found that economic growth was limited to urban areas and that rural western counties such as Mayo, Roscommon, Leitrim and Cavan have not benefited at all from the economic growth of the 1990s. The report called for strong government policies to counteract economic marginalisation and poverty in these areas.

But while the most geographically widespread poverty problem is rural, the deepest and most populated pockets of poverty and exclusion are in the urban ghettos of Dublin and other Irish cities. Dublin has numerous public housing estates like Cherry Orchard, where two-thirds of the population are under 25 yet there is not a single school, or others where the unemployment rate reaches and even exceeds 80 per cent. According to Anne Power, who has researched public housing estates throughout Europe, Ireland's estates have the lowest allocations of resources and facilities for education and leisure in Europe. Unlike other 'ghettos', where people are stigmatised according to their race, the residents of Irish public housing estates are stigmatised simply because they live there, despite the fact that they are 'white' people with similar backgrounds to the rest of the Irish population. Irish law states that public housing estates are for people who cannot help themselves, and the tenants of estates have no say in the management of their estates, which are run by bureaucrats who rarely visit them (Power 1998). A 1996 Irish government report on heroin use in these estates found that the greatest need was for sport and recreation facilities for their impoverished youth. Yet the 1998 budget – the same budget that halved the capital gains tax rate and reduced the standard corporate profit rate by 4 per cent – reduced the allocation for such facilities from I£20 million to I£1.25 million. Not only do reports of degrading conditions in these estates compare badly with the rest of Europe, they also fall far short of the public housing standards provided in other 'tiger economies' like Singapore.

The State and Poverty

The lack of state concern about its most concentrated poverty – that of its urban estates – raises the question of how the southern Irish state has reacted in general to the problem of poverty in the 1990s. We saw in Chapter 3 that the amount of economic growth in the Celtic tiger has been vastly overstated, partly because such a large part of the proceeds of growth are repatriated by TNCs and partly because an unknown part is created by TNC transfer-pricing policies. Yet there are still considerably more resources left in Ireland due to growth, much of it in the hands of the state, and how this is distributed is largely a matter of government policy.

The budgetary position of the southern Irish state has improved considerably since 1987, when it had one of the highest public- and foreign-debt to GNP ratios in the world. This has happened due to a combination of mild austerity policies, which began at that time, fortuitous shifts in foreign exchange rates, and rising tax revenues. The last of these factors is mainly due to Ireland's extremely regressive taxes, which fall heavily on working-class wage earners both through income and expenditure taxes. In addition, despite the fact that southern Irish corporate tax rates are extremely low by international standards, essentially making the state a tax haven, profits reported there have risen at such rapid rates that they have contributed to rising state revenues.

During 1990–97, the state's revenues rose by 87 per cent, or 9 per cent annually. When the different sources of revenues are distinguished, however, the class bias of taxation becomes startlingly clear. Whereas nearly three-quarters (72 per cent) of the increased revenues came from taxes on incomes and expenditure, less than a fifth (18 per cent) came from corporate profits taxes – despite the fact, as we have seen, that corporate profits made up such a large proportion of economic growth. The regressive bias of Irish taxation is especially clear with regard to capital gains tax and wealth taxes (including estate duties), which each accounted for about 1 per cent of increased revenues. Thus, the Irish state got considerably richer during the 1990s, but it was largely at the expense of the Irish working (and consuming) public. Sadly, groups such as the Irish trade unions have contributed to this inequality by encouraging a series of 'national agreements' since the 1980s that have reduced corporate taxes and given standard tax increases across the board on pay and expenditure, which left the poor and low-paid workers falling further behind (Lynch 1997).

How has the southern Irish state spent its extra cash? This is where state policy *could* have had a substantial impact on poverty. There are obvious ways the poor could have been immediately helped, through changes in taxation (such as the reduction of value-added taxes on basic consumption items which, as we have seen, was decidedly *not* done) and through government spending policies that targeted socially excluded groups of people. In 1995, the southern government announced a 'national anti-poverty strategy', about which it then consulted numerous social groups over two years. The strategy was published in 1997 by the governing 'rainbow coalition' of Fine Gael, traditionally the most economically conservative southern party, and the purportedly left-wing Labour and Democratic Left parties.[12] The government claimed that the strategy could halve the numbers of 'consistently poor' by the year 2007 through programmes of education, income maintenance and employment creation that would be targeted at the poor. It was a step forward for a government to acknowledge the importance of fighting poverty. But, of course, even its rather mild anti-poverty measures have not been implemented.

A more interesting and potentially promising approach to fighting poverty has been promoted by CORI, who propose a Basic Income policy where everyone in the state would be given a monthly income that would keep them above the poverty line. The scheme would be financed by a single tax rate on individuals and a 'social responsibility tax' on employers. It would reward previously unpaid home work, encourage further education, and promote economic equality between women and men. And it would eliminate *unemployment traps* – where people are discouraged from taking low-pay jobs (which, as we have seen, have become more and more common in Ireland) because they would lose or only marginally gain income as a result of working – and *poverty traps*, where low-paid workers find that a wage rise actually reduces their take-home pay because they pay substantially more taxes. Such anomalies are reportedly common in the Irish income tax system (Clark and Healy 1997). Such a radical programme has found support from some surprising quarters, such as the former Fine Gael Taoiseach Garret FitzGerald, who favours it because it would eliminate the peculiarities of the tax system, including not just the various poverty traps but also its inflexibility, which make it impossible to effectively target tax concessions at the lower paid. Ironically, FitzGerald argues, it is the state's improved fiscal position of the 1990s that has made this system possible, because it could now be funded by a moderate flat tax of around 45 per cent, whereas in the 1980s it would have required a tax rate of 65–70 per cent (FitzGerald 1997).

Yet the neoliberal policies which have been partly responsible for the state's increased revenues, along with the necessity of subsidising foreign capital, have kept it from instituting effective policies to fight poverty or even inequality. Year after year, the southern Irish state has avoided any serious attempts to end poverty, instead giving small increases to social welfare recipients and introducing fairly innocuous temporary job schemes for the unemployed (many of which have failed even to target the long-term unemployed). The proportion of government spending that goes on social welfare dropped from 36 per cent in 1992 to 34.5 per cent in 1996. And the proportion of GDP spent on social welfare has also fallen since 1987, despite the fact that the number of social welfare recipients has increased considerably. Despite its high unemployment and high incidence of poverty, Ireland has the lowest per capita expenditures on social welfare in the EU except for Portugal (CORI 1997).

All the while, the main recipients of government budgets have been the better-off members of society. According to CORI, who monitor the effects of government spending on different social groups, social welfare payments have fallen further below the amount necessary to provide 'a minimally adequate standard of living' while tax breaks and state transfers have effectively widened the gap between the unemployed and the highest income earners. In the decade from 1986 to 1996, for example, changes in state transfers widened the income gap between a single unemployed person and a single person receiving double the average industrial wage by I£4,960 (Pollak 1996). The state has increased the lowest kinds of social welfare payments faster than higher welfare payments, but this has only had the effect of slightly decreasing the depth of poverty, while it has failed to attack the extent of poverty or inequality. According to CORI's calculations, southern Irish governments in the mid-1990s were responsible for widening the gap in take-home pay between an unemployed couple and a couple earning I£20,000 by I£1,405 a year (Kilfeather 1997).

With each successive 'Santa Claus' budget, Irish governments appear to have favoured the rich more and more. In late 1997, the once-populist Fianna Fáil government announced another in a string of regressive budgets going back into the 1980s. It concentrated on tax cuts for the rich rather than programmes to help the poor and low-paid workers. Its major bonuses to the working class were slight decreases in income taxes, which were given in equal measure to the highest and lowest paid. Expenditure taxes, which affect the poor and low-paid workers most because they spend practically all of their income, remained high. But the major thrust under Celtic tigerhood has been to decrease taxes on the wealthy: corporate profits taxes and capital gains taxes. In late 1997, capital gains taxes were cut in half – from 40 to 20 per cent. And the corporation tax was reduced from 36 to 32 per cent, following a similar decrease in the previous year that amounted to some I£100 million in tax cuts for corporations.[13] Incredibly, while poverty remains Ireland's biggest social problem, the main fiscal commitment of all governing parties has been that corporate profits taxes should be reduced by 4 per cent per year until they fall to 12.5 per cent in the year 2006![14] It is clear that southern Irish governments have no intention of seriously addressing poverty, except through vague hopes that promoting high profits will ensure a continuation of 'economic buoyancy', in turn increasing the numbers of jobs and pulling some people out of poverty. Such hopes are by no means assured since most new jobs are extremely low paid service jobs. Thus, research indicates that a large proportion of the unemployed would be no better off if they moved into employment (Keena 1996).

Conclusions

We started this chapter with a common theme of the literature on economic development: that Taiwan and possibly South Korea indicate that it is possible to go through an economic 'take-off' without suffering higher inequality. They have grown rapidly and reduced poverty, despite the inequitable and authoritarian nature of their states. Much of the explanation for this was that equality was good business in East Asia – in Taiwan and South Korea, for example, it increased agrarian productivity and helped create more vibrant domestic markets, which were initially important for domestic industry. Land redistribution cut into the incomes of rich landholders, while the states discouraged excessive incomes for the emerging industrial elites as part of their plans for industrial efficiency. At the same time, part of the explanation is historically specific: these were poor and highly agrarian countries with very high levels of inequality, so that successful industrialisation with relatively full employment of migrants from the countryside (unlike in Latin America) meant that most workers' incomes more or less had to rise. Additionally, in the case of Taiwan the new ruling class was from the Chinese mainland, and part of its strategy to rule was to break the power of the landed indigenous class.

Singapore and the Southeast Asian 'tiger cubs', on the other hand, have experienced increasing inequality, at least partly because of their dependence on TNC investment as a basis of growth. Wages have been suppressed in order to attract TNCs, while state spending has emphasised the needs of foreign-led growth rather than the indigenous populations. Social welfare programmes have been restricted, partly to free up state resources for 'development' programmes (such as infrastructure projects and investment subsidies) and partly because they are perceived to reduce worker flexibility, which is especially attractive to inward investors. Moreover, low corporate taxes are especially attractive to TNCs, but they reduce state revenues that might otherwise be available for social welfare programmes.

Moreover, the requirement for flexible labour throughout East and Southeast Asia has created a dualistic employment structure which is highly unequal between 'core' workers in some high tech industries, and 'peripheral' workers in low-tech assembly and service jobs. The latter jobs are filled predominantly by women and migrant workers, who are least able to resist poor pay and working conditions. In times of economic recession, such workers can easily be laid off and, in the case of migrant workers, can even be expelled from the country, reducing the negative social impacts of unemployment. In 1997–98, for example, it is estimated that several million migrant workers would be expelled from Taiwan, Indonesia and Malaysia, shifting many of the adverse social consequences of economic crisis from their source country to economically marginal countries like Bangladesh.

Ireland in the late 1980s and 1990s seems to have more parallels with Singapore than Taiwan with respect to poverty and inequality. Much of its agrarian transformation, through which large numbers of people left farm work for waged employment – and which tied industrialisation to reduced inequality – had already happened during the 1970s and early 1980s. High-end incomes were also limited during the 1970s and 1980s by the dominance of TNCs, who took their high profits out of Ireland thus depressing the top end of the income distribution. But by the 1990s the agrarian transformation was largely complete, and Irish agriculture was producing with near-minimum labour inputs. The indigenous capitalist class had already been broken by the effects of free trade after Ireland joined the EC in the 1970s. Therefore, in a country where profits and high professional incomes were the basis of economic growth, where employment creation was concentrated in low-paying service jobs, and where the state was committed to fiscal policies that heavily favoured the rich, rising inequality was a fairly obvious consequence of economic growth.

Labour flexibility, which increased Ireland's attractiveness to TNCs, was assured by several mechanisms. The chronic uneven development between the south/east and the north/west of the island and the large pockets of urban unemployment not only provided a reserve of unemployed labour who could move in and out of work as employers desired but also served as a warning to labour that pliancy attracted jobs while militancy repelled them. There was a large reserve of women who were willing to enter the lower end of the job market to supply cheap and flexible labour in assembly and services. And there was a pool of emigrants and potential emigrants – both semi-skilled and highly skilled – with an established record of return immigration, who could move into the Irish labour market as jobs became available and back out again if they disappeared. Ireland's historical pattern of emigration created a group of flexible workers, very much like the foreign workers who moved into Singapore for high-tech and marginal jobs when employment was expanding, and out again during times of crisis.

The creation of a more just society, where the fruits of economic growth were distributed more equally and turned toward general social prosperity, would require a strong commitment by the state. Such a project would require effective policies to counteract inequality and poverty – progressive tax reforms, encouragement of higher pay and the kinds of radical reforms exemplified by the basic income policies discussed above. Such policies would make it harder for the south to continue attracting as many TNC projects as it attracted in the early to mid-1990s, and thus would require a shift towards a more holistic economic strategy, with a bigger role for domestic firms and the state sector. It would mean a recognition that the goal of enhancing social welfare – particularly the *re*-inclusion of socially excluded groups such as the long-term unemployed and the disabled – does not simply follow from policies that are aimed at maximising economic growth (indeed, the recent Irish experience shows that the two may be largely in opposition to each other). Such a recognition would be tantamount to social revolution in an Irish state that had been primed for economic liberalism and foreign-investment dependence since the late 1940s. It would be especially difficult in the neoliberal atmosphere of the world economy as it moves into the twenty-first century.

In the end, however, a redefinition of the goals of society is precisely what is necessary if Ireland is to break the problem of social exclusion. The very definition of poverty as a measure of how far people fall below some officially set minimum standard invites policies that merely bring impoverished people closer to the margins of subsistence. Dominant conceptions of poverty only concentrate on bringing the poorest of the population up to a bare minimum of what they need to subsist, from utter exclusion into the margins of society. As Lynch (1997) argues, adequate conceptions of poverty would have to recognise the rights of all members of society to 'participate equally' in society, including not just in society's opportunities and material benefits, but in the arena of decision making for policies that affect poverty. Clearly, the problem of poverty is also one of powerlessness. The final indictment of the 'Celtic tiger' is that economic growth may have provided the resources to begin to really tackle poverty, yet the policies that brought economic growth have made Irish policy makers *less* rather than more able to address poverty even by its more moderate definitions. Meanwhile, time is running out because these resources cannot be counted on in the long-term.

6 Tigers: An Endangered Species?

> Ní bhíonn uasal nó íseal ach thuas seal agus thíos seal.
> [Neither lordly nor lowly, but up for awhile and down for awhile.]
> (Old Irish Proverb)

This book began with a tale of success. The aim of Chapter 1 was to explain the meaning of economic tigerhood, so that we could understand what people mean when they refer to the southern Irish economy as a 'Celtic tiger'. The remarkable sustained success of Japan and the East Asian economies was explained by a model of economic development that some have termed the 'flying geese'. Many experts consider the relationship between Japan, on the one hand, and the East Asian tigers, on the other, as a much more constructive relationship than that of Western imperialism. Where Western TNCs move around the world to exploit – whether it be raw materials, labour, or consumers – Japanese corporations and their sponsoring state found mutual benefit in building up the corporations of South Korea or Taiwan so that they became junior partners in an integrated regional Asian economy. This was a dependent relationship, which strongly limited the East Asians' ability to move into the highest technologies; but it was a much more 'developmental' relationship than appears to exist in Western imperialism. Asian states played their part in constructing and managing this networked economy through their sponsorship of local capital, their planning of trading relationships and strategies for access to raw materials, and their combined 'carrot and stick' approach toward inducing export growth and technological upgrading in their national corporations.

In more recent years, new tigers such as Thailand and Malaysia appeared to be following in the wake (or 'V') of Japan and the East Asians. David Hale, the chief economist for the Zurich Insurance Group, estimated that Thailand, South Korea, Indonesia, Malaysia and the Philippines accounted for almost half of the growth in world manufacturing output since 1991 (quoted in Palat 1997).

In mid-1997, however, a severe crisis hit Asia. Some financial experts even spoke of a 'meltdown' of the Asian miracle. Beginning with the collapse of the Thai currency in early July, a series of corporate and bank failures, large currency devaluations, and stock market crashes hit nearly every major economy in Asia – from Thailand, Malaysia and Indonesia, up through South Korea and Hong Kong, and even to Japan itself. These events show how important it is to balance any discussion of the tiger 'miracles' with analysis of their limitations. Doing so also brings home the central argument of this book: that we must be careful about the unrestrained optimism that so many experts and pundits have displayed about 'miracle' economies like southern Ireland's. Undoubtedly, substantial wealth has been created in Ireland, but wealth creation that is so highly dependent on a limited range of globally organised activities is tenuous. Moreover, Southeast Asian experiences demonstrate that growth and prosperity are not the same thing, and that the former can even impede the well-being of large sections of the population.

Meltdown or Shake-out?

The popular version of the Asian crisis of the late 1990s is that it was a financial crisis. For instance, David McWilliams, senior economist at the Banque Nationale de Paris, wrote in the *Irish Times* that 'the Asian story is simply one of boom and bust stemming from bad investment and lending. Financial implosion in countries such as Indonesia, South Korea and Thailand has resulted from a lethal combination of overlending, too much investment in the wrong things and to cap it all, a rather ridiculous weakness for believing your own propaganda which in itself caused investors to look at only the most rosy scenarios for returns when placing their bets' (16 January 1988). Roger Altman, writing in the *International Herald Tribune*, blamed 'the markets' awesome power'. For him, the Asian crisis happened because foreign exchange markets 'became disenchanted' with Asia, 'flexed their muscles, and the tigers were turned into goats' (10 December 1997). In country after country, foreign exchange rates plummeted, Western investors dropped their shares as their dollar values plummeted, foreign creditors refused to roll over loans, stock markets crashed, companies defaulted on their debts, and banks crashed. Financial analysts like McWilliams or Altman give little explanation about why such 'market opprobrium' descended on East and Southeast Asia, preferring rather to sit back in awe of the power of unregulated global markets.

The main lesson the conservative business press took from the crisis was that the markets are wiser than other economic institutions. Markets 'recognised' the weaknesses of corrupt relationships between Asian states and local capital. They 'recognised' that Asian corporations had taken out too many loans to overexpand their capacities and overextend their product lines (not to mention, of course, that the same market actors – Western investors – had been going crazy for a decade buying up Asian equities to cash in on a quick buck). In some cases, this was because expansion of exports was blindly mandated by states who considered economic growth as their overriding goal. In others, it was because of corrupt relationships between the states and 'crony corporations' run by the political and family allies of the government in power. In either case, banks were listening to politicians instead of markets. They extended unsafe loans to corporations that became overburdened with perilously high debt-equity ratios. Over time, the story goes, governments continually ignored market signals and forced banks to cover bad corporate debts with new loans. Moreover, they kept their foreign exchange rates unrealistically high so that their companies could afford the expanding flows of imports they needed to produce more goods. Eventually, these corporations extended themselves too far, foolishly expanding into activities where they could not compete. The global financial markets recognised this fact, forcibly readjusted Asian exchange rates, corporations had to default on loans and, consequently, banks began to go bust. When the crash finally came it hit hard on currencies, stock markets, and financial institutions.

The lesson was one that neoliberals at institutions like the World Bank and IMF had been pushing for years: states cannot efficiently guide economies. Even smart states will eventually get into trouble, especially if their economies get too large to handle, as happened in South Korea. Economic growth, then, is not just the overriding goal of states, but is eventually their undoing *unless they recognise the need to marketise*. In most of the endangered tigers – first Thailand, then Indonesia and South Korea – the IMF stepped in with billions of dollars to bail the regimes and their banks out of crisis. But the price was one that the IMF had so successfully pushed throughout Latin America and Africa: austerity, deregulation, marketisation. The Asians, who had eluded the IMF for so many years, were finally ripe for the picking.

Writing in the *Financial Times* late in 1997, Stephen Fidler (the paper's Latin American editor) made explicit all of these parallels. He argued that Asia in the 1990s was in the same place as Latin

America in the 1980s: overburdened by debts, corrupt state–company relationships, inefficient economic 'show projects' that the countries could neither run well nor afford, and unrealistically high currency exchange rates. Once the cheap loans dried up, beginning with Mexico in 1982, one Latin American 'miracle' after another went into prolonged economic collapses that experts referred to as Latin America's 'lost decade'. Fidler wondered aloud whether the Asians, too, were experiencing a debt crisis that would reverse their previous economic gains for years (Fidler 1997).

Much of this explanation, however, is superficial. Asia in 1997 faced an economic crisis, not merely a financial one. True, a major effect of the crisis *in the West* was that investors had to rapidly pull out of Asia once the local currencies began to devaluate. For years, the Western business press has pushed an analysis that equates stock markets with economies (so much so, for instance, that the global TV network CNN regularly refers to its stock market and money reports as 'the consumer news'). But currency and stock market crashes were symptoms of the Asian crises, not their cause. Debtors failed to repay their debts *not* because they were corrupt governments led by elites who had wastefully gobbled up cheap credit – the common pattern in Latin America a decade earlier – but because they were manufacturers who could no longer sell all of their products. Many of them had expanded on the basis of economic signals and past experience, as entrepreneurs regularly do, but they failed to foresee (as entrepreneurs also regularly do) that there were limits to the demand for their products. Asian producers, by and large, depended on the US as the major market for their expanded manufactures. By the 1990s, however, American consumers could no longer purchase what Asia produced. Finding a solution to this limitation would involve considerable economic restructuring in Asia and world-wide, something which often follows from economic crisis.

Asia's crisis, then, largely indicated its economic *strength* rather than its weakness. It was a fairly normal periodic crisis of overextended capitalism, as the global economy had surely become in the wake of 1989 and the end of the Cold War. Andre Gunder Frank cleverly summarised this ironic situation, arguing that 'the present crisis in East Asia does NOT reflect the "meltdown" of the East Asian "miracle" but just the opposite: it reflects the decline of the US and the rise of East Asia in the world economy'. As evidence, Frank cited the fact that all previous world-wide recessions after the Second World War began in the US, but 'this is the FIRST major recession of modern times to START in Asia and to spread from there to other parts of the world economy'.[1]

Tigers, TNCs and other Foreign Investors

The market limitations of export-led 'development' or 'industrialisation' in a liberalised global economy were examined long ago by Samir Amin (1976). It worried him that so many countries were trying to achieve industrialisation through the back door by attracting foreign direct investment. Indeed, they had been encouraged to do so by several decades of a an American 'open door' policy, beginning with Truman's Point Four programme for the south, which paralleled the Marshall Plan in Europe. *Direct foreign investment* by transnational corporations (TNCs) soon became an extremely important source of industrial investment for many late-industrialising countries in the 1960s, especially in Latin America. From the American point of view, the original intention was to gain access to critical raw materials, often in former European colonies (Bunker and O'Hearn 1993). But over time, American and European manufacturers began directly investing in new subsidiaries around the world, making components and assembling their final products. Many observers referred to the alarming rise of TNC manufacturing investment in the Third World as a 'new international division of labour' where cheaper peripheral labour for the first time was significantly drawn into industrial production for the First World (Frobel et al 1980).

Amin recognised that foreign investment produced temporary high rates of growth in the recipient countries, but he argued that these growth rates began to collapse once the investment matured and inward investment flows began to slow. His reasoning was straightforward: TNCs invest abroad mainly to get access to new export markets, especially the developed markets of other industrial regions. They are not usually interested in building up the local markets where they invest – to the contrary, they want to keep down production costs to cheapen their exports. This tends to limit their workers' collective consuming power. Moreover, to the extent that localities must 'open up' their economies so that TNCs can operate more easily, their markets are penetrated by foreign suppliers thus reducing the local demand available to domestic firms. Another concern about foreign projects was that they were separate from the rest of the economy, existing in 'enclaves' where they did little or nothing to encourage the growth of indigenous industries. For all of these reasons, export-led development is necessarily dependent on core markets, especially those of Europe and North America. And the TNC-dominated variety of export-led development is particularly vulnerable. Unless there are strong internal markets to act as safety valves, downturns in core markets translate into local recession – TNCs relocate or restructure and domestic exporters cannot sell their products.

Many elements of this story were in my own explanation of Ireland's deep recession and unemployment boom of the 1980s (O'Hearn 1989). TNCs that invested in Ireland in the 1970s and early 1980s created immediate short-term economic growth, but they also created externalities that reduced economic growth rates in the long-run. Import penetration decimated local production. There were few linkages between the more dynamic but externally controlled TNC sectors and the stagnant local economy. When global recession and restructuring caused the TNCs, on which Ireland depended, to disinvest, the Irish economy went into a tailspin that was beyond the reach of domestic economic policy.

The East Asian tigers, however, successfully managed these problems of market dependence for at least several decades. South Korea and Taiwan were partly protected from global market fluctuations because their expansion was based on domestic industries rather than on direct TNC investment. They suppressed wages to a degree, thus enabling their corporations to compete in export markets. Such wage suppression *could have* exacerbated East Asian dependence on export markets by reducing the vibrancy of their domestic markets. This would have been a serious problem, indeed, since these countries used production for domestic markets as a hothouse to improve their manufacturers' ability to graduate into export markets. But due to factors discussed in Chapter 1, such as their military-strategic importance to the US in the Cold War, both South Korea and Taiwan were able to protect their local markets so that they could be used to their maximum degree to supplement demand for national products. To the degree that such protection will be more difficult in the liberalised conditions of the 1990s and beyond, this may be a bigger problem for the East Asians in the future than it was in the past.

Singapore used a somewhat different strategy – one of diversity – to decrease its market vulnerability. The EDB in Singapore skilfully identified the emerging global growth sectors and targeted their energies on attracting firms from those sectors. They adeptly managed their role as an *export platform* for TNCs, maintaining high flows of new FDI by attracting a diverse geographic range of projects from North America, Asia, and even Europe. But they also diversified very early on into financial services, becoming an Asian leader, and then into integrated production and services in infrastructure (for example, transport, communications, distribution). Thus, Singapore balanced its dependence on foreign investments with its own thriving domestic activities. This distinguished Singapore from other Southeast Asian economies that had high rates of TNC direct investment – those economies were dependent on a much more limited basket of exports to a more limited set of customers, and had little in the way of vibrant domestic manufacturers to balance the foreign corporate sector. In this respect, they more closely resemble the southern Irish economy.

By the 1990s, global conditions had changed considerably. Following the Uruguay Round of GATT and other measures, the global economy was considerably liberalised under the regulation of the new WTO and other supranational bodies. Moreover, the East Asians no longer had special dispensation to protect their domestic markets since the end of the Cold War and the opening up of economies such as China's and Vietnam's. This increasing global liberalisation made it even more imperative that corporations from each major economic region maintain a presence in every market since it is harder for core powers to build up their own zones of economic influence as guaranteed markets. Indeed, this was how I explained the emergence of the 'Celtic tiger' in the 1990s (Chapter 3): American corporations made major moves to increase their presence in the European market; they tended to agglomerate their new projects to take advantage of the flexibility this allowed; and Ireland was fortunate enough to receive a major share of American-owned electronics projects in Europe because they agglomerated around other major firms such as Intel.

In the scramble for market share, every major producer of cars or computers tries to produce and sell as many units of their product as they can in each market. But this increases their vulnerability to problems of insufficient market demand. As they and their competitors produce more of their product globally than people can buy, prices fall and stocks of unsold goods build up. This is precisely what happened to Asian productive networks in the 1990s – from the large Japanese and East Asian firms to their subsidiaries and subcontractors in Southeast Asia – as they were unable to sell enough of their products, especially in the West. As a consequence, their profits fell and many companies closed, although their capacities generally remain intact. Ironically, Singapore's strategy of diversification rather than protection left it less vulnerable to the demand crisis of the 1990s, since it had already adapted to global liberalisation and depended less on protection to assure its conditions for expansion.

Countries like Thailand fared the worst. Just like other tigers, exports are its 'engine' of economic growth. But its exports are highly concentrated in TNC-controlled sectors, and that was where the crisis began. Thai exports in September 1996 were more than 9 per cent below the same month in 1995. Overall, Thailand had zero export growth in 1996, and negative growth in 1997 due to insufficient global demand in sectors like electronics and textiles. Other Asian countries also experienced difficulties in exports and this precipitated the 'financial crises' and currency devaluations that swept the region.

Viewed in these terms, an increasing number of observers predicted that many of the Asian economies would re-emerge strongly from their economic crisis. Falling exchange rates, encouraged by IMF receivership, cheapened Asian exports, making them more attractive in Western markets and enabling them to sell more there. Moreover, devaluation made imports less attractive in Asia, ironically having the perverse effect (from the point of view of the US and Europe) of turning regional Asian consumption back inward. As Palat argues, far from creating a 'lost decade' as happened in Latin America, the 1997 crisis was more likely to encourage a renewed industrial boom in Asia, as European and American companies moved their manufacturing operations there to take advantage of vastly reduced (in dollar terms) costs.[2] If such shifts were widespread, it would mean renewed pressures of unemployment in the West.

Of course, such changes would impact differently in different parts of Asia. As leading industrial economies, Japan and the original 'tigers' were most likely to re-emerge as leading industrial powers. The economic future of later industrialisers like Thailand and Indonesia is less certain. Unlike Japan and East Asia before them, these economies are practically at the tail end of the 'V' of the flying geese. Thus, they depend to a much greater degree on foreign TNC investments while their domestic industries are far less advanced (despite the emergence of such show projects as the Malaysian Proton car project). The most dynamic industrial producers in Thailand, Indonesia or Malaysia are mostly controlled by Japanese, South Korean or American corporations, either directly or through their extensive subcontracting networks. Where a Taiwanese or South Korean firm that makes parts for Japanese cars may be a large company that makes other things as well, the Thai company that makes parts for the same Japanese firm is unlikely to have the expertise to make other things – it is dependent on its foreign buyer. The Southeast Asian firms that are not dependent are usually less viable than similar Japanese or East Asian companies, and often corrupt. In Indonesia, for instance, scores of state-sponsored monopolies are run by ex-President Suharto's relatives, from Tommy Suharto's national car project (run by a company with no experience in car manufacture), to Tutut Suharto's toll roads and mass transit railway in Jakarta. Southeast Asia then, despite its rapid growth, appears to be far more dependent and thus more economically vulnerable than East Asia.

The major concern for the countries of Southeast Asia, therefore, is whether they can attract enough foreign investment to regain acceptable economic growth rates, or whether they will continue to lag, as the Latin American countries did in their 'lost decade'. Structurally, the 'tiger cubs' of Southeast Asia appear to be caught in a squeeze in their abilities to attract TNC projects and subcontracts. On the one hand, devalued currencies and rising unemployment made their labour much cheaper after 1997, which in turn makes them more attractive to potential investors. Yet Asia as a whole has a large labour surplus, and heavy competition for foreign investment from China, Vietnam and South Asia will make it difficult to recover a large and consistent enough flow of foreign projects to ensure their previous level of 'dependent development'. There are many more 'geese' at the tail of the 'V' than at its head. On the other hand, the Southeast Asian economies have severe shortages of skilled labour such as engineers and technicians, so it will be difficult for them to attract many more higher-tech TNC projects.

Ireland

What parallels can we draw for Ireland from these global changes, crises, and probable outcomes in other 'tiger economies'? Let us quickly run down what we have established about the southern Irish economy with respect to its recent period of high economic growth. This will allow us to assess the social and economic impacts of economic growth in the 1990s.

First, rapid Irish growth has been overwhelmingly concentrated in exports by TNC-dominated sectors. Within this, growth has been dominated by exports generated by American electronics and pharmaceutical firms. As I argued in Chapter 3, this is largely a result of the fact that the IDA attracted key manufacturing projects like the computer processor firm Intel, which like all major electronics companies was looking for a European base to gain access to the EU market. Scores of companies agglomerated around Intel to capture the advantages of proximity in this age of 'flexible specialisation'. Since Intel, the south of Ireland has attracted a third of American manufacturing investments in the EU. Additionally, top American pharmaceuticals companies have come to Ireland, not just to be near other such firms but also to take advantage of Ireland's tax haven in an economic sector that is notorious for its transfer pricing practices. Twelve of *Fortune* magazine's top 20 American electronics corporations – and each of its top 10 pharmaceutical companies – have at least one plant in Ireland. Additional wealth has been created in activities that are tied to these expansions, particularly construction and financial/property speculation.

Second, while *economic growth* has been primarily in foreign-owned manufacturing, *employment growth* has been overwhelmingly in services. TNCs have created relatively little employment, despite the high publicity profile of the jobs they create. Services, on the other hand, have accounted for the vast majority of new jobs in the 1990s, half of which were routine service jobs like clerical workers, hotel workers and shop assistants and another third of which were (mostly semi-skilled) 'technical workers'. By and large, the quality of work created by Irish tigerhood has been low, with job security, conditions of employment, and pay at substandard levels. By European standards, Ireland had low levels of part-time and contract work before 1990, but the proportion of such 'atypical' work among new Irish jobs has been the highest in the EU. While skill shortages have emerged for engineers and other trained personnel, most Irish people must compete for unskilled or semi-skilled service jobs in sectors like tourism and retail, 70 per cent of which have gone to women.

Third, investment has been surprisingly low for such a rapidly growing economy. As we saw in Chapter 3, private investment fell by more than a third between 1990 and 1994 and the fall was especially large in manufacturing – the sector that has driven southern Irish export growth and overall economic growth! The share of manufacturing investment in total capital investment fell to 16 per cent in 1996, despite the fact that industry accounted for 60 per cent of GDP growth. Southern Irish investment rates have been the lowest in the EU during the 1990s, despite the rapid increase in the presence of TNCs. As a result, some experts have referred to the Irish experience of the 1990s as 'investmentless growth'.

Finally, consumption has risen at a much lower rate than economic growth, while inequality and poverty have risen. Both private and public consumption stagnated in the first half of the 1990s, the first because the share of earned incomes fell rapidly relative to profits, and the second because the state restrained its spending after the late 1980s. The share of consumption in GDP fell from 78 per cent in the mid-1980s to 70 per cent in the mid-1990s, although it recovered some in 1996. While overall consumption has stagnated relative to economic growth, however, there has been a rapid rise in conspicuous consumption such as property speculation and luxury car purchases, and this reflects increasing inequality during the 1990s.

Thus, Irish tigerhood is characterised by a rather strange set of contradictory results: high growth of TNC production and exports *without* correspondingly high investments or job creation in manufacturing; concentration of employment growth in services *without* correspondingly rapid growth of service provision; and rapid overall economic growth with stagnant investment, sluggish or spotty consumption growth, and rising inequality. How does this compare to other tigers, and what are the implications of the differences or similarities? This comparative question is especially important since so many of the Asian tigers, especially the more recent industrialisers like Thailand and Indonesia, collapsed so severely in the late 1990s. Does their demise in any way foreshadow similar problems in Ireland? Does Ireland have any safety valves against collapse, or are there even factors that might make its collapse *deeper* or *more severe* than those of Asia?

In terms of liberalisation, increased competition for export markets, and possible sources of crisis little has changed to Ireland's position in the 1990s despite its 'tiger' status. In some ways its position has disimproved since southern Irish economic growth depends more than ever on the state's ability to attract TNCs and, in turn, on the TNCs' ability to expand their exports to European markets. Moreover, these companies are concentrated more than ever in terms of both their geographical and sectoral origins: they are American-based TNCs making computers and pharmaceuticals. Thus, Ireland is most vulnerable to precisely the phenomena that created the Asian crisis of the 1990s: the limitations of core demand for the products that are produced there, although in this case it is European demand for American products rather than American demand for Asian products.

Many economists have begun to argue that East Asia's 'fix' for their crisis was the crisis itself: falling exchange rates cheapen Asian goods and make them more saleable abroad, while Asian labour is cheaper and thus more attractive to Western investors. Unlike East Asia, however, Ireland has no such 'fixes' for a demand crisis. Its exchange rates are tied within the EU, and from the late 1999 it will trade in the single EU currency. In these circumstances, the demand for products made in Ireland is at the whim of currency movements that are determined elsewhere. The cost of imports, of course, is also determined elsewhere. Even if a devalued dollar substantially improved the competitive position of American products in Europe, for instance, under European Monetary Union this would increase the costs of Irish labour and services to American companies and could hinder a full recovery of American production in Ireland.

Hints of Asian-style global changes impacted Ireland in 1997, although they would take some time to reach full strength. In late 1997 and 1998 the Irish punt rapidly fell in value relative to all other Western currencies. It fell by 15 per cent relative to sterling, from parity at the beginning of 1997 to £0.85 at year's end. And it fell by even more against the US dollar, from $1.64 to $1.37. The Irish Central Bank admitted that the punt would continue to fall rapidly against the major currencies in 1998 and that it could do little to stop this mini-freefall. Although the devaluation was mostly due to adjustments of currencies in the run-up to European Monetary Union, it made some commentators aware of the vulnerability of the Irish economic miracle.

Also in late 1997, global demand problems and changing Asian conditions began to affect Ireland's ability to attract TNCs. The computer firm Seagate decided to move its major disk-drive manufacturing plant in Clonmel (County Tipperary) to Asia, creating a loss of 1,400 jobs. It also halted planned expansion of its operations in Derry, in the north of Ireland. Seagate's management cited lower production costs in Asia as the reason for its decision. AST, a major computer manufacturer, announced plans to cut its global workforce by a third, including the probable closure of its Limerick plant. Other cutbacks due to sluggish global demand included layoffs in the software giant Microsoft. Very dark clouds appeared to be gathering in 1998, despite the fact that major expansion by companies like Dell computers appeared to ensure that above-average economic growth would continue for a time.

The vulnerability of the Irish economy was shown most vividly in late February of 1997, when the share price of its most important TNC, Intel, fell by a quarter in less than one week. Intel admitted that it (along with the rest of the high-tech electronics sector) was suffering from long-term global structural problems. Demand for personal computers was near saturation point, with prices falling drastically and consumers demanding lower-cost, low-profit products. Moreover, more computer companies were supplying their products on a flexible, made-to-order basis, causing instability of demand for suppliers of components. Computer companies reporting losses or drastically reduced profits for the first quarter of 1998 were precisely those that have driven the Celtic tiger: Intel, Compaq, Motorola, Hewlett-Packard. Industry analysts were predicting that if computer companies expanded their output in the future, they would have to do so with virtually no revenue growth and, at best, zero earnings growth. On the face of it, such a profits squeeze suggests that companies would have to move more production offshore in order to reduce costs. But, given the downward readjustment of Asian costs after 1997, along with the fact that TNCs locate in Ireland mainly for market access and tax advantages rather than low costs, it is hard to imagine that Ireland would retain its share of such a cost-induced outward expansion.

Ireland's ability to attract and maintain foreign projects could be restricted even more with the expansion of the EU early in the twenty-first century. The *new* EU periphery in Eastern Europe will provide extremely attractive low-wage sites with highly educated labour forces from which American and Asian investors can gain free access to the EU market. The numbers of firms choosing Asia over Ireland might be limited by the fact that most TNCs locate in Ireland primarily to gain duty-free access to the EU rather than to reduce their labour costs. Obviously they would lose this advantage if they moved all of their production facilities to Asia. But the vast overdependence of the southern Irish economy on US electronics and pharmaceutical firms will leave it extremely weak in the face of any new international crisis of demand for their products, especially as Asia re-emerges as the world's manufacturing powerhouse.

Similarly to Singapore in Asia, the southern Irish state has used its advantageous geographic position – Ireland as a gateway to Europe and Singapore as a gateway to Asia – as the basis of its strategy of 'industrialisation by invitation'. For American firms seeking access to European markets Ireland provides a relatively well-educated, low-cost, English-speaking labour force without a threat of militant trade unionism; a free enterprise oriented state that interferes minimally in business, except to subsidise it; and free trade both inward (for industrial inputs) and outward (to European markets). Add in specific benefits like capital grants and, most especially, tax-haven status for manufacturers with free profit-repatriation, and the southern Irish economy has been able to attract an impressive share of the large inflows of American direct investment into Europe. Like Singapore, Ireland is a classic example of an *export platform*: foreign companies locate relatively labour-intensive assembly operations there, importing the vast proportion of material inputs, exporting virtually all of their product, and amassing rather large profits which they subsequently take out of the country.

Playing the export-platform game requires adept management, as has been displayed by agencies such as the EDP in Singapore and the IDA in the south of Ireland. Indeed, Irish strategies of identifying emerging foreign investors appear to follow Singapore's with a lag. But there is a crucial difference in the reasons why each country introduced new policies or targeted new sectors of investment. Singapore generally changed its strategies to manage economic 'success'. It had to identify new strategies or target new sectors when bottlenecks or 'ceilings' were met in old strategies or sectors. It targeted financial services, for example, because it had attained full employment and needed to shift growth to sectors that did not require as much labour. The same is true of its attempts to upgrade manufacturing by attracting less labour-intensive projects, although this kind of strategy is difficult because host countries often must 'take what they are given' by way of TNC investment.

Ireland shifted its foreign investment targets, on the other hand, to manage economic failure. Electronics was targeted because Ireland could not attract enough foreign investment in traditional industrial sectors to assure acceptable economic growth rates or job creation. Financial services were targeted when foreign manufacturing investment slowed. In each case, despite rapid emigration, Ireland had a large labour surplus and the jobs created by TNCs could not provide enough jobs for the unemployed. In the late 1990s, after nearly a decade as Europe's leading growth economy, Ireland still has one of Europe's highest unemployment rates and its worst long-term unemployment problem. Unlike Singapore, then, Ireland has never been able to attract 'enough' foreign investment to assure full employment. Until the 1990s, it was never even able to secure enough to ensure rapid economic growth.

Ireland's narrow dependence on American TNCs makes a return to the dark days of the 1980s a strong possibility. But several years of rapid economic growth have brought very real changes to the south of Ireland. Massive amounts of wealth have been created, and some of this rapid increase in resources has gone to the southern Irish state, dramatically improving its fiscal position.

Since future growth can never be assured on the basis of TNCs, such temporary windfalls must not be squandered, but must be used for two purposes: strengthening future economic sustainability and improving the position of the Irish people as a whole, especially the most needy and economically marginalised. To what degree have the opportunities of rapid growth been exploited to make a better and more sustainable Irish society? This relates to the broader basic question that critical development analysts have asked for some time: is economic growth equivalent to prosperity?

Sustainability

There are many conceptions of sustainability. Here I refer simply to a 'weak' non-ecocentric conception, where acceptable levels of economic growth can be maintained over time (the criteria of ecological sustainability is a tougher and, in many ways, far more important one to fulfil). I have considered the present basis of Irish growth to be unsustainable because it depends on a continuous increase in exports by foreign corporations, a factor over which the Irish state has no control, apart from the IDA's ability to attract and hold TNC projects. The IDA has been very successful in this regard during the 1990s, but ultimately will be unable to maintain its success rate as the expanding EU periphery increases competition for foreign investment, as key skills become scarce in Ireland, and as global contractions and shake-outs inevitably hit TNC operations in Ireland.

Study after study – from the 1982 'Telesis report' to the 1992 Culliton report – has found that the key factor which is necessary for future sustainability of the Irish economy is the creation of strong *indigenous* sectors. These are the very sectors that have been neglected in the frantic search for more TNC investors. The Asian experience, especially that of Singapore, demonstrates clearly that dependence on foreign entities must be balanced by strategic government intervention to help create more sustainable indigenous technological capabilities. Such intervention and investment requires, first, money and resources – precisely what the southern Irish state has acquired as a result of the economic changes of the 1990s. Yet even a financially flush Irish state has still eschewed any direct role in helping create a more vibrant and sustainable indigenous economy (O'Sullivan 1995).

One might argue that an exception to this evasion has been education, where the southern Irish state invested heavily for two decades in creating more technical skills, especially in engineering. Yet this skill formation has been driven by the perceived future needs of incoming TNCs, rather than by a strategic conception of the skill base that would be required for creating dynamic economic clusters that might be the basis of a sustainable indigenous economy. Here, again, we find important differences from the more economically successful education policies in East Asia.

In the Irish context, however, it would be mistaken to assert that the creation of vibrant indigenous sectors requires no more than money or even the will to intervene by a developmental state. The rules of the EU and, increasingly, the neoliberal rules of the world economy after the Uruguay Round of GATT, have removed from states like Ireland the very instruments that would make effective intervention possible. Under EU rules Ireland has little control of its trade, and is unable to use the mechanisms that were used so successfully by East Asian states to encourage and regulate their local industries. Ireland can use low taxes to attract foreign industries, but cannot discriminate in taxes to encourage promising activities while discouraging others. Nor can it selectively protect its local market – which is, admittedly, very small – as a way of cushioning indigenous industries against shocks of global recession or strengthening nascent industries until they can compete abroad. Under European Monetary Union, small states have no control of exchange rates and limited control of interest rates. In short, the very concept of a 'developmental state' has little relevance in the European periphery today because states have none of the instruments at their command that would allow them to be 'developmental'.

Consequently, it is imperative that movements of the EU periphery organise to demand new European rules that allow their states to implement developmental policies that are currently disallowed, just as peripheral regions world-wide urgently need to unite to reverse global liberalisation. Moreover, such peripheral movements would need to pressure the EU for a new technology policy where major innovative research and design projects would be located in the periphery instead of being confined to core states as they have been heretofore (see O'Hearn 1993a).

Such changes of EU practice and regulation are generally required if peripheral European regions are to achieve acceptable levels of sustainable development, rather than competing amongst themselves for foreign investment. Yet the Irish context also provides specific requirements and opportunities for economic sustainability. The most important of these is the removal of the economic partition of the island. Obviously, an all-Ireland economy would be in the interests of the north, which has suffered as a peripheral region of a declining British economy. The north of Ireland is shackled in its ability to develop an effective response to EU integration since London follows its own European agenda, and this seldom accords with and often clashes with its interests in Europe. The recent 'mad cow' scare – under which northern Irish beef exports were banned from Europe along with British exports, despite the fact that they came from another island – is but the most obvious example.[3] The north has been similarly hampered in numerous other respects, including EU fishing regulations and, most importantly, industrial promotion policies.

The south of Ireland also has much to gain from all-island integration. The artificial restriction of cross-border economic relations restricts its strategic economic options along with the north. Unnecessary transactions costs result from separate economic administrations and transport and energy networks. Additional costs arose when the Irish punt entered the European Monetary System in 1979, unlinking its value from the pound sterling, and this problem will be exacerbated after Ireland enters the European Monetary Union in 1999 and Britain does not. An all-island economy would substantially reduce transactions costs and enable Irish producers to take advantage of scale economies that would arise from an enlarged Irish market. Hutton (1994), Bradley (1996) and others have suggested that an all-island economy would create new possibilities for north–south growth corridors, industrial clusters and state economic initiatives that would improve the environment for an emerging indigenous economy. While they may be overoptimistic, some experts estimate that as many as 75,000 new jobs could be created by full Irish economic integration (see Munck and Hamilton, forthcoming). As Bradley says with respect to creating a dynamic indigenous Irish economy, 'if ever there was a good case for the Northern and Southern private and public sectors to co-ordinate their initiatives this is it' (1996:142).

Dependence, Growth and Prosperity

Sustainable growth is one problem that will be difficult to solve; perhaps, impossible to solve without basic changes to the way the EU and global economies limit the developmental options and instruments of small states. Yet southern Irish growth has remained rapid for a longer time than most experts would have predicted in the early 1990s. Ironically, the longer these rapid growth rates continued in the late 1990s, the more people began to question whether the Celtic tiger was improving the life-style of many Irish people. Inequality and poverty have increased, as we saw in Chapter 5, along with the numbers of Irish workers who receive low pay. Irish ghettos remain places of utter degrading poverty, isolated from 'respectable' Irish society. Ireland's GDP grew by 80 per cent between 1977 and 1994, but two social scientists who developed a 'Social Progress Index' – based on 15 factors ranging from infant mortality to drug use to housing needs and medical coverage – found that its 'social progress' had increased by less than 1 per cent over the same period (Clark and Healy 1996).

People want to know why these things should be so during an economic 'miracle'. Perhaps the most common answer was to personalise issues of poverty, low pay and inequality: Irish capitalists are too greedy and unwilling to pay decent wages; Irish workers are lazy, unwilling to obtain qualifications, unwilling to work hard enough to 'earn' a decent income. Reports of skill shortages in higher-paying occupations added to such personalised explanations: if people would only educate themselves plenty of job openings would be there to turn growth into widespread prosperity.

Of course, there were elements of truth to some of these perceptions. Capitalists *are* greedy by definition. They will, by and large, pay low wages if they can get away with it. Many Irish people *are* unwilling to take up jobs that pay too little to make it worth leaving social welfare. As a consequence, most of those who take such work are supplementary family wage earners. There *are* serious skill shortages for some engineering jobs, although these shortages would number in the hundreds or thousands instead of the tens of thousands. But the main underlying reasons why economic growth has increased inequality, poverty and low pay are systemic, not personal. They are the results of an Irish state that keeps its hands off of business in order to attract foreign investment. The resultant unregulated capitalism has intensified social inequalities in ways that have not happened in some of the other 'tiger economies'.

Since the 1960s, Ireland has built an economic system that depends on foreign manufacturing projects for growth. Attracting these projects requires low taxes and a hands-off government attitude toward business. TNCs must be allowed to get on with their own business with a minimum of government interference or they simply won't come. Given such a liberal environment, they can accumulate substantial wealth, as they have done in the 1990s.

But they have never created substantial numbers of jobs. At best, as in the 1990s, they helped create a general level of economic activity that induced the creation of thousands of jobs in services and construction. But in these sectors – as in foreign assembly-type manufacturing and teleservices – most of the jobs are low paying with poor conditions of employment.

Given the 'free enterprise' ethic, whereby Irish governments hope to attract foreign companies, how could it be any different? Where the state keeps its hands off of business for the sake of foreign investors, local firms – often but not always working on a thin margin of profitability – take advantage by paying low wages. The result is increasing duality between higher-paid core workers in manufacturing and some areas of finance, and low-paid insecure workers in services, construction and manufacturing assembly.

Under these conditions, the state could ameliorate conditions of low pay and poverty through enhanced social welfare, more progressive taxation policies and other moderate social measures. But, as we saw in Chapter 5, the southern Irish state failed even this test, despite the fact that it went into the end of the 1990s with nearly twice as much annual revenue as it entered the decade. In budget after budget, the state ignored the needs of the marginalised sections of the population, preferring instead to distribute the fruits of growth unequally in favour of the richer segments of society.

The rationale was one which pits economic growth *against* social prosperity. Low corporate taxes are a main cause of rapid Irish economic growth – US TNCs have chosen Ireland primarily because its tax breaks are much more beneficial than anywhere else in the EU. If low taxes are the source of growth, the state seems to reckon, then lower taxes should bring yet more growth, a sort of insurance policy against future stagnation of the kind Ireland has experienced so often before. Successive Irish governments, made up of political parties from the right to the moderate left, committed themselves to reduce taxes on profits and wealth until they reach uniformly low rates in 2006. Despite the warning signs of increasing inequality and poverty, Irish governments have consciously chosen growth and exclusion over prosperity and inclusion.

Again, comparison with Asia is useful, even though Ireland is very different from Singapore or Taiwan. Taken as a whole, economic 'tigers' that depend on TNCs have experienced rapidly rising inequality, while those with more dynamic indigenous sectors have experienced either falling or less rapidly rising inequality. The connection may be indirect. Rising inequality does not appear to happen primarily because foreign corporations pay low wages.

In Ireland and Singapore, foreign corporations pay some higher wages (to their core workers) and some low wages (to peripheral production-line workers). Yet wages that are low by TNC standards, at least in electronics as opposed to textiles and clothing, are often higher than wages in services and informal sectors. The more important connection between foreign dependence and inequality appears to be an indirect one: in periods of rapid economic growth most of the jobs that are created are low-skilled jobs in low-paying sectors such as services, many of which service the TNCs. Where the goal is to attract foreign companies, the incidence of low pay and inequality can increase dramatically (in Singapore, low wages are set by the state while in Ireland they are set through a combination of the market and corporatist national wage agreements). This is especially true if wealth concentrates in one sector of the economy and jobs in another, as has happened in Ireland. There appears to be a connection between rising inequality and dependence on foreign investment in economies as disparate as Singapore, Ireland, and Thailand.

On the other hand, tiger economies like Taiwan that have not depended on foreign corporate investment as a source of growth have avoided this apparent connection between rapid growth and inequality. In such East Asian states, a larger part of growth has been turned into the domestic economy – wealth has not concentrated as much in as few sectors. In addition, some East Asian states have introduced programmes to improve working-class standards of living, not out of the goodness of their hearts but because social welfare makes economic sense. It increases investment and helps the state to manage labour resources, turning young workers into training programmes for new economic sectors as new needs are perceived.

At the bottom end, however, migrant workers have been treated with the same contempt throughout Asia as they are generally treated in the West. They are excluded from many welfare schemes. They are the low end of labour flexibility, brought in as they are needed at the lowest wages and then discarded when no longer needed. In 1998, the Asian tigers announced that they would be shedding millions of migrant workers – two and a half million migrants were to be expelled from Southeast Asia and up to a million from South Korea. Countries such as Bangladesh faced severe social and economic dislocation as a result of these expulsions. But in many of the 'tigers' and 'tiger cubs' this was the awful price of assuring some level of material welfare for their populations at the expense of others.

Since Ireland has never experienced a labour shortage, it has not exploited cheap migrant labour to any major extent (although, for the first time, Celtic tigerhood appears to have attracted a significant number of extremely low paid migrant workers in the catering industry). Rather, it has achieved labour flexibility by using its own migrants and return migrants. In poor economic times, Irish emigrants flee the country in droves, while each period of economic boom induces some to return. With key labour markets nearby and others made closer by modern transport, this pattern of 'shuttle migration' has become socially unsettling (Mac Laughlin 1994).[4]

What Next?

As Ireland approached the end of the 1990s, many of its financial experts were reverting to the state of mind of the early 1990s, before it experienced its few years of rapid economic growth. They began to question whether the Irish miracle was indeed just a flash in the pan between two more normal periods of relative economic stagnation. An economist from an Irish stockbrokers caught the mood early in 1998 by writing in the *Irish Times* that the Celtic tiger should be shot!

Even the original cheerleader of Irish success, the former Irish Taoiseach Garret FitzGerald, began to worry in his regular column in the *Irish Times*. 'Well before the time when the Celtic Tiger sobriquet was invented,' he wrote, 'I have been offering in this column a consistently cheerful and upbeat economic analysis. But we have now reached a point at which it is necessary to say there is a possibility ... that our run of good fortune could abruptly end' (24 January 1998).

What appears to have brought on most of this scepticism was not a sudden analysis of the origins and dynamics of the Celtic tiger, as I have attempted in this book, but a financial crisis that was beginning to look too much like what was happening to the Asian tigers across the globe. As the Irish currency collapsed in Asian style, and inflation loomed on the horizon, people began to ask questions about sustainability.

At about the same time, the Irish government went a step too far in its pandering to the rich, who were already the 'winners' from Celtic tigerhood. In the run-up to the 1998 state budget, government sources led economic journalists to believe that the fiscal fruits of growth would be given back to the neediest sections of the population in the form of tax cuts and social programmes. Even middle-of-the-road economists thought this was right – after all, Ireland was now a 'rich European country' according to the common wisdom, so it was about time it began to look after those who had been left behind. In the event, the government did a U-turn. It gave tax breaks to the wealthy speculators and businesses that were paying low wages, instead of the workers who were receiving them. A sense was growing that the Irish state was squandering its riches. State television and radio ran programmes about low pay and social exclusion. A bishop asked in the *Irish Times* whether 'we really want a country where the only good is profit?'

Many people began to wonder if they were living not in a Celtic tiger, but in a *Celtic crocodile* – an economy that eats rather than nurtures its young and its weak. With economic crisis possibly looming on the horizon, time was running out for the state to use some of the proceeds of economic growth to ease the pain of the mass of poor that had been created in the 1980s and augmented in the 1990s.

If tigers are not for the people, who *are* they for? As always, there is a huge gap between the rhetoric of capitalism – whose proponents claim that today's riches for a few will become tomorrow's prosperity for all – and the reality of a class system that excludes so many people who work hard for a living, who work hard in the home, or who simply cannot get paid work. In today's global economy, more than ever, regions like Ireland are forced to follow a neoliberal path or face economic and political exclusion from the major economic coalitions of Europe, North America and Asia. If they are smart and lucky, their observance of the neoliberal way and their cunning at out-competing other countries that are in the same boat, can bring rewards in the form of economic growth, or *dependent development*. But the Irish experience of the 1990s shows clearly that such growth leaves masses of people untouched or, in some cases, in a worse state than they were in before it appeared on the scene.

Perhaps it is not too late for the southern Irish state to turn some of its new-found wealth to reduce inequality. Perhaps it can feel confident enough about the economy to impose even some mild reforms like a minimum wage, tax reductions for the low paid, and even a mild basic incomes policy. More likely, it appears, this state like all others that depend on stronger economic powers to generate wealth, will balk at any meaningful change for fear that such change would threaten its ability to attract the foreign companies on which it has staked its economic future.

Despite the fall of actually existing communism, working classes in the industrialised countries of the world still face the project of creating a just society where labour is properly rewarded for its work, where the value of unpaid work is recognised, and where decisions about what to produce and consume are made according to the usefulness of goods and services (including their disuse to environments and the sustainability of human life) and not the narrow calculations of profitability, and where no groups are excluded from the material wealth of society or from decisions about the quality of life. This project is even greater for people in late industrialising and economically marginalised regions, where there is a seeming conflict between what is required for growth and what is required for social and economic justice. The experience of dependent tigers like southern Ireland points out more than ever the precarious nature of a system where an economy must attract foreign companies in ever greater numbers in order to maintain growth. In their attempts to lubricate the way for these companies, states take decisions that are in conflict with prosperity for large sections of their populations. In the short run, it is imperative to understand why economic growth has taken so many people even further from prosperity. This false equation must be broken if we are to force such states to turn resources to the needs of their people instead of pandering to the desires of the wealthy investors and potential investors.

In the long run, the experience of the *other* tigers – those who have not depended on foreign companies to create wealth – indicates that sustained economic growth requires more active policies than the Irish regime has pursued. It requires nuanced policies by a developmental state, strategically selecting among protection and openness and open to taking direct state action where private capital fears to tread. But these regimes have also achieved such goals at the cost of freedom and democracy, and especially with the suppression of the very forms of popular organisation and mobilisation that are necessary for the masses of people to win back some of the fruits of growth. Although Ireland has not faced this kind of authoritarianism, the prerequisites of growth there have undermined popular organisation. The more successful the IDA has become in attracting TNCs, the weaker popular organisations and trade unions have become at the heights of the economy where they are always unwelcome, and the less input they have had on public policy.

In such circumstances, mobilisation may have to take new forms, and incorporate sections of the population that have often been ignored by traditional working-class movements. In the long run, there are people who are debating, organising, preparing for a transformation of the global economy, so that some form of just and sustainable system can be achieved – a 'new common sense', as Santos (1995) puts it, borrowing from Noam Chomsky – where struggles for emancipation and prosperity are not turned, as they have been in the past into new forms of oppression and inequality. In the meantime, however, we must seriously mobilise to ensure, when momentary periods of economic 'success' are achieved, that a fair share of the fruits of such 'tigerhood' are used to improve the well-being of the masses of people in society, and especially the poorest and weakest. Momentary surges in available resources *can* be used for middle-range improvements of the social economy: to create basic incomes programmes to bring people out of poverty, to fund programmes that revalue socially useful work that is presently devalued and unpaid or underpaid, to create education not only for more engineers but to provide real chances for the marginalised and the long-term unemployed. A mild 'national anti-poverty strategy' was mooted at the height of Ireland's recent tigerhood. Irish governments implemented this already modest strategy only in the most watered-down terms, while increasing tax benefits to the rich. There is no excuse for the fact that the fruits of Irish economic growth were not used to implement real anti-poverty measures with teeth. Countries cannot afford to let such opportunities pass them by.

Notes

Chapter 1

1. Kevin Gardiner (1994). The 'four Tigers' – South Korea, Taiwan, Hong Kong and Singapore – are also referred to as the four 'dragons'. Either term, or the more general term 'tiger economy', derives from the East Asian symbols of power and dynamism: the tiger for the Koreans and the dragon for the Chinese.
2. Angela Long, 'Survey of Ireland (2): the boat has stayed afloat', *Financial Times*, 25 May 1994.
3. 'NICs' usually includes Malaysia, Thailand and Indonesia, and sometimes even China and the Philippines. Obviously, this is a more disparate group even than the original four tigers, so the concept of 'new NICs' is especially vague.
4. Economic growth is measured here by GDP. The per capita figures are for 1965–89 (Chowdhury and Islam 1993:14, 8).
5. Although the concept of the 'developmental state' has become popular in recent years (see, for example, Johnson 1987, Wade 1992, Evans 1995), it is largely based on much earlier works by writers such as Gerschenkron (1962) and Polanyi (1944).
6. In terms of the following discussion, most European companies appear to follow strategies that are closer to the US than to Japanese patterns, although they also exhibit more variation and appear to have adapted more features of Japanese strategies of 'flexibility' than have most North American companies.
7. This is part of a general strategic linkage between industrial investment and trade strategies by Japanese state agencies like the Ministry for International Trade and Industry (MITI). Not only its industrial investment strategies, but also Japanese resource investment strategies are specifically aimed to support industrial accumulation. On the industrial end, this may mean creating new market demands for Japanese products in semi-peripheral regions. On the resource end, it often means encouraging other states to undertake mining and other resource investments that will assure a steady and cheap supply

of raw materials to Japanese industry. For more on this resource strategy, see Bunker and O'Hearn (1993).

8. This pattern is not without precedent in the West: a similar strategy was behind the Marshall Plan after the Second World War, when the US attempted to reconstruct European industry so that its revived markets could consume the products of American industry. Yet this strategy was never extended to poorer regions that would be analogous to a South Korea or Taiwan.
9. This does not include the petroleum sector.
10. These figures actually refer to the broader sector of metal products and machinery, which is now dominated by electronics (United Nations, various years).

Chapter 2

1. Flann O'Brien got one thing wrong. The reason the US investors supposedly promoted the sago forests in Ireland was to employ the Irish at home, so that they would not emigrate to the United States. At the time he wrote, this appeared possible, since the initial 'feel-good factor' of prosperity in the 1960s had reversed chronic Irish emigration to net immigration. Soon, however, when foreign investment proved inadequate to create adequate employment, rampant emigration to the US returned and has remained since.
2. Department of Industry and Commerce, 'Memorandum for submission to the government on Paragraph 7 (Industrial Development) of Statement of Government Policy', 22 October 1951. S11987B. An earlier list was compiled in 1945. See Department of Industry and Commerce, 'Memorandum on industrial development for An Taoiseach', October 1945. S11987B. (Reference numbers beginning with 'S' refer to files in the Irish Public Records Office, Dublin. Those beginning with 'P' refer to files in the archives of the University College Dublin.)
3. Department of Finance (T.K. Whitaker) memorandum, 'Financial Policy', 26 November 1949. P35c/47.
4. Letter from J.E. Corrigan, Chief of ECA Mission to Ireland, to Minister for External Affairs Sean MacBride, 7 December 1949. P35c/47.
5. Foreign fixed capital investment in manufacturing during 1960–82 is estimated by multiplying IDA grants given to each

company in each year by the normal grant/investment ratio for each type of grant in each sector (for example, new investment grants, re-equipment grants). IDA data are available for projected capital grants and capital investments in each year. Under the assumption that grants are paid out as a proportion of actual investments at the original projected rates of grants to assets, the actual grant payments to foreign companies may be multiplied by the appropriate factor to reach an accurate estimate of foreign capital investment. Data after 1983 were directly computed by the IDA and made available to the author.

6. In order to maximize the positive publicity from new investment the government always announced projects along with a figure for 'approved jobs'. In practice, TNCs on average created only about half as many actual jobs as the initial figure of 'approvals'. It was in the interests of both parties to inflate these figures – the IDA and Irish government, in order to create the impression that they were creating more employment than was actually true, and the TNCs in order to justify larger grants from the IDA.
7. The data in this and the following paragraphs are from unpublished IDA employment surveys, supplied to the author. The 15 largest companies included 14 sheltered companies: 3 in the cement and glass sector, 3 newspapers, 3 dairy co-ops, 3 other food firms, and 2 state firms. The other company produced carpets.
8. Profit rates refer here to profits as a proportion of sales.
9. Data from the US Commerce Department's *Survey of Current Business* have consistently shown since the 1970s that American companies' profits in Ireland have been substantially higher than their average profits elsewhere. Although comparable data are not available for Irish corporate profit rates before 1983, they were certainly much lower then, as they were after 1983.
10. Until the 1980s, entering TNCs were given a tax holiday on all profits gained from exports (since the most important foreign sectors export more than 98 per cent of their product, this amounted to a complete tax holiday). After the EC ruled that the Irish tax laws were illegal because they discriminated against non-exporters, the Irish government changed to a flat 10 per cent profits-tax rate for all manufacturers. This compares with a 40 per cent profits-tax rate in Britain.
11. Kieran Kennedy argues, to the contrary, that the important indicator of linkages and their effect on the local economy is

not their *proportion* relative to total TNC output but their *absolute* amount. Thus, while TNCs have not increased the proportions in which they purchase local inputs relative to their output, they have increased their absolute purchases because their output has expanded rapidly. Kennedy's focus on absolute linkages, however, is something of a red herring, since the developmental effects of TNCs should be measured in dynamic terms if they are to have much meaning. Although material purchases by TNCs have risen in absolute terms, they are still quite low and their rate of growth is inadequate to constitute significant indigenous industrialisation (as is shown by the low growth rates and profit rates of indigenous Irish industry). Moreover, their failure to grow as a proportion of TNC materials purchases indicates that Irish companies still provide only basic inputs and have not expanded into providing more technically demanding components. See Kennedy (1991).

12. Estimates of unemployment in Ireland can vary considerably, depending on the means of counting the unemployed (for example, surveys or unemployment registers) and the definitions of employment or unemployment, which frequently change. A definitional change in 1977, for example, reduced recorded unemployment rates by as much as 15 per cent. Subsequent changes further reduced the official rate. None the less, official unemployment statistics for 1985 counted 18 per cent of the labour force as unemployed.
13. Quoted from confidential Ministry of Commerce memorandum, 'Industrial Development and Unemployment in Great Britain', 15 September 1958 (Public Records Office of Northern Ireland).
14. As well as liberalising the north's investment attraction programmes, Britain also considerably increased its subsidies of major Northern manufacturers, such as Harland & Wolff and Shorts. This did not halt deindustrialisation, but was an important way of maintaining support among the loyalist working class.
15. It should be noted that similar losses were incurred in the southern clothing and textiles sectors after Britain and Ireland joined the European Community in 1973. The difference, however, was that the south had already broken from its dependence on these sectors with policies that enabled it to attract new US investors, on which it now came to depend.
16. In the 1990s, the English share of inward manufacturing investment in the 'UK' rose to more than 80 per cent, with

Scotland receiving about 10 per cent and Wales about 5 per cent of inward investment (Hamilton 1992).

Chapter 3

1. The logic behind the PPS system of comparing national incomes makes sense: foreign exchange rates do not reflect national price levels, so that comparing national incomes at foreign exchange rates distorts the buying power of a given level of national income. On the other hand, there are some serious problems with the way that the PPS accounts are calculated. One of these is that they are highly dependent on wage rates, especially for the calculation of the price levels of public goods. Thus, while it may be true that services and public goods are provided more cheaply in poorer countries because of the low wages paid to providers of these goods and services, it is also true that their populations are less able to consume these goods and services because of their lower wages. Another problem with comparing national incomes in terms of PPS is that it may be biased by changes in the composition of GDP between its uses: personal expenditures, public goods, fixed capital formation and net exports. In the Irish case, there has been an extreme movement in the composition of GDP over the recent period of 'convergence', away from consumption and investment and toward the export surplus. Consumption fell from 74 per cent of GDP in 1990 to 70 per cent in 1996 while the surplus of exports over imports rose from 4.7 per cent to 11 per cent of GDP. We will return to the implications of this for popular welfare in Chapter 5. Finally, GDP is calculated both as a flow of incomes and a flow of output. In the Irish case, real GDP has risen more rapidly when calculated by incomes (this should not be confused with personal incomes, which have risen more slowly than GDP) than when calculated by output.
2. In one 18-month period during 1994–95, the following major companies announced new investment projects in Ireland: Digital, 3 Com, Seagate, Hewlett-Packard, Apple, AMP, Silicon, Motorola, NEC, Quantum, Analog Devices, Creative Technology, Dell, Xilinx and Sensormatic (*Irish Times*, 19 October 1995).
3. Murphy (1994) adds cola concentrates to his list of key American-dominated sectors that have dominated recent Irish

economic activity, referring to the 'three Cs' of computers, chemicals and Cola. In an earlier article, McAleese (1988) compared Coca-Cola and Pepsi to the Irish dairy industry, pointing out that the two American cola companies with 150 workers export more from Ireland than the dairy industry, with 11,000 workers. While the apparent profit-shifting activities of the soft drinks sector are outrageous, however, it has not been as important as computers and pharmaceuticals in the economic growth spurt of the 1990s.

4. The ten companies involved (in order of greatest sales) were Apple, Dell, Microsoft, Digital, Coca-Cola, Amdahl, Pepsi, Schering Plough, Pfizer and Northern Telecom.
5. For discussion of more evidence on transfer pricing, see Emmanuel and Mehafdi (1994:56–62).
6. For example, the southern Irish state, with its 10 per cent profits-tax rate, must attract investment yielding three times as much profits as it would attract with a 30 per cent rate. The British experience shows that it is possible to attract a large share of foreign investment (half of the investment entering the EU) even with 40 per cent tax rates, although many structural features of the British economy are attractive to foreign investors, while the Irish state may have to depend more on its tax policies to attract foreign projects.
7. All but one of the companies uncovered by Stewart are in pharmaceuticals, office machinery, health products and soft drinks.
8. Author's calculations from unpublished data supplied by the IDA and Forfás.
9. Among other things, radical Irish critics of TNC behaviour in the 1970s concentrated more on the orthodox Marxist argument that they were exploiting cheap Irish labour, without considering other possibilities such as transfer pricing (for example, Official Sinn Féin 1977). Additionally, nationalist critics concentrated on the degree to which TNCs were crowding out Irish economic elements, whether capitalist or potentially socialist. Outside of these circles, there was very little criticism of foreign investors.
10. This rapid fall in *private* investment contradicts the authors of a medium-term review for the Economic and Social Research Institute in Dublin, who argue that investment fell because the state abandoned its wasteful investment programmes after 1987 (Bradley et al. 1997). Nor does this argument explain the particularly large fall-off of *manufacturing* investment.

11. Although few observers have looked at Ireland's low investment rates, there have been some recent studies of investmentless growth. In 1996, for instance, the National Economic and Social Council was mandated as part of the national social agreement to study investment in Ireland.

Chapter 4

1. While I have concentrated here on processes whereby labour relations have become more flexible or casual, it should be remembered that there is another set of regions which flexible accumulation has passed by. As I have already noted, globalisation in the 1990s has been a process of agglomerated TNC investments. Foreign direct investment in the former Third World nearly tripled from 1990 to 1993, but 60 per cent of it was concentrated in just seven Asian countries: China, Singapore, Malaysia, Thailand, Hong Kong, Taiwan and Indonesia. As a result, vast areas in Africa and Latin America have been *marginalised*, receiving an insignificant share of foreign investments and accounting for a shrinking proportion of world trade. Their populations, as a result, have been impoverished, and often suffer from chronic subsistence crises and famines.
2. This was a play on the famous 'Dutch disease', where a single booming sector crowds out others, with a net result of economic stagnation. Barry and Hannan concentrate on the effects of exchange rates on indigenous sectors, although they admit that domestic decline could also be a result of Irish-owned firms' inability to compete in conditions of free trade, either in local or export markets. This was an argument that I raised some time ago (O'Hearn 1989). An additional implication of dependence on TNCs is that average wages may be tied partly to rising productivity which, as we have seen, is almost entirely concentrated (indeed, possibly distorted upward) in the foreign sector. Since wage rises have tended to be about equal in foreign and domestic firms, and since domestic firms tend to be much more labour-intensive, this could have a severe negative impact on domestic competitiveness, just as it enhances TNC competitiveness.
3. National level wage bargaining appears to have been more important in determining working class than managerial or professional pay. A study by the *Industrial Relations News* (1992)

found that basic pay for 71 per cent of manual workers and 55 per cent of clerical workers was determined primarily at the national level, while the same was true for only a third of managers and professionals. Pay for most managers and professionals was determined either through company-level or individual bargains.

4. This phrase is borrowed from the title of Peadar Kirby's recent critique of inequality and poverty in Ireland (Kirby 1997).

Chapter 5

1. This chapter title is borrowed from Cliff Taylor, 'Celtic Tiger Perceived to be Neglecting Some of Her Cubs,' *Irish Times*, 20 June 1997.
2. These quotes are all from separate year-end reviews in the *Irish Times*, 28 December 1996. They are taken from, respectively, Colm Keena, 'Spend, spend, spend'; Bernice Harrison, 'If you had it in '96, boy could you blow it'; Jack Fagan and Orna Mulcahy, 'Boom, boom, boom'; and Fintan O'Toole, 'In the land of the Emerald Tiger'.
3. Traditional Marxism defines social class by one's access to productive assets, like machinery and raw materials. Workers must sell their labour to capitalists because they have no independent access to these assets. More recent Marxian approaches, however, distinguish between those who do or do not have access to knowledge assets, which either gives them access to or excludes them from certain positions in production. In the view of some Marxists, this puts such analysts closer to the understanding of class advanced by followers of Max Weber, who saw one's market position in terms of status and skills as a most important determinant of one's class. See, for example, the debates on class in Eric Wright (1989).
4. The distribution of profits between foreign and domestic capital affects intra-country inequality because a greater degree of profit repatriation leaves fewer profit incomes within a country and, therefore, 'reduces' inequality as measured there. Of course, the disposition of profits also has an effect on international inequality. The higher the level of profits that goes to TNCs and is repatriated, the more wealthy the core regions in the world economy become.

5. This basic distribution of factor income shares is very similar for some time before 1985. Earlier years have been excluded here for the sake of brevity.
6. For simplicity, I will refer throughout to 'investment' rather than the more formal category of the national income accounts, 'gross domestic fixed capital formation'. There is also a category for the 'value of physical changes in stocks'. This is a very small component of national income, however, so changes in stocks have simply been included under 'investment' in the following analysis. This does not significantly affect the conclusions of the analysis.
7. This begs the question for now of whether consumers are wealthy, middle income or poor. I will return to this issue in the subsequent section on the distribution of individual incomes.
8. Such rising inequality will not significantly change the income shares of different groups of income earners in such a short period, although small changes may be apparent. On the other hand, the rate of income growth may be significantly different between higher- and lower-income workers. Unfortunately, since most southern Irish income data are collected by household, the changes may be further blurred, since women working in peripheral jobs may none the less raise *family* incomes by a significant amount even though their individual incomes are quite low.
9. The OECD defines low pay as hourly or weekly earnings that are less than two-thirds of the median earnings in a country (OECD 1976).
10. Other measures of 'depth of poverty' show that it fell during 1987–94 (Combat Poverty Agency 1997b:35). Yet a closer look shows that the depth of poverty fell after 1987 because that was a particularly bad year for farming, with many farmers reporting zero or low incomes. After that year, the numbers of low-income small farmers in Ireland fell and incomes rose for the remaining farmers. This is the main factor explaining the reduction in the deepest poverty after 1987.
11. It has seemingly become a trend for states to target the most socially marginalised for welfare cuts, in relative or even in absolute terms. The British Labour Party, for instance, was responsible for making drastic cuts in benefits for lone parents in 1997, a policy originally mooted by the Tories but carried through by Tony Blair. Plans were to follow this with cuts for the disabled. Thus, the whole island of Ireland appears to be

becoming a worse place for socially excluded groups like lone parents, the disabled and the elderly.

12. The national anti-poverty strategy was published under the title *Sharing in Progress*.
13. This applies to non-manufacturing companies. Manufacturers already benefit from a standard 10 per cent profits-tax rate, which the Irish state has guaranteed at least until the year 2025.
14. The 12.5 per cent rate applies to all trading profits, although non-trading profits will be reduced to 25 per cent. In addition, it is unclear whether manufacturers will remain taxed at their present 10 per cent rate, or will be included in the 12.5 per cent category.

Chapter 6

1. Frank's analysis is contained in a contribution to an Internet debate on the East Asian crisis on the World Systems Network <wsn@csf.colorado.edu> (November 1997).
2. Palat also predicts that the re-emergence of the Asian economies will take a different form. Not only will many crony firms be discouraged by the structural reforms that the IMF has demanded, but an increasing presence of global corporations in large sectors will weaken the ability of national states and agencies to play the active developmental co-ordinating role that they achieved in the early 'tiger' decades.
3. Here I cannot resist paraphrasing the arch-unionist politician Ian Paisley, who asked the British government to seek an EU exception for the north from the British beef exports ban on the basis that 'we're British but our cows are Irish'.
4. Only in the mid-1990s did significant numbers of non-Irish immigrants arrive on the island, but they have tended to be part of a large political-economic migration from places like Turkey and Bosnia to the EU and have a minimal impact on the Irish labour market.

References

Adelman, Irma and Cynthia Morris (1973) *Economic Growth and Social Equity in Developing Countries* (Stanford, CA: Stanford University Press).

Amin, Ash (1992) 'Big firms versus the regions in the Single European Market', in M. Dunford and G. Kafkalis (eds), *Cities and Regions in the New Europe* (London: Belhaven Press), pp.127–49.

Amin, Samir (1976) *Accumulation on a World Scale* (New York: Monthly Review).

Amsden, Alice (1989) *Asia's Next Giant: South Korea and Late Industrialization* (Oxford: Oxford University Press).

Amsden, Alice (1994) 'Why isn't the whole world experimenting with the East Asian model to develop?: review of *The East Asian Miracle*', *World Development* 22:4, pp.627–33.

Arrighi, Giovanni (1995) *The Long Twentieth Century* (London: Verso).

Arrighi, Giovanni, Satoshi Ikeda, and Alex Irwan (1993) 'The rise of East Asia: one miracle or many?', in Ravi Palat (ed.), *Pacific-Asia and the Future of the World-system* (Westport, CT: Greenwood) pp.41–66.

Balassa, Bela (1988) 'The lessons of East Asian development: an overview', *Economic Development and Cultural Change* 36 (third supp.), pp.S273–S290.

Baran, Paul (1957) *The Political Economy of Growth* (New York: Monthly Review).

Barrett, Richard and Martin Whyte (1982) 'Dependency theory and Taiwan: analysis of a deviant case', *American Journal of Sociology* 87:5 (March), pp.1,064–1,089.

Barry, Frank and Aoife Hannan (1995) 'Multinationals and indigenous employment: an "Irish disease"?', *Economic and Social Review* 27:1, pp.21–32.

Bell, Daniel (1974) *The Coming of Post-Industrial Society: A Venture in Social Forecasting* (London: Heinemann).

Bello, Walden (1993) 'The Asia-Pacific: trouble in paradise', *World Policy Journal* 10:2 (Summer), pp.33–40.

Bernard, M. and J. Ravenhill (1995) 'Beyond product cycles and flying geese: regionalization, hierarchy, and the industrialization of East Asia', *World Politics* 47:2, pp.171–209.

Bond, Larry (1997) 'Unemployment and Poverty' in *Prioritising Poverty* (Dublin: Combat Poverty Agency), pp.27–34.

Borkowski, S.C. (1992) 'Organisational and international factors affecting multinational transfer pricing', *Advances in International Accounting* 5, pp.173–92.

Borooah, Vani (1993) 'Northern Ireland – Typology of a Regional Economy', in Paul Teague, *The Economy of Northern Ireland: Perspectives for Structural Change* (London: Lawrence and Wishart).

Bradley, John (1996) 'An island economy: exploring long-term economic and social consequences of peace and reconciliation in the island of Ireland', Forum for Peace and Reconciliation, Consultancy studies no. 4 (Dublin: Stationery Office).

Bradley, John, John FitzGerald, Patrick Honohan and Ide Kearney (1997) 'Interpreting the recent Irish growth experience' in David Duffy et al., *Medium-term Review: 1997–2003* (Dublin: Economic and Social Research Institute), pp.35–66.

Bunker, Stephen and Denis O'Hearn (1993) 'Strategies of economic ascendants for access to raw materials: a comparison of the United States and Japan' in Ravi Palat (ed.), *Pacific-Asia and the Future of the World-system* (Westport, CT.: Greenwood), pp.83–102.

Callan, Tim, Brian Nolan, Brendan Whelan, Christopher Whelan, and James Williams (1996) *Poverty in the 1990s: Evidence from the Living in Ireland Survey* (Dublin: Oak Tree Press).

Carter, Charles (1957) 'The Irish economy viewed from without', *Studies* 46:182 (Summer).

Chandler, Alfred (1962) *Strategy and Structure: Chapters in the History of the Industrial Enterprise* (Cambridge, MA.: MIT Press).

Chandler, Alfred (1990) *Scale and Scope: the Dynamics of Industrial Capitalism* (Cambridge, MA: Belknap Press).

Chowdhury, Anis and Iyanatul Islam (1993) *The Newly Industrialising Economies of East Asia* (London: Routledge).

Clark, Charles and John Healy (1997) *Pathways to a Basic Income* (Dublin: Conference of Religious in Ireland).

Colgan, J. and E. Onyemadum (1981) 'Spin-off companies in the Irish electronics industry', *Journal of Irish Business and Administrative Research* 3:2 (October), pp.3–15.

Combat Poverty Agency (1997a) 'Poverty in Ireland: The Facts', Poverty Briefing no. 6 (Dublin: Combat Poverty Agency).

Combat Poverty Agency (1997b) 'Poverty, social exclusion and inequality in Ireland' in *Sharing in Progress: National Anti-Poverty Strategy* (Dublin: Stationery Office), pp.25–89.

Commission of Inquiry (1936) *Final Report of the Commission of Inquiry into the Civil Service, 1932–5* (Dublin: Stationery Office).

Compston, Hugh (ed.) (1997) *The New Politics of Unemployment: Radical Policy Initiatives in Western Europe* (London: Routledge).

CORI (1997) *A question of choices* (Dublin: Conference of Religious in Ireland).

Courtney, Damien (1995) 'Demographic structure and change in the Republic of Ireland and Northern Ireland' in Patrick Clancy, Sheelagh Drudy, Kathleen Lynch, and Liam O'Dowd (eds), *Irish Society: Sociological Perspectives* (Dublin: Institute of Public Administration), pp.39–89.

Cumings, Bruce (1984) 'The origins and development of the Northeast Asian political economy: industrial sectors, product cycles, and political consequences', *International Organization* 38:1 (Winter), pp.1–40.

Curtin, Chris, Trutz Haase, and Hilary Tovey (1996) *Poverty in Rural Ireland: A Political Economy Perspective* (Dublin: Oak Tree Press).

Cypher, James (1979) 'The internationalization of capital and the transformation of social formations: a critique of the Monthly Review school', *Review of Radical Political Economics* 11:4 (Winter).

Department of Industry and Commerce (1933) *Census of Industrial Production, 1926, 1929* (Dublin: Stationery Office).

Deyo, Frederick (ed.) (1987) *The Political Economy of the New Asian Industrialism* (Ithaca, NY: Cornell University Press).

Dunning, J.H. and R.D. Pearce (1985) *The World's Largest Industrial Enterprises 1962–1983* (London: Gower).

Durkan, Joe (1995) 'Economic growth 1987–1993/94' in Central Statistics Office, *Proceedings of Conference on Measuring Economic Growth* (Dublin: Central Statistics Office) pp.33–43.

Emmanuel, Clive and Messaoud Mehafdi (1994) *Transfer Pricing* (London: Academic Press).

Eolas (1989) *Electronics Manpower Study: Trends in the Irish Electronics Manufacturing Industry up to 1995* (Dublin: Eolas).

European Commission (1996) *The Economic and Financial Situation in Ireland: Ireland in the Transition to EMU* special issue of *European Economy* (Brussels: European Commission).

Evans, Peter (1987) 'Class, state, and dependence in East Asia: lessons for Latin Americanists' in Frederick Deyo (ed.), *The*

Political Economy of the New Asian Industrialism (Ithaca, NY: Cornell University Press), pp.203–26.

Evans, Peter (1995) *Embedded Autonomy* (Princeton, NJ: Princeton University Press).

Fei, John, Gustav Ranis and Shirley Kuo (1979) *Growth with Equity: The Taiwan Case* (Oxford: Oxford University Press).

Fidler, Stephen (1997) 'Might Asia lose a decade?' *Financial Times* (27 November).

FitzGerald, Garret (1997) 'The basic income system has merit', *Irish Times* (12 April).

Forbairt (1996) *National Software Directorate Irish Software Industry Survey, 1995: Results* (Dublin: Forbairt).

Forfás (1995) 'Employment in industry and international services hits 10 year high', 1994 review statement (Dublin: Forfás).

Forfás (1996) *Annual Survey of Irish Economy Expenditures* (Dublin: Forfás).

Foster-Carter, Aidan (1997) Letter to the editor, *Financial Times* (9 December 1995).

Frank, Andre Gunder (1969) *Latin America: Underdevelopment or Revolution*? (New York: Monthly Review).

Frobel, Folker, Jurgen Heinrichs, and Otto Kreye (1980) *The New International Division of Labour* (Cambridge: Cambridge University Press).

Gardiner, Kevin (1994) 'The Irish economy: a Celtic tiger', in *Ireland: Challenging for Promotion*, Morgan Stanley Euroletter (31 August), pp.9–21.

George, Susan (1992) *The Debt Boomerang* (London: Pluto Press).

Gerschenkron, Alexander (1962) *Economic Backwardness in Historical Perspective* (Cambridge, MA: Harvard University Press).

Gill, Colin, Therese Beaupain and Hubert Krieger (1993) *Workplace Involvement in Technological Innovation in the European Community. Volume II: Issues of Participation* (European Foundation).

Gold, Thomas (1986) *State and Society in the Taiwan Miracle* (New York: M.E. Sharpe).

Goodman, James (1996) *Nationalism and Transnationalism: The National Conflict in Ireland and European Union Integration* (Aldershot: Avebury).

Greenhalgh, Susan (1988) 'Supranational processes of income distribution' in Edwin Winckler and Susan Greenhalgh (eds), *Contending Approaches to the Political Economy of Taiwan* (New York: M.E. Sharpe), pp.67–100.

Grice, Kevin and David Drakakis-Smith (1985) 'The role of the state in shaping development: two decades of growth in Singapore', *Trans. Inst. Br. Geogr.* 10, pp.347–59.

Griffith, Arthur (1918) *The Sinn Fein Policy* (Dublin).

Grimwade, N. (1989) *International Trade* (London: Routledge).

Haggard, Stephen (1990) *Pathways from the Periphery: The Politics of Growth in the Newly Industrializing Countries* (Ithaca, NY: Cornell University Press).

Hamilton, Douglas (1992) *Inward Investment in Northern Ireland*, report no. 99 (Belfast: Northern Ireland Economic Council).

Hamilton, Nora (1982) *The Limits of State Autonomy: Post-revolutionary Mexico* (Princeton, NJ: Princeton University Press).

Hill, Richard Child and Kuniko Fujita (1995) 'Product cycles and international divisions of labor: contrasts between the United States and Japan' in David Smith and József Borocz, *A New World Order? Global Transformations in the Late Twentieth Century* (Westport, CT: Praeger), pp.91–108.

Hobday, Mike (1994a) 'Technological learning in Singapore: a test case of leapfrogging', *Journal of Development Studies* 30:3 (April), pp.831–58.

Hobday, Mike (1994b) 'Export-led technology development in the four dragons: the case of electronics', *Development and Change* 35, pp.333-61.

Huff, W.G. (1995) 'What is the Singapore model of economic development?' *Cambridge Journal of Economics* 19, pp.735–59.

Hutton, Will (1994) *Britain and Northern Ireland, the State We're In: Failure and Opportunity* (Belfast: Northern Ireland Economic Council).

ICTU (1993) *New Forms of Work Organisation: Options for Unions* (Dublin: ICTU).

ICTU (1994) *Managing Change: Review of Union Involvement in Company Restructuring* (Dublin: ICTU).

ICTU (1996) *Minimum Standards for Atypical Work* (Dublin: Irish Congress of Trade Unions).

IDA (1995) 'IDA end-year statement' (Dublin: IDA).

Isles, K.S. and N. Cuthbert (1957) *An Economic Survey of Northern Ireland* (Belfast: HMSO).

Jacobson, David (1996) *New Forms of Work Organisation in Ireland: An Annotated Bibliography*, research papers no. 9, Dublin City University Business School.

Jacobson, David and David O'Sullivan (1994) 'Analyzing an industry in change: the Irish software manual printing industry', *New Technology, Work and Employment* 9:2, pp.103–14.

Jenkins, Rhys (1987) *Transnational Corporations* (London: Methuen).

Jeon, Jei Guk (1995) 'Exploring the three varieties of East Asia's state-guided development model: Korea, Singapore, and Taiwan', *Studies in Comparative International Development*, 30:3 (Fall), pp.70–88.

Johnson, Chalmers (1987) 'Political institutions and economic performance: the government-business relationship in Japan, South Korea, and Taiwan', in Frederick Deyo (ed.) *The Political Economy of the New Asian Industrialism* (Ithaca, NY: Cornell University Press) pp.136–64.

Kearney, H.F. (1959) 'The political background to English mercantilism, 1695–1700', *Economic History Review* 11, pp.484–96.

Keena, Colm (1996) 'Religious group critical of report on tax and welfare', *Irish Times* (6 August).

Kennedy, Kieran (1991) 'Linkages and Overseas Industry' in Anthony Foley and Dermot McAleese (eds), *Overseas Industry in Ireland* (Dublin: Gill and Macmillan), pp.82–105.

Kennedy, Kieran and Brendan Dowling (1975) *Economic Growth in Ireland: the Experience since 1947* (Dublin: Gill and Macmillan).

Kilfeather, Frank (1997) 'CORI condemns budget as lost chance', *Irish Times* (24 January).

Killeen, Michael (1979) 'The electronics revolution: Its impact on Ireland', address to the Royal Institution of Chartered Surveyors (December), mimeo.

Kirby, Peadar (1997) *Poverty Amid Plenty: World and Irish Development Reconsidered* (Dublin: Trócaire).

Kohli, Atul (1994) 'Where do high growth political economies come from? The Japanese lineage of Korea's "developmental state"', *World Development* 22:9, pp.1269–93.

Koo, Hagen (1987) 'The interplay of state, social class, and world system in East Asian development: the cases of South Korea and Taiwan' in Frederick Deyo (ed.) *The Political Economy of the New Asian Industrialism* (Ithaca, NY: Cornell University Press), pp.165–81.

Labour Force Survey (various years) (Dublin: Stationery Office).

Lee, William Keng Mun (1997) 'Foreign investment, industrial restructuring and dependent development in Singapore', *Journal of Contemporary Asia*, 27:1, pp.58–70.

Lim, Linda (1983) 'Singapore's success: the myth of the free market economy', *Asian Survey* 23, pp.752–64.

Lucey, Katherine (1996) 'Ireland's software industry poised for next leap', *Irish Times* (9 December).

Lynch, Kathleen (1997) 'Inequality, social exclusion and poverty' in Combat Poverty Agency, *Prioritising Poverty* (Dublin: Combat Poverty Agency), pp.51–68.
McAleese, John (1988) 'Chasing the phantom in the Irish accounts', *Business and Finance* (24 March), pp.11–13.
McCormick, Thomas (1989) *America's Half-Century* (Baltimore, MD: Johns Hopkins University Press).
Mac Laughlin, Jim (1994) 'Emigration and Peripheralization of Ireland in the Global Economy', *Review* 17:2 (Spring), pp.243–73.
McMichael, Philip (1996) *Development and Social Change: A Global Perspective* (Thousand Oaks, CA: Pine Forge).
Mangan, Oliver (1994) 'No longer a joke', *Davy Stockbrokers Weekly Market Monitor* (Dublin, 22 July).
Marx, Karl and Friedrich Engels (1971) *Ireland and the Irish Question* (Moscow: Progress Publishers).
Mason, Edward et al. (1980) *The Economic and Social Modernization of the Republic of Korea* (Cambridge, MA: Harvard University Press).
Meenan, James (1970) *The Irish Economy Since 1922* (Liverpool: University of Liverpool Press).
Mjøset, Lars (1993) *The Irish Economy in a Comparative Institutional Perspective* (Dublin: NESC).
Munck, Ronaldo (1993) *The Irish Economy: Results and Prospects* (London: Pluto Press).
Munck, Ronaldo and Douglas Hamilton (forthcoming) Politics, the economy and peace in Northern Ireland', in D. Miller (ed.), *Rethinking Northern Ireland: Culture, Identity and Colonialism* (Harlow: Longman).
Murphy, Anthony and Brendan Walsh (1996) 'The incidence of male non-employment in Ireland' *Economic and Social Review* 25:5 (October), pp.467–90.
Murphy, Antoin (1994) *The Irish Economy: Celtic Tiger or Tortoise?* (Dublin: Money Markets International).
Murphy, Antoin (1995) 'The two-faced economy' in Central Statistics Office, *Proceedings of Conference on Measuring Economic Growth* (Dublin: Central Statistics Office), pp.17–32.
NESF (1994) *Ending Long-term Unemployment*, report no. 4 (Dublin: National Economic and Social Forum).
NESF (1996) *Long-term Unemployment Initiatives*, opinion no. 3 (Dublin: National Economic and Social Forum).
NIEC (1983) *The Duration of Industrial Development Assisted Employment*, report no. 40 (Belfast: Northern Ireland Economic Council).

Nolan, Brian and Gerard Hughes (1997) 'Low pay, the earnings distribution and poverty in Ireland', Working Paper no. 84 (Dublin: Economic and Social Research Institute).

O'Brien, Ronan (1985) 'Technology and industrial development: the Irish electronics industry in an international context', in Jim Fitzpatrick and John Kelly (eds), *Perspectives on Irish Industry* (Dublin: Irish Management Institute).

O'Connell, Philip (1997) 'The Irish labour market', Working Paper no. 81 (Dublin: Economic and Social Research Institute).

O'Dowd, Liam (1995) 'Development or Dependency? State, Economy and Society in Northern Ireland' in Patrick Clancy, Sheelagh Drudy, Kathleen Lynch, and Liam O'Dowd (eds), *Irish Society: Sociological Perspectives* (Dublin: Institute of Public Administration), pp.137–77.

OECD (1976) *Public Expenditure on Income Maintenance* (Paris: OECD).

OECD (1992a) *Ireland: Country Report* (Paris: OECD).

OECD (1992b) *Economic Outlook*, no. 51 (Paris: OECD).

O'Hearn, Denis (1989) 'The Irish Case of Dependency: An Exception to the Exceptions?', *American Sociological Review*, vol. 54, no. 4 (August), pp.578–96.

O'Hearn, Denis (1990a) 'The road from import-substitution to export-led industrialization in Ireland: Who mixed the asphalt, who drove the machinery, and who kept making them change directions', *Politics and Society* (March), pp.1–38.

O'Hearn, Denis (1990b) 'TNCs Intervening Mechanisms and Economic Growth in Ireland: A Longitudinal Test and Extension of the Bornschier Model', *World Development* (March), pp.417–29.

O'Hearn, Denis (1993a) 'Global competition, Europe and Irish peripherality', *The Economic and Social Review*, vol. 24, no. 2 (January), pp.169–97.

O'Hearn, Denis (1993b) 'Strategies of economic ascendants for access to raw materials: a comparison of the US and Japan' (with Stephen Bunker), in Ravi Palat (ed.), *Pacific-Asia and the Future of the World-System* (Greenwood Press, 1993), pp.83–102.

O'Hearn, Denis (1994a) 'Innovation and the world-system hierarchy: British subjugation of the Irish cotton industry, 1780–1830', *American Journal of Sociology* 100:3 (November 1994), pp.587–621.

O'Hearn, Denis (1994b) *Free Trade or Managed Trade: Trading between Two Worlds* (Belfast: Centre for Research and Documentation).

O'Hearn, Denis (1995a) 'Global restructuring, TNCs and the "European periphery": what has changed?' in Jozsef Borocz and David A. Smith, *A New World Order? Global transformation in the late 20th century* (Westport, CT: Greenwood).

O'Hearn, Denis (1995b) 'Global restructuring and the Irish political economy', pp.90–131 in Patrick Clancy, Sheelagh Drudy, Kathleen Lynch, and Liam O'Dowd (eds.), *Irish Society: Sociological Perspectives* (Dublin: Institute of Public Administration).

O'Hearn, Denis (1996) 'Irish linen in the changing world-system', in Marilyn Cohen (ed.), *The Warp of Ulster's Past: Interdisciplinary Perspectives on the Irish Linen Industry, 1700-1914* (Manchester: Manchester University Press and St. Martin's Press), pp.161–90.

O'Hearn, Denis (forthcoming) 'Would you rather be dependent on a winner or a loser? The two Irish economies compared', in James Anderson and James Goodman (eds), *Dis/Agreeing Ireland: Contexts, Obstacles, Hopes* (London: Pluto Press).

O'Malley, Eoin (1989) *Industry and Economic Development: the Challenge for the Latecomer* (Dublin: Gill and Macmillan).

O'Malley, Eoin (1992) 'Industrial structure and economies of scale in the context of 1992' in John Bradley, John Fitzgerald and Ide Kearney (eds), *The Role of the Structural Funds* (Dublin: ESRI), pp.203–49.

Ó Riain, Seán (1997) 'The birth of a Celtic Tiger', *Communications of the ACM* 40:3 (March), pp.11–16.

O'Sullivan, Mary (1995) 'Manufacturing and global competition' in J.W. O'Hagan (ed.), *The Economy of Ireland: Policy and Performance of a Small European Country* (Dublin: Gill and Macmillan), pp.363–96.

O'Toole, Fintan (1996) 'In the land of the Emerald Tiger', *Irish Times* (28 December).

Page, John (1994) 'The East Asian miracle: an introduction', *World Development* 22:4, pp.615–25.

Palat, Ravi (1997) 'A lost decade for Asia?' *The Hindu* (December 12).

Paukert, Felix (1973) 'Income distribution at different levels of development: A survey of evidence', *International Labour Review* 108:2–3, pp.97–125.

Peillon, Michael (1982) *Contemporary Irish Society* (Dublin: Gill and Macmillan).

Perkins, Dwight (1994) 'There are at least three models of East Asian development', *World Development* 22:4, pp.655–61.

Perrons, Diane (1992) 'The regions and the Single Market' in M. Dunford and G. Kafkalis (eds), *Cities and Regions in the New Europe* (London: Belhaven Press), pp.170–94.

Pettman, Ralph (1992) 'Labour, gender and the balance of productivity: South Korea and Singapore', *Journal of Contemporary Asia*, 22, pp.45–56.

Polanyi, Karl (1944) *The Great Transformation* (Boston, MA: Beacon).

Pollak, Andy (1996) 'Budget effect to "widen poverty gap"', *Irish Times* (25 January).

Porter, Michael (1990) *The Competitive Advantage of Nations* (New York: Free Press).

Power, Anne (1998) *Estates on the Edge* (London: Macmillan).

Quigley, George (1992) 'Ireland – an island economy', speech to Confederation of Irish Industry, Dublin, 11 February, mimeo.

Ramesh, M. (1995) 'Economic globalization and policy choices: Singapore', *Governance* 8:2 (April), pp.243–60.

Ritzer, George (1996) *The McDonaldization of Society* (Thousand Oaks, CA: Pine Forge).

Roche, Patrick and Esmond Birnie (n.d.) *An Economics Lesson for Irish Nationalists and Republicans* (Belfast: Ulster Unionist Information Institute).

Roche, William (1995) 'The new competitive order and the fragmentation of industrial relations in Ireland', address to IBEC Annual Employee Relations Committee (November).

Rostow, Walt (1960) *The Stages of Economic Growth* (Cambridge: Cambridge University Press).

Rowthorn, Bob (1981) 'Northern Ireland: an economy in crisis', *Cambridge Journal of Economics* 5, pp.1–31.

Rowthorn, Bob (1987) 'Northern Ireland: An Economy in Crisis' in Paul Teague (ed.), *Beyond the Rhetoric: Politics, Economy and Social Policy in Northern Ireland* (London: Lawrence and Wishart) pp.111–35.

Rowthorn, Bob and Naoimi Wayne (1988) *Northern Ireland: The Political Economy of Conflict* (London: Polity Press).

Sachs, Wolfgang (ed.) (1992) *The Development Dictionary: A Guide to Knowledge as Power* (London: Zed Books).

Santos, Boaventura de Sousa (1995) *Toward a New Common Sense: Law, Science and Politics in the Paradigmatic Transition* (New York and London: Routledge).

Sheehan, Maura and Mike Tomlinson (1996) 'Long-term unemployment in West Belfast' in Eithne McLaughlin and Pádraic Quirk, *Policy Aspects of Employment Equality in Northern Ireland*

(Belfast: Standing Advisory Commission on Human Rights), pp.51–88.
Shirlow, Pete (1995) 'Transnational corporations in the Republic of Ireland and the illusion of well-being', *Regional Studies* 29:7, pp.687–705.
Shoup, Lawrence and William Minter (1977) *Imperial Brain Trust* (New York: Monthly Review).
Sinn Féin the Workers Party (1977) *The Irish Industrial Revolution* (Dublin: Repsol).
Smith, David (1997) 'Technology, commodity chains and global inequality: South Korea in the 1990s', *Review of International Political Economy* 4:4, pp.734–62.
SNP (1996) 'Ireland to overtake UK by the year 2000: "Scotland can become tiger economy of Europe"', Scottish National Party news release, 27 September.
So, Alvin and Stephen Chiu (1995) *East Asia and the World Economy* (Thousand Oaks, CA: Sage).
Soon, Teck-Wong and William Stoever (1996) 'Foreign investment and economic development in Singapore: a policy-oriented approach', *Journal of Developing Areas* 30 (April), pp.317–40.
Stewart, J.C. (1988) 'Transfer pricing: some empirical evidence from Ireland', *Journal of Economic Studies* 16:3, pp.40–56.
Tan, Gerald (1993) 'The next NICs of Asia', *Third World Quarterly* 14:1, pp.57–71.
Tang, H.K. and K.T. Yeo (1995) 'Technology, entrepreneurship and national development: lessons from Singapore', *International Journal of Technology Management* 10:7/8, pp.797–814.
Taylor, George (1996) 'Labour market rigidities, institutional impediments and managerial constraints: some reflections on the recent experience of macro-political bargaining in Ireland', *Economic and Social Review* 27:3 (April), pp.253–77.
Telesis Consultancy Group (1982) *A Review of Industrial Policy*, report no. 64 (Dublin: National Economic and Social Council).
Thurow, Lester (1992) *Head to Head: the Coming Economic Battle among Japan, Europe, and America* (New York: Morrow).
Townsend, Peter (1987) *The International Analysis of Poverty* (New York: Harvester Wheatsheaf).
United Nations (various years) *Yearbook of National Accounts Statistics* (New York: United Nations).
Vernon, Raymond (1971) *Sovereignty at Bay: The Multinational Spread of U.S. Enterprises* (New York: Basic Books).

Wade, Robert (1992) 'East Asian economic success: conflicting perspectives, partial insights, shaky evidence', *World Politics* 44, pp.270–320.

Wallerstein, Immanuel (1991) *Geopolitics and Geoculture: Essays on the Changing World-system* (Cambridge: Cambridge University Press).

Walsh, Jim (1997) 'Children and Poverty' in *Prioritising Poverty* (Dublin: Combat Poverty Agency), pp.18–26.

Wheeler, J.E. (1990) *Hearings on Tax Underpayments by Foreign-owned US Subsidiaries* (Washington, DC: House Ways and Means Oversight Sub-Committee of the United States House of Representatives).

Whitaker, T.K. (1948–49) 'Ireland's external assets', *Journal of the Statistical and Social Inquiry Society of Ireland* 18, pp.192–211.

Wickham, James (1993) *New Forms of Work in Ireland: An Analysis of the 'New Forms of Work and Activity' Data Set* (Dublin: European Foundation for the Improvement of Living and Working Conditions).

World Bank (1993) *The East Asian Miracle: Economic growth and public policy* (Oxford: Oxford University Press).

World Bank (various years) *World Development Report* (Washington, DC: World Bank).

Wortzel, L.H. and H.V. Wortzel (1981) 'Export marketing strategies for NIC and LDC-based firms', *Columbia Journal of World Business* 16:1 (Spring).

Wright, Eric (1989) *The Debate on Classes* (London: Verso).

Index

Index compiled by Auriol Griffith-Jones